From New Christians to New Jews:
Seventeenth-Century Spanish Texts
in Defense of Judaism

Juan de la Cuesta Hispanic Monographs

Series: *Estudios judeoespañoles «Samuel G. Armistead y Joseph H. Silverman»*, 10

FOUNDING EDITOR
Tom Lathrop†
*University of Delaware*

EDITOR
Michael J. McGrath
*Georgia Southern University*

EDITORIAL BOARD
Vincent Barletta
*Stanford University*

Annette Grant Cash
*Georgia State University*

David Castillo
*State University of New York - Buffalo*

Gwen Kirkpatrick
*Georgetown University*

Mark P. Del Mastro
*College of Charleston*

Juan F. Egea
*University of Wisconsin - Madison*

Sara L. Lehman
*Fordham University*

Mariselle Meléndez
*University of Illinois at Urbana - Champaign*

Eyda Merediz
*University of Maryland*

Dayle Seidenspinner-Núñez
*University of Notre Dame*

Elzbieta Sklodowska
*Washington University in St. Louis*

Noël Valis
*Yale University*

# From New Christians to New Jews: Seventeenth-Century Spanish Texts in Defense of Judaism

*by*

MATTHEW D. WARSHAWSKY
*University of Portland*

## Juan de la Cuesta
Newark, Delaware

On the cover: *View of the Sephardic and Ashkenazi Synagogues in Amsterdam*, by Gerrit Adriaenszoon Berckheyde, 1682. Musée d'art et d'histoire du Judaïsme, Paris, on permanent loan from the Musée de Picardie, Amiens.

No portion of this book may be reproduced in any form without permission from the publisher. For permission contact: libros@juandelacuesta.com.

Copyright © 2024 by Linguatext, LLC. All rights reserved.

Juan de la Cuesta Hispanic Monographs
An imprint of Linguatext, LLC.
103 Walker Way
Newark, Delaware 19711 USA
(302) 453-8695

www.JuandelaCuesta.com

MANUFACTURED IN THE UNITED STATES OF AMERICA

ISBN: 978-1-58871-405-3

Table of Contents

Acknowledgments ................................................................................... 9

A Note about Spelling and Translations ............................................... 13

Introduction ........................................................................................... 15

1   "All True, All Holy, All Divine": Jewish Identity in the Polemics
    and Letters of Isaac Orobio de Castro ............................................ 25

2   "May Your Holy Inspiration Call Me in the Desert": New Jewish
    and Baroque Identity in the Poetry of João Pinto Delgado .......... 48

3   "There Is No Greater Nobility than Sublime Virtue": Converso
    Identity in the Poetry of Antonio Enríquez Gómez ...................... 81

4   "One God, One People, and One Law": *Las excelencias de los hebreos*
    of Isaac Cardoso as a Defense of Judaism through a Spanish-
    Portuguese Lens ............................................................................. 112

5   "O Israel, If You Were to Return to God, How Quickly You Would
    Show Yourself Redeemed": The Literary and Spiritual Journey of
    Miguel (Daniel Levi) de Barrios ................................................... 132

6   "Your Grace, Lord, Will Sustain Me": A Transatlantic Perspective on
    Psalms in *Espejo fiel de vidas* of Daniel Israel López Laguna ........ 163

Conclusion ........................................................................................... 189

Works Cited ......................................................................................... 193

Index .................................................................................................... 203

*For* THERESA, SIENNA, *and* JACOB,
*with love and gratitude.*

Acknowledgments

I AM PLEASED TO thank many individuals whose support and assistance helped me to research and write this book over a period of more than ten years. At the University of Portland, I am grateful to the Summer Undergraduate Research Experience (SURE) Program of the College of Arts and Sciences and its director, Academic Associate Dean Jacqueline Van Hoomissen, for the opportunity to conduct research with students in 2020 and 2021 about two of the authors discussed in the book. Catherine Wojda, Joshua Henderson, and I immersed ourselves in *Espejo fiel de vidas* by Daniel Israel López Laguna and the context of its production in late 1600s/early 1700s Jamaica, publishing our work in *International Journal of Undergraduate Research and Creative Activity*. Arielys Morffiz González, Fabi Zeller-Márquez, and I delved into religious poetry of Miguel (Daniel Levi) de Barrios and the Sephardic community of Amsterdam that nourished it, publishing our findings in *Reinvention: An International Journal of Undergraduate Research*. I thank all four students for their commitment to our projects as well as their insights that broadened my understanding of the works we studied.

I would also like to thank Heidi Senior, Diane Sotak, and especially Stephanie Michel, reference librarians at the Clark Library of the University of Portland, for connecting me with databases and other online links related to the study of crypto-Jews. Interlibrary loan librarians Cindy Blanding and Christopher Wiley-Smith expedited my requests for books and journal articles, and Head of Collection Services Christina Prucha ordered new titles related to the subject of the book that I requested for the library's collection.

I am grateful to the University of Portland for a Butine Faculty Development grant during the summer of 2017 and a research sabbatical during the spring semester of 2022. The Butine award provided time to research and write an article about the poetry of João Pinto Delgado that became the basis of chapter 2, while the sabbatical enabled me to complete chapters 3 and 5 as well as many tasks needed to prepare the manuscript for publication. I also thank the University of Portland for generously underwriting the subvention for publishing the manuscript through faculty development funds and an additional Butine award in 2023.

Between 2020 and 2023, I participated in a research-and-writing group with the following colleagues from across the College of Arts and Sciences at the University of Portland: Brandy Daniels, Alexa Dare, Christin Hancock, Molly Hiro, Anne Santiago, Kristin Sweeney, and Rachel Wheeler. I have appreciated the support and friendship of this group and have found inspiration in hearing about the challenges and successes that they have shared.

At Juan de la Cuesta Hispanic Monographs, I thank editor Michael McGrath for his enthusiastic reception of the idea for this book and for accepting the manuscript, as well as Michael Bolan for publishing it. I am especially grateful to outside reviewer Michael McGaha for reading the entire manuscript, identifying errata, and suggesting a more elegant title.

Additionally, with his typical generosity, Michael McGaha answered all my queries regarding translations of quotations and made very helpful comments and corrections so that these passages communicated the sense of the original Baroque Spanish. Michael also shared his personal copies of a bound facsimile edition of *Academias morales de las musas* of Antonio Enríquez Gómez and *De la cárcel inquisitorial a la sinagoga de Amsterdam*, by Kenneth Brown. As grateful as I am for Michael's help, I am equally thankful that our conversations about converso poets provided an opportunity to nurture a friendship that has lasted over two decades.

At The Ohio State University, Elizabeth B. Davis introduced me to Spanish Golden Age poetry in her graduate class on this topic and directed my dissertation on several works by Antonio Enríquez Gómez. Laura Leibman suggested Daniel Israel López Laguna as a research topic and shared a PDF version of *Espejo fiel de vidas*. Likewise, her presentations about early modern Jews in the Caribbean to my class at the University of Portland on Latin American Jewish literature and culture have shone a new light on this topic for students and me. Kenneth Brown offered helpful comments to my article about Enríquez Gómez in a special edition of *Calíope* in 2011 addressing the poetry of converso authors that became the basis for part of chapter 3 of this book. In a series of emails, he also explained his preparation of the synoptic edition of "Romance a Lope de Vera" in *De la cárcel inquisitorial*. Claude Stuczynski shared his chapter, "Ex-*Converso* Sephardi New Jews as Agents, Victims, and Thinkers of Empire: Isaac Cardoso Once Again," which situated the work of Cardoso in the context of diasporic Iberian New Christians returned to Judaism. When I was first researching Cardoso, Hernán

Matzkevich Rodrigues sent me a digitized PDF of *Las excelencias de los hebreos*. The late David Gitlitz made timely suggestions about sources to consult and encouraged my research. My good friend Natan Meir kindly listened to updates about the progress of the book and offered helpful advice during our runs and walks in Portland.

Several individuals met with my student collaborators and me in the Summer Undergraduate Research Experience in conversations that helped bridge the Covid era and the 1600s. Ainsley Cohen Henriques, founding president of the Jamaican Jewish Genealogical Society, brought Jewish history in Jamaica to life for us. Ruth Fine discussed her work on Daniel Israel López Laguna and offered feedback for our ideas about the poet. Julia R. Lieberman shared insights about the allegorical plays of Miguel de Barrios and the environment in which they were written.

I am grateful to several journals for helping me strengthen my arguments in articles that, with additional revisions, form the basis of five of the six chapters in this book. Prior versions of chapter 1 appeared in *Journal of Jewish Identities*, vol. 11, no. 2, 2018, pp. 267–87; of chapters 2 and 3 in *Calíope: Journal of the Society for Renaissance and Baroque Hispanic Poetry*, vol. 24, no. 1, 2019, pp. 29–53, and vol. 17, no. 1, 2011, pp. 97–124, respectively; of chapter 4 in *Pacific Coast Philology*, vol. 55, no. 2, 2020, pp. 191–211; and of chapter 6 in *American Jewish History*, vol. 107, no. 2/3, 2023, pp. 553–73.

Finally, I would like to acknowledge my mother Elizabeth Warshawsky, my father of blessed memory David H. Warshawsky, my sisters Beth Ricanati and Kittie Warshawsky and their families, and my family in Oregon for their support and love. I am especially thankful to my wife Theresa Burks and our children Sienna and Jacob for encouraging me during my extended figurative residence in the 1600s, and with love and gratitude dedicate *From New Christians to New Jews* to them.

A Note about Spelling and Translations

GENERALLY, THROUGHOUT THE BOOK I have modernized the spelling of citations of original texts for ease of reading, especially when doing so does not affect pronunciation, and have standardized capitalization of words in these citations. Likewise, unless otherwise indicated, translations are my own, although as mentioned in the Acknowledgments, Michael McGaha provided invaluable assistance regarding some of the more difficult ones. Any remaining errors in the translations are mine.

# Introduction

THE EXPULSION OF THE Jews from Spain in 1492 and their forced conversion in Portugal five years later produced several consequences that the monarchs who authorized these decisions, Fernando and Isabel in Spain and Manoel in Portugal, surely did not anticipate. First, crypto-Judaism persisted over multiple generations among some *conversos*, or New Christians, that is, converts to Christianity of Jewish origin who remained in the Iberian Peninsula or traveled to the respective overseas territories of Spain and Portugal. Trial records from Inquisition tribunals on both sides of the Atlantic corroborate the authenticity of this secret Judaism among conversos and their descendants whom these courts prosecuted as heretics as late as the 1700s. In fact, small pockets of vestigial crypto-Judaism have survived to the present day, notably in Portugal, as well as in former Spanish-Portuguese American territories, long outlasting the demise of the Inquisition during the 1800s. In recent decades, some adherents of this belief system have openly reclaimed their Jewish faith.[1] Second, during the 1600s, many descendants of the forced converts of the 1490s who had remained in Spain and Portugal traveled to (and in some cases from) port cities in the Ottoman Empire, Western Europe, and colonial Latin America, among other places. Broadly speaking, in Ottoman lands of the eastern Mediterranean, these conversos joined already established Jewish communities, many of which themselves had grown due to the arrival of the original exiles from Spain in 1492. In the western diaspora—especially, but not limited to, Venice, Livorno, Bordeaux, smaller cities and towns in southwest France, Nantes, Rouen, Hamburg, Amsterdam, London, several Caribbean islands colonized by England and Holland, and Dutch settlements in Suriname and Brazil—the emigres

---

[1] See the Society for Crypto-Judaic Studies for the study of crypto-Judaism of Iberian origin in historical and contemporary contexts. The author is a former board member of the Society and served as vice-president of its conference program between 2013 and 2015.

established communities of fellow conversos, where in many instances they participated in a process of rejudaization in the context of their Spanish and/or Portuguese origins.²

This transformation of New Christians into "New Jews" emphasized the differentiated status of such individuals in both Iberian and Jewish history, in part by showing the impact of decades of separation from normative Judaism and of Inquisitorial Spain and Portugal on their faith once they could express it freely.³ Indeed, commenting on this process regarding Amsterdam, where during the 1600s conversos established the most important center of such returnees to Judaism in northern Europe, James Amelang notes, "The history of Judaism had been marked by few occasions in which converts to Christianity, much less their descendants, were able to return to their ancestral religion" (142). Frequently, the belief in a shared ethnicity, as well as ties of kinship, commerce, and language with the Iberian world, characterized this return, as much as and occasionally more than a recovered religious identity alone. For example, conversos and former conversos communicated amongst themselves in Portuguese and Spanish, thus fostering separateness within their new locales while also reflecting pride in their Iberian origin. In Amsterdam and elsewhere in their diaspora, these individuals typically used Portuguese for day-to-day business and synagogue affairs, and Spanish for literary expression, especially of Jewish identity (Amelang 142; Bodian, *Hebrews of the Portuguese Nation* 92). These linguistic tendencies confirm the contradictory nature of converso identity. On one hand, Portuguese and Spanish were the languages of Inquisition tribunals that in some cases had prosecuted them or family members; on the other, writing literary works in

---

2   *Sephardim* is also a term that describes Jews of Iberian background, including to the present day, based on a verse in the book of Obadiah that states, "the Jerusalemite exile community of Sepharad shall possess the towns of the Negeb" (Obad. 1.20). Regardless of the possible geographical location of Sepharad elsewhere, Iberian Jews referred to Spain by this name and called themselves Sephardim (see Vernet Pons for discussion of the term Sepharad).

3   The term "New Jew" describes Iberian conversos post-1492 who, despite having practiced Jewish rites incompletely or not at all in Spain and Portugal, could become openly practicing Jews in Sephardic communities beyond the Iberian Peninsula, especially in Western Europe during the 1600s. Yosef Kaplan has used this term in a number of his publications describing ex-conversos returned to Judaism, for example, in "Wayward New Christians" 27, 30, 38, 39. See also Y. Kaplan, *From Christianity to Judaism* 326–77, for a discussion of challenges in this transition facing such former New Christians as well as the communities where they settled.

Spanish showed how they sought to ennoble these texts by adhering to poetics esteemed in the Spanish literary Golden Age of the Baroque era.[4]

Against this background, *From New Christians to New Jews: Seventeenth-Century Spanish Texts in Defense of Judaism* studies poetry, polemics, and a play that six New Christian authors published during the 1600s and early 1700s. Examining the hybrid nature of these writers as emergent or New Jews who used literary language of Catholic Spain to communicate their experiences as conversos and to varying degrees former conversos, the book shows how they were Iberian and Jewish at a time when the Inquisitions of Spain, Portugal, and their colonies prevented such identities from coexisting openly. Through its analysis of selected works of Isaac Orobio de Castro, João Pinto Delgado, Antonio Enríquez Gómez, Isaac Cardoso, Miguel de Barrios, and Daniel Israel López Laguna, the study shines a light on authors who have not been considered canonically Spanish, despite writing texts that in many ways conform to Baroque literary techniques. Likewise, it seeks to position them as Jewish authors, notwithstanding the Catholic milieu in which they grew up and to which one (Enríquez Gómez) returned. In so doing, the book calls attention to the resilience all six showed by overcoming Inquisition-inspired fear through their spiritual and geographic mobility, and the redemption they claimed by asserting through their texts a once forbidden Judaism.

Adding to the works of Miriam Bodian, Kenneth Brown, Emily Colbert Cairns, Ruth Fine, Yosef Kaplan, Laura Leibman, Michael McGaha, Timothy Oelman, Ronnie Perelis, Kenneth Scholberg, Yosef Yerushalmi, and others who have studied converso writers of the post-1492 era, *From New Christians to New Jews* focuses on texts of converso and former converso authorship as examples of Baroque Spanish literature written beyond the Inquisitorial sphere but reflective of its impact. In so doing, the study bears witness to this oft-marginalized worldview, showing how these six writers created an emergent Jewish sense of self rooted in their knowledge of Spanish literary practices and of the Inquisitorial societies from which they came. That they did so across a wide geographical landscape and despite the eclipse of Judaism in Iberian lands at that time testifies to the reach and cohesiveness of this identity. Finally, by studying texts of these authors in the context of their production, *From New Christians to New Jews* also aims to broaden

---

4   The Spanish literary Golden Age of the 1500s and 1600s, especially in poetry, theater, and prose, should not be confused with the Hebrew Golden Age of medieval Spain of the 1000s and 1100s, an era of comparable cultural richness, especially in poetry and philosophy. For the Hebrew Golden Age, see Gerber, *The Jews of Spain* 60–89; and Menocal 100–11, 158–73.

awareness of the early modern Western Sephardic diaspora within the fields of Iberian studies, including in a transatlantic sense, and Jewish studies, as well as for a general audience interested in these disciplines.

Each chapter of the book focuses on the literary output of a distinct author representative of this diaspora and active principally during the mid- to late-1600s, and as far as the early 1700s in the case of López Laguna. These six subjects reflect the influence of their upbringing in a religiously inflexible society through works that span open advocacy for Judaism to laments about injustice and suffering. In its study of these works, *From New Christians to New Jews* also argues for greater recognition of their authors as exemplars of early modern transatlantic literature, whether they wrote letters and polemics common to religious debates; poetry whose forms typified the Spanish Baroque, including sonnets, epic poems, and narrative ballads; or, in one case, an allegorical play that affirms not the Eucharist, as this genre of religious theater typically did, but Judaism.

Chapter 1 analyzes three letters of Isaac Orobio de Castro to fellow converso Juan de Prado and two tracts addressed to Huguenot and Catholic opponents to show how, responding to the nearly secular Judaism of his first adversary and the Christianity of the others, Orobio evinced a faith unimpeachably Jewish. The chapter also studies how Orobio's early years affected his interactions with Prado, but in reverse: just as Inquisitorial Spain persecuted Orobio as a crypto-Jew, the community in Amsterdam that he joined could not reconcile the deism of Prado to its understanding of Judaism. This idea of history inverted is visible in Orobio's privileging of Judaism in the longer tracts, in which knowledge of Christianity helped him defend Jewish beliefs.

Chapter 2 studies the influence of the Spanish Golden Age on poems that João Pinto Delgado published in France to show how they express a Jewish voice that would have been forbidden in Spain and Portugal. Analyzing texts treating themes from the books of Esther, Lamentations, and Exodus, the chapter explores how Pinto Delgado communicates a Jewish identity, regardless of the extent to which he could live openly as a Jew in France. Additionally, by comparing his poetry with works of Jorge Manrique, Fray Luis de León, and Luis de Góngora, the chapter proposes that the Jewish perspective of Pinto Delgado coexisted with a Spanish literary one.

Antonio Enríquez Gómez was the only one of the six authors discussed in this book to return to the Iberian Peninsula. The autobiographical aspect and the breadth of his writing illumine the worldview of someone literally and figuratively in and out of Spain and its poetic trends as he strove to create a space for himself in the literary culture of the country during the mid-1600s. Chapter 3 investigates how Enríquez Gómez fashions this space in three poetic texts of his exile in France, although not to look for signs that their author was a crypto-Jew. Rather, the chapter proposes that in these poems he advocates a world of greater transparency, tolerance, and individual free will, all issues of special importance to a New Christian whose family suffered Inquisition trials, who sued the tribunal, and who died in Inquisitorial custody.

Chapter 4 explains how, in *Las excelencias de los hebreos* (*The Excellences of the Hebrews*), Isaac Cardoso uses examples from Iberian Jewish history to vindicate Judaism as a religion and people "apart" at a time when both no longer officially existed on the Iberian Peninsula. He does so by cataloging ten "excellences" of Jews and then disproving ten groundless but persistent "calumnies" against Jews and New Christians. His meticulous study shows the extent of Cardoso's Jewish knowledge despite his having lived half his life deprived of this identity, as well as how awareness of the unjust treatment of Jews and conversos in Spain and Portugal contributed to his emergent Jewish sense of self.

In the allegorical play *Contra la verdad no hay fuerza* (*Nothing Can Stand Up to The Truth*), Miguel (Daniel Levi) de Barrios memorializes three conversos burned for crypto-Jewish heresy at the conclusion of the auto de fe of June 29, 1665, in Córdoba, Spain.[5] Chapter 5 discusses autobiographical references in several works of Barrios to show how his own life story led him to extol the three for their faith; examines an eyewitness account of the auto de fe that made them (in)famous as well as poetry from the introductory pages of *Contra la verdad* contemplating this fame; and then analyzes the play to show how Barrios uses an *auto sacramental* (sacramental act), a canonical literary genre of Spanish Catholicism, to assert a Jewish identity.

Chapter 6 shows how in his paraphrase of Psalms, *Espejo fiel de vidas que contiene los Psalmos de David en verso* (*Faithful Mirror of Lives That Contains the Psalms of David in Verse*), Daniel Israel López Laguna encapsulates the transatlantic reach of the Spanish-Portuguese Jewish diaspora in the early 1700s. Emphasizing resilience and redemption in his reworking of the biblical book, López Laguna reflects his transatlantic travels and spiritual trajec-

---

5   The auto de fe (act of faith), was a ceremony, usually public, at which the Inquisition pronounced sentence against individuals accused of heresy and other practices regarded as deviant from faithful Catholicism. When imposed, capital sentences of garroting and burning at the stake or burning while the victim was still alive were carried out at a separate location immediately afterward.

tory from living as an apparent secret Jew to openly practicing Judaism. The chapter explores the influence of this geographical and religious journey in the poems by examining how López Laguna repeatedly mentions the *peregrino*, or wanderer; praises the chosen status of the Israelite people; beseeches God to protect conversos against enemies symbolizing the Inquisition; and disparages talebearers representative of Inquisitorial informants.

The conclusion reflects on the preceding case studies in order to show the importance of the worldview that they evince to Jewish identity of Iberian origin at a time of its eclipse on the Peninsula and to Spanish literary trends of the Baroque era. It also suggests how this worldview continues to speak to readers today, symbolized poignantly by the opening of a synagogue in the birthplace of one of the authors.

In light of the aforementioned structure of the book, a condensed summary of the establishment of the Sephardic community of Amsterdam and its Iberian and Jewish characteristics during the 1600s can contribute historical context to the worldviews of the six authors whom *From New Christians to New Jews* studies.[6] More connections link them to this city than to any other, confirming its role as a focal point in the transatlantic Spanish-Portuguese Jewish diaspora of the seventeenth century. Pinto Delgado, Orobio de Castro, and Barrios all immigrated to Amsterdam. The text of Cardoso analyzed in this book was published there. Barrios mentioned in one of his poetic miscellanies the martyrdom of a Spanish convert *to* crypto-Judaism, Lope de Vera y Alarcón, whom Enríquez Gómez celebrated in a *romance*, or ballad, also treated in this book. Finally, López Laguna published his paraphrase of Psalms in the Spanish-Portuguese community of London, many of whose members had come from Amsterdam after Jews could return to England starting in the 1650s.

Financial woes resulting from the imperialism and seemingly incessant military expenditures of Spain's Habsburg monarchs contributed to increased emigration of New Christians from there and even more from Portugal. This trend prevailed especially during the sixty-year period between 1580 and 1640, when Spain annexed the crown of its smaller neighbor. The increased diaspora of conversos even reached Spain's and Portugal's New

---

6   For a detailed explanation of the formation and functioning of the Sephardic community of 1600s Amsterdam, see Bodian, *Hebrews of the Portuguese Nation*; and Swetschinski, *Reluctant Cosmopolitans*. Also see Bodian, "The Formation of the Portuguese Jewish Diaspora," for a concise account of the arrival of Spanish Jewish emigres into Portugal at the end of the 1400s and the subsequent emergence of Portuguese Jewish and converso communities outside Portugal.

World colonies, despite an official—albeit not uniformly enforced—prohibition on travel there by New Christians.[7] In this context, early in the seventeenth century, the Duke of Lerma, the *valido,* or favorite minister, of King Felipe III, agreed to accept 170,000 cruzados from Portuguese conversos in exchange for granting them permission to leave Spain and Portugal. Prior to this bribe lifting the prohibition on travel, New Christians wishing to travel outside the Iberian Peninsula might serve as ship's crew or captain (Gerber, *The Jews of Spain* 179–80), and in the case of Portuguese conversos, obtain a license to trade in the Indies if the Spanish crown deemed them necessary to overseas commerce (Cross 152–53). The subsequent Twelve Years Truce of 1609–1621 between Spain and Holland further stimulated emigration by enabling Portuguese converso merchants to participate in Amsterdam's trade with Dutch colonies in the East and West Indies (Bodian, *Hebrews of the Portuguese Nation* 26), as well as position them to form commercial networks with New Christians in these and other overseas outposts.

Then, during the 1620s, Gaspar de Guzmán, Count-Duke of Olivares, who was the *valido* of Felipe IV, invited Portuguese converso bankers to Madrid in order to help solve Spain's debt woes. Soon a substantial number of Portuguese conversos were living in Spain and forming important mercantile connections with other New Christians throughout the Mediterranean world, northern Europe, and beyond. The greatest period of Portuguese immigration to Amsterdam, and that which pertained to the arrival of Pinto Delgado, Barrios, and Orobio, occurred during the mid-1600s. Ironically, as Jonathan Israel has shown, events outside Portugal contributed to this increase: the loss of the Dutch enclave in northeast Brazil, where Sephardim were involved in the sugar trade; the flight of Jews from Venice on account of war with the Ottoman Empire; and increased Inquisitorial persecution of Portuguese New Christians in Spain after the end of that country's unification with Portugal in 1640 (51). Israel also emphasizes economic considerations above religious ones in the establishment of the Sephardic community of Amsterdam, noting that the commercial activities of Iberian Jews (and

---

7    The case of Miguel de Cervantes *might* be an example of the difficulties New Christians experienced trying to travel to the Americas due to their background. Michael McGaha has argued that the denial of Cervantes's applications for appointments in the Spanish Indies in 1582 and 1590, despite his exemplary military service and subsequent captivity, contributes to the "compelling circumstantial evidence" of the author's converso background ("Is There a Hidden Jewish Meaning in *Don Quixote?*" 173).

former New Christians) in Spain's and Portugal's American territories positioned them well in the Dutch city as it became a center of trade.

When Portuguese conversos established a toehold in Amsterdam in the 1590s, the city was already a center of mercantile importance in northern Europe. The community formed by the new arrivals likewise derived its prosperity from commerce, not only through the dealings of great merchants whose homes the Dutch artist Romeyn de Hooghe represented in prints, but more commonly those of New Christians of lesser economic prestige who worked as traders, speculators, brokers, lenders, and ship owners, among other professions (Bodian, *Hebrews of the Portuguese Nation* 3–4). Economically, the Portuguese conversos, and subsequently ex-conversos become Jews, traded with fellow Portuguese New Christians throughout their diaspora, which stretched from port cities in northern Europe and the Mediterranean basin to India and Dutch holdings in the Americas. These networks developed in part due to the participation of Iberian conversos within and beyond Spain and Portugal in those countries' relatively new trade in "rich" commodities highly valued in Europe, including sugar, coffee, tobacco, spices, and precious stones (Israel 45–47). At the same time, while the Dutch encouraged the participation of the Iberian newcomers in these commodities, they did not allow this new community to join "most guild and retail occupations," excepting wholesale commerce (Bodian, *Hebrews of the Portuguese Nation* 60). In other words, the Sephardim could contribute to the growing prosperity of Amsterdam without threatening it.

On the one hand, then, the foundation of Amsterdam's converso community rested on mercantile ties between New Christians who traded in lucrative goods throughout the Iberian (especially Atlantic) world, regardless of prior secret Judaism and desire to live openly as Jews in the Dutch city. On the other hand, the new community also forged a religious identity, apart from its economic one, that was rooted in rabbinic Judaism and connected to the Iberian Peninsula. This aspect of the community's foundation grew out of how conversos, aware of or having lived through Inquisitorial prosecution, understood their settlement in a place free of the dreaded tribunal. As Miriam Bodian notes, "the organizing notion in these stories [of the establishment of Amsterdam's converso community] was that of restoration ... the escape from enforced conformity to a false belief system, and a return to the true ancestral faith" (*Hebrews of the Portuguese Nation* 19–20). While not all New Christians came to Amsterdam intent on such a spiritual journey, this notion of restoration and return describes accurately the trajectory of five of the six authors in *From New Christians to New Jews*, from secret

Judaism in Spain and Portugal to open Judaism in diaspora. Regardless of whether the sixth, Enríquez Gómez, might have practiced Judaism amongst the converso community of Bordeaux, he certainly expressed a converso perspective in works written there before his return to Spain.

Thus, in Spain and the places of their subsequent diaspora, including Amsterdam, the "Portuguese" formed a distinct social grouping that combined economic, religious, and increasingly, ethnic characteristics, with the result that many Spanish Old Christians conflated the terms Portuguese, New Christian, and Jew.[8] While Old Christians in Iberia used the term "nation" to disparage conversos, however, New Christians referred to themselves as a "nation" in a positive sense, creating communities whose members formed bonds rooted as much in ethnicity as religion. Due to this sense of ethnic difference, "those of the [Portuguese] Nation" (*os da nação*) of the 1600s encompassed conversos in Iberian lands who might be practicing Catholics; others there who were secret Jews; still others who might be a combination of both; and, notably for the focus of this book, conversos of diaspora, many of whom might have returned to Judaism. A clear example of this shared identity in action was the *Dotar*, short for Santa Companhia de dotar orfans e donzelas pobres (Sacred Society for Dowering Orphans and Poor Brides). This organization was founded in Amsterdam in 1615 to provide dowries to orphaned and poor girls throughout the Sephardic diaspora in northern Europe and, significantly, to conversos residing in Catholic territories (Bodian, *Hebrews of the Portuguese Nation*, 135–36).[9] Thus, a question addressing the potential conflict confronting a community such as this one, whose identity stood on ethnicity and religion, seems particularly relevant: "How were they to reconcile the traditional Judaism they craved, with the dynamic Iberian culture that was their secular life and with the new horizons of thought and action to which they also aspired?" (Popkin 21). The lives and works of the six authors discussed in the following pages provide one answer, as their experiences living as Catholics in Spain and Portugal would inform the various degrees of Jewish identity that their writings express.

---

8   In the early modern period, the term "Old Christian" described an individual in Spain or Portugal whose lineage supposedly was free from Jewish or Muslim ancestry.

9   I thank Miriam Bodian for her assistance with the translation of the term *Dotar*.

# 1
# "All True, All Holy, All Divine": Jewish Identity in the Polemics and Letters of Isaac Orobio de Castro

DURING THE 1600S, THE physician and polemicist Isaac Orobio de Castro exemplified the diverse intellectual elite of New Christian Portuguese immigrants to Amsterdam who became New Jews while maintaining their Iberian cultural identity. Prior repression of his Jewish identity led Orobio, once established in the Dutch republic, to engage in polemics with Protestant, Catholic, and, in the case of Juan (Daniel) de Prado, converso thinkers, in which he expounded Judaism as a divinely inspired faith and legitimated what for him was its superiority to Christianity. Additionally, in his epistolary correspondence with Prado, Orobio successfully cataloged the ways in which the deistic beliefs of his fellow former New Christian fell outside accepted Jewish teachings of the time, even as such beliefs foreshadowed an incipient transition to Jewish identity not rigorously bound to biblical teachings. The following pages outline the peripatetic life that brought him to Holland. They then consider the three responses of Orobio to Prado in order to demonstrate how Orobio's view of Judaism—as the bearer of a divine law that an all-powerful God gave to the Jewish people, esteemed above other peoples—prompted him to criticize sharply the heterodox views of his friend for denying the unique status of this religion. The last part of the chapter examines the treatises *La observancia de la divina ley de Mosseh* (*Observance of the Divine Law of Moses*) and part 1 of *Prevenciones divinas contra la vana idolatría de las gentes* (*Divine Forewarnings against the Vain Idolatry of Gentiles*) that he directed, respectively, to Huguenot and Catholic opponents, as documents that assert a Jewish identity by attacking foundational teachings of Christianity.

FROM IBERIA TO AMSTERDAM AND FROM HIDDEN TO OPEN JUDAISM
Isaac Orobio de Castro was born in Bragança, Portugal, ca.1617, to Manuel Alvares de Orobio and Mencía Fernández Núñez, New Christians whose own ancestors likely were Jews expelled from Spain in 1492. While still in his youth, Orobio, whose baptismal name was Baltasar Alvares de Orobio, joined his family and many other Portuguese conversos in reversing the exile from Spain imposed upon their forebears. At the Universities of Osuna and Alcalá he studied medicine, despite the purity of blood statutes in Spain that officially excluded conversos from advancement in this and other fields, including religious and military orders, university colleges, and the law.[10] Orobio married an apparently Old Christian woman, Isabel Pérez de la Peña, and they and their children resided in several cities throughout the southern part of the country. In 1654, officers of the Holy Office of the Inquisition (*Santo Oficio de la Inquisition*, i.e., the "Spanish Inquisition") used hearsay testimony to arrest, detain, and try Orobio, his mother, three sisters, and a brother-in-law for such crypto-Jewish heresies as fasting at the approximate time of Yom Kippur, reading prayers from a book sent by a relative in Italy, and belittling images worshipped by Catholics. While evidence of circumcision would seem to have confirmed his Jewish identity, the Inquisition in 1656 reconciled Orobio upon his admission to having lived as a secret Jew for more than two decades.[11] Despite the seriousness of their heresies, Orobio and his family emerged from the Holy Office relatively unscathed, obtaining freedom from incarceration and from wearing the penitential sackcloth of the *sambenito* (likely short for *saco bendito*, or holy sackcloth) within two years.

As secret or crypto-Jews, Orobio and his family belonged to that group of conversos in Spain, Portugal, and the territories of these kingdoms who tried to practice increasingly vestigial remnants of Judaism, despite the dan-

---

10   In truth, however, when the statutes were enforced, they tended to affect only families containing an individual whom the Inquisition had punished; otherwise, "they [statutes] were always controversial and never widely accepted," and in many cases, New Christians managed to evade them (Kamen, *The Spanish Inquisition* 312; see also 301–27).

11   "Reconciliation" was a euphemistic term used to describe the readmission to the Catholic Church of individuals convicted of heresies grave indeed, but whom the Inquisition did not regard as unrepentant or recidivist. The conditions of this return were somewhat misleading, however, because the reconciled heretic could suffer penalties including confiscation of goods, flogging, and sentence rowing on the royal galleys. See Gitlitz, *Secrecy and Deceit* 21–22; and Kamen, *The Spanish Inquisition* 248–54.

ger and subsequent illegality of doing so. While Iberian Jews had converted under duress throughout their history—such as to Catholicism under the Visigoths in the seventh century and to Islam under the Almohads in the twelfth—the number of such conversions increased dramatically in 1391 as a result of Church-inspired pogroms that Old Christians carried out across Spain. Later, crypto-Judaism established stronger roots in Portugal for at least three reasons. First, nearly all the Jews forcibly baptized in 1497 had left Spain five years previously for refusing to abandon their Judaism, so they were unlikely to forsake it now. Second, King Manoel I then agreed not to examine the religious practices of the *novos-cristãos* (New Christians) for twenty years. According to Jane Gerber, he did so to recognize the claim of these conversos that the unexpected and cruel elements of their conversion made necessary an extended time during which they could adapt to their new religion (*The Jews of Spain* 142). Finally, an Inquisition only began functioning in Portugal nearly forty years after the forced conversions. This history perhaps helps explain the specifically Portuguese origin of the Sephardic community of Amsterdam; despite having practiced Jewish rites incompletely in Portugal—and in Spain, if they returned there before leaving Iberia, as in the case of Orobio—these individuals grew up in families imbued over several generations with a degree of Jewish identity.[12]

At the same time, the identity of such crypto-Jews was a fluid construction that varied over time and even within a specific person. For this reason, David M. Gitlitz proposed that we "visualize the conversos along the spectrum that runs from wholly Christian to wholly Jewish, recognizing that even the two polar designations admit a wide variety of beliefs and practice" (*Secrecy and Deceit* 84). He then described four typologies, with their various subcategories, according to which conversos formed their self-identity: Christians, Jews, vacillators and syncretists, and skeptics (84–90). Writing as a Jew in Amsterdam, Orobio clearly identified with "observant Judaizers" along such a spectrum, who despite the syncretism of their beliefs, considered "their particular brand of Judaizing as very much akin to the normative Judaism practiced outside the Iberian Peninsula" (Gitlitz, *Secrecy and Deceit* 87). Thus, early in *La observancia de la divina ley de Mosseh*, Orobio makes a statement that possibly refers to this group of conversos still in Spain and Portugal: "If God were to order Israel, presently in a condition impossible for keeping the Law, to observe it, Israel would not be able to sin, nor would

---

12  For a summary of the emergence of Iberian crypto-Judaism in the face of expulsion, conversion, and the establishment of the Inquisition in Spain, see Warshawsky, *The Perils of Living the Good and True Law* 13–42.

it sin, even though it were not to adhere to it" ("Si estando ya en estado imposible de guardar la Ley, Dios se la mandase observar, no podría ni pecaría aunque no la guardase"; 13). These words describe a reality for many New Christians, whose conversion forced them to contravene their ancestral Judaism, but who nevertheless considered themselves Jews despite baptism and the impossibility of practicing much of their true religion. Nevertheless, despite having practiced Jewish rites incompletely or not at all in Spain and Portugal, these individuals could return to Judaism openly in Sephardic communities beyond the Iberian Peninsula, as the case of Orobio himself demonstrates.

By 1660, Orobio and his family decided to travel north through France via a route commonly followed by other conversos, residing briefly in Bayonne and Toulouse before establishing permanent residence in Amsterdam in 1662. The more tolerant environment of that city permitted Orobio, his wife, and children to participate in the process of what Bodian has called "rejudaization" (*Hebrews of the Portuguese Nation* 96–131). They took Hebrew names, with Baltasar becoming Isaac; his wife Isabel, now known as Esther, publicly converted; and their five children—Moses, Hannah, Rebecca, Abraham, and Sarah—received a Jewish upbringing and subsequently married spouses of Iberian converso origin. In addition to his writings as polemicist, Orobio held leadership positions in the Jewish community supporting the sick and the poor and overseeing the religious education of young men. He died in 1687, at approximately age seventy. His wife, who lived for nearly another quarter century, would be laid to rest beside him in the Portuguese-Jewish cemetery at Ouderkerk.[13]

The path that Orobio and his family followed in Amsterdam exemplified several essential features of rejudaization there, including creation of a Jewish self-identity; study of Torah, albeit a privilege reserved for men and boys; and endogamous marriage. Moreover, circumcision assumed importance as a "rite of passage" and tangible evidence of a "return" to Judaism, all the more important due to the misguided view of some conversos that without circumcision a Jew was not bound by the other commandments (Bodian, *Hebrews of the Portuguese Nation* 97–98). Rejudaization also involved guidance in bridging a gap between the newly arrived conversos' belief in the Law

---

13 Y. Kaplan, *From Christianity to Judaism: The Story of Isaac Orobio de Castro*, is the source of the biography of Orobio in the preceding two paragraphs. In particular, see 80–95 for Orobio's treatment at the hands of the Inquisition, and 107–09 and 207–08 for the integration of his family into the Jewish community of Amsterdam.

of Moses and the actual practice of its tenets, all but impossible in Inquisitorial Spain and Portugal. Such guidance was all the more necessary because, as Bodian notes while commenting on the preoccupation with salvation on the part of Judaizing conversos, many secret Jews had fashioned their identity according to a framework and even liturgy learned in church. That they did so confirms an apparent antithesis by which "a determined rejection of a repressive social order [was] accompanied by an unwitting embrace of some of its deepest impulses" (*Hebrews of the Portuguese Nation* 101). Of course, not all converso emigres to Amsterdam were willing to submit themselves to the rigorous process that the Mahamad (council of elders) had established to immerse them in Judaism as a daily experience lived in and out of the synagogue. Some refused to pay communal taxes or chose to live among Christians. Perhaps most memorably, others, including Prado, the first opponent of Orobio discussed below, rejected the rabbinic teachings of the Portuguese-Jewish community and espoused views that challenged communal authority, which threatened the upstanding reputation of ex-conversos in the Dutch republic (Bodian, *Hebrews of the Portuguese Nation* 112–18).

### Epistolary correspondence with Juan de Prado

While most of his works are extant only in manuscript form, scholars of Orobio have published editions of the three texts of 1663–1664 that this chapter studies. The first of these is actually a series of three letters directed to Prado, a converso of similar background to that of Orobio, against whom the Mahamad of Amsterdam had issued a *herem* (censure and/or expulsion) in 1657, for having professed heretical beliefs and taught them to his students.[14] Of the tracts comprising this correspondence, only the three letters Orobio wrote in response to letters from Prado survive. The initial and longest one, "Epístola invectiva contra Prado" ("Letter inveighing against Prado"), written probably in 1663, illuminates the contrasting spiritual paths followed by two recent New Christian arrivals to Sephardic Amsterdam: one who became a defender of rabbinic Judaism, and one whose belief in the supremacy of natural over divine law imperiled the orthodoxy of this community. The second

---

14   Portuguese Sephardic Jews in Amsterdam formed the first Mahamad in 1639 as a way to unify governance of their three synagogues, partly in response to increased immigration of Ashkenazim, or Jews from central and eastern Europe, to the city. While the original seven-member board was comprised of individuals chosen from among the *parnasim*, or community leaders, subsequent Mahamad elected their own successors, thus concentrating power in the hands of this elite ruling group (Bodian, *Hebrews of the Portuguese Nation* 50–51).

letter, "Carta apologética" ("Apologetic Letter"), is important as much for its autobiographical clues as for its portrayal of the conflicted emotions of Orobio regarding the wayward beliefs of his friend. In the third letter, Orobio responds to three questions of Prado in a way that shows a halakhic understanding of Judaism that did not align with what Daniel M. Swetschinski, commenting on the heterodox beliefs of several individuals in Amsterdam's Portuguese-Jewish community, has suggested was Prado's "inclination, perhaps, toward cosmopolitanism" (*Reluctant Cosmopolitans* 276).[15]

The similar trajectories of the life stories of Orobio and Prado in the Iberian Peninsula contrasted with the subsequent divergence of their beliefs and even whereabouts once both had left Spain. Born ca. 1612 into a Portuguese family that had settled in the town of Lopera, in southern Spain, Prado (originally Prados) met Orobio when they were students of medicine and theology at the University of Alcalá in the mid-1630s. At this time, both were secret Jews; in fact, in meetings with other conversos, Prado translated passages of the Bible from Latin to Spanish "in order to convince them that Mosaic Law was the true law" (Y. Kaplan, "Intellectual Ferment" 304). However, upon meeting Orobio again, in 1643 in Lopera, where he was now practicing medicine, Prado also evinced belief in the tenets of deism. This theology represented a threat to traditional Jewish teachings by privileging natural law over the elect status of Israel, lessening the role of God and rabbinic teachings in human activity, and even claiming that the Law of Moses and the Hebrew scriptures were not of divine origin.[16] Prado further evinced the beliefs that would run him afoul of the Mahamad in Amsterdam fifteen years later, when he claimed not only that people could reach God by observing the laws of nature, but also that Jews, Muslims, and Christians should

---

15   The complete title of "Epístola invectiva" in its final form was "Epístola invectiva contra Prado, un Philósopho Médico que dudava o no creya la verdad de la divina Escritura, y pretendió encubrir su malicia con la afectada confesión de Dios y la ley de la naturaleza." My translation of the beginning of this title cites Y. Kaplan, *From Christianity to Judaism* 152. The second letter was entitled "Carta apologética del Dr. Ishack Orobio de Castro al Doctor Prado" and the third "Carta al hijo del Doctor Prado." In *Spinoza et le Dr. Juan de Prado*, Israel S. Révah, a French scholar of Iberian Sephardim in post-1492 Western Europe, published the entire first discourse of "Epístola invectiva" and fragments of the second, third, and fourth ones; as well as "Carta apologética" and "Carta al hijo del Doctor Prado." My citations to these letters refer to Révah's versions of them.

16   For more information about deism, see Y. Kaplan, "Intellectual Ferment" 306–07; Swetschinski, *Reluctant Cosmopolitans* 271–73; and Yovel, *Spinoza and Other Heretics* 75.

all be able to achieve salvation because their respective religions strove to make them conscious of God. Nevertheless, Prado, his wife Isabel, and his mother left Spain in 1652 not because of these convictions, but due to fears of another run-in with the Inquisition. They spent two years in Rome after Prado convinced the archbishop of Seville, recently named cardinal, to appoint him as personal physician, then a year in Hamburg, before arriving in Amsterdam in 1655 (Y. Kaplan, *From Christianity to Judaism* 126).

The deistic thinking that Prado avowed threatened the efforts of the Mahamad of Amsterdam to inculcate Jewish teachings in a community composed of many individuals recently escaped from the Iberian Inquisition. Scarcely a year after arriving in this environment, Prado agreed to read a statement before the governing board in the synagogue attesting to the position to which deism had led him and his willingness to revoke it. Whereas, according to this acceptance of guilt, before he had shown "little enthusiasm in the service of God and his holy Law" ("por aver mostrado poco zelo no servicio de Deus e de sua s[an]ta Ley"; Révah, *Spinoza* 57), now he sought forgiveness and promised never to relapse into similar offenses.[17] The fact that Prado read this mea culpa a few days after the Mahamad issued its censure on July 27, 1656, against Benedict (Baruch) Spinoza, the community's most infamous thinker, shows the extent to which the ruling council enforced its understanding of normative Judaism by censuring individuals whose own views doubted or fell outside this worldview. Despite being welcomed back, in less than six months, Prado relapsed into unbelief in traditional Jewish teachings, prompting community leaders to impose censure that they said would only be lifted were he to move overseas. "Relapse" in this case describes the unwillingness of Prado to abide by his admission of guilt despite having promised to forswear beliefs the Mahamad considered heretical.[18] The unwillingness of members of the Mahamad to countenance avatars of "skepticism and heterodoxy" such as Spinoza and Prado, as well as Uriel Da Costa and Daniel Ribera, indicates "not their piety or stringency, but their rejection of the principle of individual freedom of conscience" for the sake of stability and conformity (Bodian, *Hebrews of the Portuguese Nation* 122, 118).

---

17    Révah quotes the *Livro dos Acordos da Naçam: Anno 5398–5440*, written in Portuguese.

18    Likewise, in Inquisition parlance, a *relapso* was a convicted heretic who recurred to forbidden beliefs and practices after renouncing them at an auto de fe. When enforced, the penalty for such a *relapso* was death by burning at the stake.

Prado refused such a drastic measure as moving overseas, and instead settled in Antwerp, from where, with the aid of his son David, he tried to compel the Mahamad to overturn its decision. Principally, he claimed that Rabbi Saul Levi Morteira, founder of a yeshiva, or academy for religious study, called Keter Torah ("Crown of the Law"), had set a trap by using students from the school for the poor where Prado taught Latin to collect incriminating information about his deism. These lessons provided a means for one of the students, Jacob Monsanto, to lead Prado to describe deistic beliefs such as the following: "he said that there is no reason why we should believe in Moses any more than we believe in Mohammed.... He also says that the world was not created but has always existed in the same form and will continue to exist forever" (qtd. in Yovel, *Spinoza and Other Heretics* 72). Not surprisingly, then, throughout his correspondence with Prado, Orobio had to tread a fine line between avoiding direct contact, per the conditions of the ban, and reaching out in order to persuade his friend to renounce his heretical views. Such a task could not have been easy, given that Prado was a new kind of Jew for the 1600s: someone who identified as a Jew without necessarily adhering to the many rabbinic laws whose observance the identity had traditionally required.

In the end, the correspondence between Orobio and Prado did not achieve its salutary effect, because Prado had become "a faithless Jew clinging to his people and severed from them at the same time" (Yovel, *Spinoza and Other Heretics* 72). In fact, such was his sense of isolation that Prado attempted to procure, unsuccessfully, the assistance of the Inquisition so that he might return to Spain, despite having been a secret Jew there and the tribunal's persecution of his wife and her family. Perhaps as a consequence of this isolation, Prado fell into a dissolute lifestyle that culminated in 1669 in his own death due to a fall from a horse while on his way to wed one woman after apparently promising marriage to another. Nevertheless, despite this ignominious end and the fact that, as Natalia Muchnik observes, Prado was a converso unwilling to be either Jewish or Christian, and as such, possessor "of an identity in perpetual construction" ("d'une identité en perpétuelle construction"; 521), his very fluidity prefigured a transition to a broader sense of Jewish selfhood.[19]

---

19  Muchnik situates Prado within the emergence and expression of both orthodoxy and heterodoxy among the community of Iberian New Christians, many of whom had been secret Jews in Spain and Portugal, that became openly Jewish "ex nihilo" in Amsterdam during the 1600s (497). For a colorful description of the morally lax lifestyle of Prado in his final years, see Barrios, *Desengaño* XVIII in *Coro de*

Orobio divides "Epístola invectiva" into a prologue and four *discursos* (arguments) in order to discredit his erstwhile friend, who would deny to the Jewish religion its unique status in the eyes of God. The prologue is especially important for the way in which he differentiates himself from Prado by describing how New Christians recently arrived in Amsterdam respond in contrasting ways to the rabbinic Judaism taught there. Individuals in the first group, including Orobio,

> ... use all their will in loving the divine Law, [and] they try (as much as the strength of their understanding reaches) to learn what is necessary in order to observe conscientiously its sacred teachings, laws, and ceremonies, which due to captivity itself they and their ancestors forgot. They listen humbly to those who, having been raised in Judaism and learned the Law, are able to explain it.

> ... emplean toda su voluntad en amar la divina Ley, procuran (cuanto alcanza la fuerza de su entender) aprender lo que es necesario para observar religiosamente los sagrados preceptos, fueros y ceremonias que, con el mismo cautiverio, olvidaron ellos y sus mayores. Oyen humildes a los que, por haberse criado en el judaísmo y aprendido la Ley, pueden explicarla. (Révah, *Spinoza* 89)

On the other hand, Prado belonged to a second group of New Christians who reach Amsterdam equally ignorant of Judaism, but conceited due to their knowledge of secular sciences. As a result, once they begin to learn about their ancestral faith,

> ... vanity and pride do not allow them to receive education in order to come away from ignorance; it seems to them that they fall from esteem as learned men if they allow themselves to be taught by those who truly are learned in the holy Law; they feign great knowledge in order to contradict that which they do not understand, even though it be all true, all holy, all divine.

---

*las musas* 355–61. Barrios introduces the poem by writing, "Divine justice punishes Dr. Juan de Prado, teacher of false dogmas, who did not have more religion than that which was agreeable to his body" ("Castiga la divina justicia al doctor Juan de Prado, maestro de falsos dogmas, que no tenía más religion que la que convenía a su cuerpo"; 355). Révah includes the poem in *Spinoza* 70–74.

> ... no les permite su vanidad y soberbia recibir doctrina para salir de la ignorancia; paréceles que descaecen del crédito de doctos, si se dejan enseñar de los que verdaderamente lo son en la Ley santa; afectan grande ciencia en contradecir lo que no entienden, aunque todo verdadero, todo santo, todo divino. (90)[20]

Freedom from such arrogance permits Orobio to embrace Judaism, whereas the egotism of Prado has led him to reject it. At the same time, the dichotomy also shows the extent to which, for Orobio, the roots of Jewish religious authority lie in long-held teachings from the past; Prado would disregard this authority and any legitimacy derived from its biblical origin.

In the first discourse, Orobio opposes the deistic tenet that no one theology brings its believers closer to God, instead affirming the divinity of the Torah and explaining the origin of the elect status of the Jewish people manifested in this work. Further legitimizing the written law is, for Orobio, its conformity with natural reason; as an example, he claims in chapter 3 of the discourse that the first lesson the Torah teaches is "the existence of God, God's independent essence, God's eternity" ("la existencia de Dios, su esencia independiente, su eternidad"; 98).[21] Yet in contrast to this truth, there exist minds of "such harmful nature that have been persuaded to not believe it [the truth of God's existence] ... and although there is nothing so certain nor a truth so certain as divine existence, with all that, he who wants to remain an atheist will not be evidently convinced to the contrary" ("de tan maligna naturaleza que se han persuadido a no creerlo ... y, aunque no hay cosa tan cierta ni verdad tan infalible como la divina existencia, con todo, quien quisiera quedar ateísta, no será evidentemente convencido a lo contrario"; 98).

Presumably referring to Prado, in chapter 6, Orobio criticizes such minds for thinking that the works of God can be reduced to human comprehension. Against this desire to compartmentalize the divine, he asserts that God effected creation in ways unknowable to humanity, so that "all creatures are sufficient signs of the omnipotence of God; it does not require other evidence in order to be believed" ("bastantes indicios son todas las criaturas de la omnipotencia de Dios, no necesita de otra prueba para ser creída"; 105).

---

20  The words "all true, all holy, all divine" in the title of the current chapter come from this citation, as testament to Orobio's faith in the "Holy Law" of Judaism.

21  Orobio organized each of the four arguments of *Epístola invectiva* into specific chapters. Citations to chapters in my analysis of this work refer to sections of its first argument.

Orobio concludes this letter emphasizing the chosen status of the Israelite people, perhaps as a direct rebuttal to Prado's claim of the superiority of natural law to divine law. After stating in the subheading of chapter 11 that "denying the sacred writings [Torah] and God is the same thing" ("negarla y negar a Dios es una misma cosa"; 119), Orobio emphasizes the centrality of the divine, reminding his addressee that God "formed man [humanity] in God's likeness, so that, imitating the creator, people would act with the integrity owed to the heroic nature of God's intellectual and perfect nature" ("lo formó a su semejanza para que, a su imitación, obrase con la rectitud debida a lo heroico de su intelectual y perfecta naturaleza"; 119, 121–22).

The second letter of Orobio to Prado, "Carta apologética del doctor Ishack Orobio de Castro al doctor Prado" ("Apologetic Letter of Doctor Isaac Orobio de Castro to Doctor Prado"), shows the conflict its writer felt regarding his friend's heterodoxy while also revealing aspects of his own crypto-Judaism in Iberia.[22] For example, at the beginning of the document, speaking of Prado, Orobio notes "the repeated and continued experiences of his good will and desire for my success, without forgetting the favors and assistance" ("repetidas y continuadas experiencias de su buena voluntad y deseo de mis medras, sin olvidar los favores y asistencias") he received from him during their youth, but such help notwithstanding, is unable "to stop condemning his [Prado's] disordered opinions" ("dejar de abominar sus desordenados dictámenes"; 130). The letter's real interest lies in its catalog of the many books on Christian theology Orobio read in Spain, leaving no doubt that regardless of whatever Jewish rites he practiced secretly, as a converso his literary formation was Christian in content. Some of these texts include Latin translations of the Bible by Xantes Pagnino and Benito Arias Montano; the *Fortalitium Fidei* (*Fortress of Faith*) of Alonso de Espina; and works of Paul of Burgos, St. Thomas Aquinas, John Calvin, and Martin Luther, among others.[23] Explaining his choice of texts and thoroughness reading them, he

---

22   "Apologetic" in the title of this letter should be understood not as an expression of regret, but more as a justification of the superiority of the law of God, in this case Judaism, to the law of nature, as expressed in deism.

23   The Italian Dominican Santes Pagnino (Pagnini) published *Veteris et Novi Testamenti nova translatio* in 1527, while the Spanish philologist Benito Arias Montano supervised the Antwerp Polyglot Bible of 1568–73. Alonso de Espina was a fifteenth-century Spanish Franciscan cleric of possible converso origin who authored the anti-Jewish *Fortalitium fidei*. Paul of Burgos, also known as Pablo de Santa María, like Espina a converso who became a Catholic theologian, authored the *Scrutinium Scripturarum*, a well-known anti-Jewish tract of 1400s Spain.

wrote, "the theological, scholastic works of Christians . . . I studied with all care, *ex professo* [as a profession], in order to know how the others believe and how I had to believe, and today I try to do the same with respect to our ancient teachers" ("las materias teológicas, escolásticas de los cristianos . . . estudié con todo cuidado, *ex professo*, para saber cómo creían los otros y saber cómo yo había de creer, y hoy procuro lo mismo en nuestros antiguos doctores"; 132). The letter also speaks of the difficulty of living as a Christian in Inquisitorial Spain during the seventeenth century: "I never feigned it well, and thus it was discovered that I was not but a Jew" (mas nunca lo fingí bien y así se descubrió que no era sino judío"; 133); and shows the author earned his bona fides as a polemicist based on interactions with scholars in Toulouse and Amsterdam (136).

Orobio then returns to the controversy with Prado, asserting that Prado cannot be saved in deism, since "whoever loves it [the divine Law], whoever believes it, whoever fears God . . . are the people of God, protected in so many ages with the highest providence, a wise and discreet people, even in the opinion of Gentiles, and wise according to the judgment of God himself" ("quien la ama, quien la cree, quien teme a Dios . . . son pueblo de Dios conservado por tantas edades con altísima providencia . . . pueblo sabio, pueblo discreto, aun en opinión de las gentes, y sabio por sentencia del mismo Dios"; 137). Toward the end of the letter, he recurs to his own heartfelt faith in order to convince his friend of the truth of Judaism. In words showing Orobio's spiritual constancy throughout his journey to Judaism, he writes, "I am a Jew, because since Abraham, Isaac, and Jacob, I am an Israelite . . . I keep the Law of God because [God] gave it to my parents at Sinai and my ancestors have kept it to this very day" ("yo soy judío, porque desde Abraham, Ishack y Jacob, yo soy israelita . . . Guardo la Ley de Dios porque la dio a mis padres en Sinaí y la han guardado mis ascendientes hasta este día"; 139–40). Given that, according to Orobio, God "will always receive the penitent sinner" ("siempre recibe al pecador arrepentido"), not just on Yom Kippur, Prado need not wait to cry out for God's mercy (140–41). Once again, Orobio evinces the conflict in which his friendship with Prado placed him and a desire to correct the latter's heretical views. Nevertheless, in a religious environment intolerant of dissent, Orobio privileges established doctrine over nonconformity; hence, while admitting the mutual affection between himself and Prado, he also writes, "but I cannot pay back your fondness with more precious coin than in repeated persuasions of the truth [of the divine Law]." ("mas no puedo satisfacerlos [los afectos] con más preciosa moneda que en repetidas persuasiones de la verdad"; 141).

As its title indicates, Orobio addressed "Carta al hijo del doctor Prado" ("Letter to Doctor Prado's son") to the latter's son, David de Prado, because conditions of the father's censure forbade direct communication with him. The letter consists of replies to Juan de Prado concerning the following three questions: the dissension of opinions among people whose souls are formed of the same material; the importance of free will in decision-making, regardless of the opinions of others; and the innocence of wrongdoers whose ignorance makes them unaware that they have strayed from "the true path" ("el verdadero camino"; 151). In his responses, Orobio addresses Prado's rejection of both Hebrew Scriptures and the divine law contained therein. First he treats what for him is the fallacy of Prado's claim that "no man is obligated to one religion more than to another, that the path to pleasing God is indifferent, and that, consequently, there is no divine Law, but only human reasons that each one holds divine" ("no está el hombre obligado a una religión más que a otra, que es indiferente el camino para agradar a Dios y que, consiguientemente, no hay Ley divina, sino medios humanos que cada uno tiene por divinos"; 147). Orobio is unable to accept the dangerous relativism underpinning this worldview, because doing so would repudiate Israel's elect status. He therefore explains to Prado why his friend should shun both Christianity and Islam: the first relies on blind faith without recourse to thought or reason, while in the Koran, Prado will not find cause for abandoning the Law given to the Jews at Sinai (148–49).

Orobio ends the letter by differentiating between those who err due to ignorance and those who err due to malice. An individual in the first category, whose ignorance leads to sin, will inhabit a type of limbo, neither saved nor condemned, whereas a transgressor in the second will incur punishment corresponding to the malicious act committed, because unlike the ignorant one, this person never showed a "good intention and true desire to serve God" ("buena intención y verdadero deseo de servir a Dios"; 152). While Orobio does not say directly to which, if any, category he believes Prado pertains, one would hope the first, but fear the second. Even without recourse to Prado's words themselves, Orobio's responses in these three aforementioned letters confirm the extent to which Prado represented a threat to the orthodoxy of a community built on strict observance of rabbinic tradition. Yet, some strands of Judaism today, especially those less bound to a literal reading of the Torah than the Portuguese-Jewish community of 1600s Amsterdam, would likely grant someone such as Prado the space to argue for a more secular identity, as well as for the legitimacy of other faiths, without impugning his own Jewish identity.

### La observancia de la divina ley de Mosseh

Jacobo Israel Garzón, a Spanish writer and proponent of Sephardic culture, issued in 1991 an edition of the second polemical work under consideration in this chapter, reproducing an edition prepared in 1925 at Coimbra, Portugal, by Moisés Bensabat Amzalak. Dating to approximately 1670, *La observancia de la divina ley de Mosseh* recounts Orobio's debate with a Huguenot theologian about such questions as the limits of original sin, the appearance and role of the Messiah as an agent of salvation, and the relationship between God and the Israelites. Orobio did not describe the circumstances or locale in which he wrote this response, although Yosef Kaplan states that he did so in Amsterdam after having surreptitiously received the polemic from his French adversary (*From Christianity to Judaism* 239–40).[24] Moreover, despite writing during a period of messianic fervor among diasporic Jewish communities, Orobio did not support Sabbatai Zevi (or Sevi), a Sephardic Jew from Smyrna (Izmir, Turkey) who, exploiting his kabbalistic knowledge and the hunger of Jews for redemption, in 1665 proclaimed himself the Messiah. In response to the renown that this claim brought him throughout the Ottoman Empire, within a year its leaders compelled Zevi to renounce his messiahship and convert to Islam, on pain of death. Perhaps in part for this reason, no reference to Sabbateanism appears in *La observancia de la divina ley de Mosseh* despite the work's treatment of salvation.

The antithetical ways in which the ex-converso recently returned to Judaism and the Huguenot preacher regard original sin and the role of the Messiah comprise the substance of *La observancia de la divina ley de Mosseh*. Orobio contrasts the worldview of his Protestant opponent, according to which the fall from grace represents the sins of all humanity that only the death of Christ on the cross can redeem, with a vision of humanity in which individual agency plays a more active role and God forgives sins without messianic intervention. Denying the depiction of Adam as personification of the sinful actions of future generations, Orobio states:

---

24  In the same place Kaplan also discusses the possibility that Orobio might have been in Toulouse when he first saw the treatise of his unnamed opponent, but that he must have authored a response from Amsterdam, due not only to the more tolerant environment of the Dutch city but also to references to it in the text. The complete title of the treatise is *Respuesta a un escrito que prezentó un predicante francés a el autor contra la observancia de la divina ley de Mosseh* (*Response to a Text that a French Preacher Presented to the Author against the Observance of the Divine Law of Moses*).

... the sin of Adam did not corrupt anybody other than Adam ... the children of Adam were not even in the world [at the time of his sin] and therefore they could not sin against God, and thus, as grace is not hereditary, disgrace cannot be inherited, if the children did not continue in the sins of Adam.

... el pecado de Adam no corrompió a otro que a Adam ... los hijos de Adam en el tiempo que él cometió el pecado, aun no estaban en el mundo y consiguientemente no pudieron pecar con Él, y así como la gracia no es hereditaria, la desgracia no se puede heredar, si los hijos no perseverasen en los pecados de

Adam. (Orobio, *La observancia* 2–3)

Orobio also rebuts the Huguenot preacher by describing God as a "most loving father" ("padre amantísimo") whose promise of redemption leaves the Christian vision of the Messiah irrelevant (74). Similar to a loving but firm parent, God does not turn a blind eye to the immoral conduct of children; however, given that the divine is a merciful entity, "if man shows contrition [for the offending behavior], divine justice will be satisfied and mercy will have its place" ("si tuviere contrición, será satisfecha la divina justicia, y tendrá su lugar la misericordia"; 23).

Orobio further represents the potential relationship between God and humanity in a manner that seems applicable to our times by saying, in effect, that God helps those who seek to help themselves through divine aid and repentance and punishes those who do not mend their ways (23). Repeatedly the polemicist counters the Huguenot preacher by asserting the everlasting character of the alliance between God and the Israelite people, regardless of whether the latter comport themselves poorly or well (83). Like a recalcitrant child whose parent nevertheless does not cease to love him or her, so "Israel always was deaf to the voices of its Lord God, but with all that, God says, God will have mercy on God's people" ("siempre estuvo sordo a las voces del Señor su Dios, mas con todo dice que tendrá misericordia de su pueblo"; 88). When Orobio states that Jews do not understand the death of the Christian Messiah because they do not think it necessary that Jesus die for the redemption of humanity, he expresses a view of God as an entity that creates a space for humans to participate more directly in their own redemption. He closes the work by leaving clear the privileged status of the Israelites because, when their redemption occurs, all will believe that God "fulfilled [God's] word to [God's] people" ("cumplió su palabra a su pueblo"; 98), who have been the "true Church" ("verdadera Iglesia") of God for more than three thousand years (101). Not only does Orobio assert the superiority of Judaism to Christianity here, but as a former New Christian living as a Jew, he also claims absolution for conversos previously forbidden to practice that religion in Iberian lands and now able to do so.

### *PREVENCIONES DIVINAS CONTRA LA VANA IDOLATRÍA DE LAS GENTES*

In 2013, the Italian scholar Myriam Silvera brought forth a critical edition of the first part of *Prevenciones divinas contra la vana idolatría de las gentes*, a work written in all probability between 1668 and 1675.[25] This text grew in part from what Gianni Paganini in his forward calls an "intersecting triangular focus" ("fuoco incrociato triangolare"; x) connecting Catholic, Jewish, and Calvinist cultures in a place where the writing of polemical, often anti-Christian, literature was possible, at least in manuscript form. In the prologue and subsequent twenty-nine chapters of the work, Orobio attacks Catholic Christianity and defends Judaism forcefully by, among other arguments, stating that the Torah warned the Jewish people against beliefs such as idol worship, the tripartite notion of the divine, incarnation, and the messiahship of Christ. Denial of this last claim was particularly important because secret and now formerly secret Jews such as Orobio "possessed an esoteric metaphysical key: they knew that the true way to salvation was not through Christ but through the Law of Moses" (Yovel, *Spinoza and Other Heretics* 19). These claims allowed Orobio to move from asserting the elect status of Judaism by negating the heterodoxy of Prado in the letters, to doing so here by deprecating Catholicism through his knowledge of the Hebrew Bible.

Orobio states the hypothesis of the work in its subtitle: *Prevenciones divinas* "proves" ("pruébase") that God forewarned the Jewish people in the Torah of "everything that would be invented in Christianity" ("que todo cuanto se había de inventar en el cristianismo"), so that, thus alerted, they would not accept "such defects" ("tales errores") in this invention (3). In the prologue, Orobio writes that the impetus for the work came from friends who asked him to publish his response to an unnamed "great authority" regarding the content of several debates that he (Orobio) had conducted with Carmelite friars. In these debates, forming the basis of *Prevenciones divinas*, Orobio, notwithstanding his perhaps disingenuous claim of "limited understanding" ("corto ingenio"), refutes what for him is the idolatry of Christi-

---

[25] The author reviewed this edition of *Prevenciones divinas* for *Sephardic Horizons* vol. 4, no. 3, 2014.

anity that the Carmelites, "well learned and taught in their Gentile theology" ("bien doctos e instruidos en su teología gentílica"), have described (14). One way to understand how Orobio contrasts differences between Judaism and Christianity throughout the text is by organizing them into the following categories: explanation of the chosen status of Israel concomitant with the responsibility of the Jewish people to follow the teachings of Torah; criticisms of the fundamental beliefs of Christianity; and praise of the otherness of Judaism as a means of maintaining its separate identity.

In the prologue, Orobio emphasizes the covenantal obligation of Jews to adhere to the Torah while also affirming Israel's stature as a protected people. Thus, he reminds his reader, Moses told the Jewish people at the end of Deuteronomy that although disregard of divine law may cause Israel "to be destroyed and scattered, it will never be forgotten nor abandoned, but preserved until its ultimate return ("mas aunque sea esparcido, nunca será olvidado, ni abandonado, sino conservado hasta su última restitución"; 14). However, at the same time as he emphasizes the elect status of Israel in its diaspora, Orobio also laments the ongoing reality of conversions from Judaism to Christianity. So common, in his view, is the allure of this idolatry that "almost the majority of Gentiles have Jewish blood of those who, failing to keep the divine Law, submerged themselves in the waters of Christian baptism" ("casi las más gentiles tienen sangre judaica de los que, prevaricando la Ley divina, se sumergieron en las aguas del cristiano baptismo"; 17). Notwithstanding their anti-Christian bias, these words describe in part Orobio's life, given his efforts to disregard his own baptism, first by adhering to Judaism secretly in Spain and then by embracing this belief system openly in Amsterdam.

*Prevenciones divinas* repeatedly disparages Catholic Christianity for its insistence on a Trinitarian understanding of God. Citing in the prologue the declaration of God's oneness central to Judaism, "Hear, Israel, the Lord [is] your God, God is one" (from Dt. 6.4), Orobio scorns Christianity for its "tripartite representation of persons" ("triplicidad de personas") that he says results in "the immense Deity and its vastness reduced to the narrow and wretched terms of humanity" ("la inmensa Deidad y su infinitud reducida a los estrechos y miserables términos de la humanidad"; 15).[26] Further he claims in chapter 1 that Christianity consists of "three Gods" ("tres Dioses"), not one represented in three distinct ways (21–22). The polemicist argues that God made "this abhorrent error" ("este abominable error") known so

---

26  Citations of the Hebrew Bible throughout the book are from *The Jewish Study Bible*.

that Israel would "cast from itself such a perverse and detestable philosophy ("arrojar de sí tan perversa y destable filosofía"; 22). Consequently, Orobio interprets God's command that Moses make clear among his people the central tenet, "I am who I am" (Ex. 3.14) to mean "I am, and so absolute and independent is my being, that there is properly no other being than I, because all that [there] is depends on me, and my being depends on no [one] thing" ("yo soy, y tan absoluto e independiente es mi ser, que no hay otro ser proprio más que Yo, porque cuanto es depende de mí, y mi ser de cosa ninguna"; 22). Orobio writes with great prolixity on this theme because for him it suggests that the son depends for his existence on the father and that therefore, in the case of Christ, he cannot be divine.

Besides censuring its Trinitarian character, Orobio condemns other pillars of Christian belief throughout the work. He rejects the incarnation of God, asserting in chapter 2 that not even Moses, "the most holy, the most pure of all men" ("el más santo, el más puro de los hombres"; 26), could see God with his own eyes; and argues in chapter 5 against the doctrine of original sin, saying that this concept is the root of making innocent children pay for the transgressions of their parents (35). Subsequently, in chapter 19 he elaborates this argument by asserting that God punished but did not abandon Israel for sins of idolatry and disobedience, given that "no Jew today suffers any particular punishment for the sins of his ancestors, [because] that would be against divine justice, [and] each one is judged by God according to his deeds" ("ningún judío padece hoy alguna particular pena por los pecados de sus ascendientes, que eso fuera contra la rectitud divina, cada uno es juzgado de Dios conforme sus obras"; 118). Although not exclusive to conversos alone, this privileging of actions over lineage defined the worldview of many Iberian New Christians, for whom baptism did not erase the stigma of Jewish, and hence impure, lineage.[27]

---

27   So widespread was this stigma that even Old Christians in Spain apparently were aware of it. In both parts of *Don Quixote*, published in 1605 and 1615, Cervantes mocks this societal preoccupation with lineage through the character of Sancho Panza, Don Quixote's squire, by depicting him as a simpleton who equates being an Old Christian with being a good Christian and "a mortal enemy of the Jews." (2.8.505; when citing *Don Quixote* in this book, I quote the translation by Edith Grossman). Several times throughout the text, Sancho asserts this Old Christian identity, as for example when he says it qualifies him to be a count, in marked contrast to Don Quixote himself, who is conspicuously silent regarding his own lineage (1.21.161).

Orobio grounds much of his argument on what he calls in chapter 12 the "divine Law" of the Torah. The words of Torah, in the form in which they are written, obviate the need for the "hollow mysteries" ("vanos misterios") and "affected interpretations" (sofísticas interpretaciones") that he faults Paul and the followers of Paul of associating with the holy text (72). Additionally, just as Christian thought claims that Christ as Messiah will redeem Israel, so Orobio in chapter 22 argues for the impossibility of this claim, pointing out that the Messiah is an "irrelevant being" ("cosa impertinente") in light of the dispersion of Jews, whose observance of the Law does not depend on the Messiah (135). He further claims that only by removing "all evil inclination" ("toda mala inclinación") from their hearts and loving God in a pure way will Jews achieve such redemption, both spiritual and corporal (138); at this time God will gather them from throughout the diaspora into the land of Israel (139). Throughout these and other examples, Orobio tries to show the privileged position of Israel in the eyes of God by contrasting it with Christian teachings and by marginalizing the role of Christ.

Observance of the divine law is perhaps the most omnipresent manner that Orobio uses to confront what he regards as the idolatry of Christianity, because such obedience clearly differentiates the two faiths: "Gentiles say that God cast us out because we keep the precepts of the obedience to the Law, while God tells us that God will cast us out if we do not keep them" ("Las gentes dicen que por eso nos arrojó Dios, porque guardamos los preceptos de la Ley, y Dios nos dice que nos arrojará si no los guardamos"; 81–82). Subsequently Orobio uses the concept of a wanderer to further emphasize this dichotomy, stating that for Christians, Jews will always be "wretched wanderers" ("míseros peregrinos"), in the sense of outcasts, for not abandoning the law; while Jews think that by keeping the law their wandering will cease (88). Thus, adherence to the Torah is the most important command that Israel must fulfill in order to maintain the opposition to Christianity that, for Orobio, legitimizes Judaism in the eyes of God.

Not only does *Prevenciones divinas* declare the superiority of Israel to Christianity, but it also uses criticisms of the latter religion unthinkable were Orobio to have written them from Iberia. Thus, in the prologue, he attacks Christianity for attempting to imprison God, whose enormity exceeds heaven and earth, "into the short and foul womb of a woman" ("en el corto e inmundo vientre de una mujer"; 15). Subsequently, in chapter 6 he claims that the "false doctrines" ("falsas doctrinas") of Christianity derive from its founding by "ordinary men... from the dirtiest and lowest dregs of the republic[:] fishermen, moneylenders or publicans [rent collectors], and women of known and public unchastity and scandalous life" (" hombres vulgares . . . de la más sucia y baja escoria de la república, pescadores, oficiales, logreros o publicanos, mujeres . . . de conocida y pública deshonestidad y vida escandalosa"; 42). Orobio further inveighs against Christianity in chapter 23 for the hypocrisy with which its "ancient philosophers . . . made a great show of disdaining temporal goods" ("los antiguos filósofos de las gentes . . . hicieron grande ostentación de despreciar los bienes temporales") and of insisting on the saintliness of a life of poverty and want; instead, he claims that God rewards the bounty of the earth to a people who work assiduously and keep the divine law (145). These bold aspersions indicate Orobio's ability to use the knowledge of the religion in which he was raised as a weapon against it once he lived an openly Jewish life.

Besides fulminating against Christianity, Orobio attempts to delegitimize the figure of Christ himself. In chapter 9, he refers to the latter as "That Man" ("Aquel Hombre"; 52) and then accuses him "of wanting to show himself more devout than the extreme devotion of his Maker" ("quiso . . . mostrarse más piadoso que la suma piedad de su Hacedor"; 55). According to this reasoning, such an effort on the part of Christ justified his death, because he had tried to make himself as revered as God. Orobio in chapter 15 then denies the messianic role of Christ as bearer of divine law by stating that "the Law is not in heaven but [rather in] us" ("la Ley ya no está en los cielos sino en nosotros"; 93). Having made this claim, Orobio challenges the authority of Christ evident in the feast of Pentecost, as narrated in Acts 2, according to which Christians believe that the Holy Spirit descended on his disciples fifty days after the crucifixion. For Orobio, Christianity "must have invented [this story about . . . ] That Man" ("había de fingir que Aquel Hombre . . ."), the "false prophets" ("falsos profetas") on whom his spirit descended, and the "feigned mysteries" ("fingidos misterios") by which this descent transmitted "the intelligence of the Law" ("la inteligencia de la Ley"; 93–94). Through statements such as these, Orobio creates a space for showing how God privileged and punished the Jewish people without regard to the divinity of Christ.

Orobio further criticizes Christianity by asserting that the latter faith has usurped and corrupted central tenets of Judaism, including observance of the Sabbath, circumcision, the words of Torah, and even the name and significance of Israel itself. In chapter 11 he contrasts the original Jewish understanding of the Sabbath as a day of both rest and recognition by humans of God's work of creation during the previous six days with an attempt by Christian theologians—he mentions John Calvin—to "show that the sacred Sabbath was a symbol of their resuscitated God" ("y así enseñarían que el santo Sabat era símbolo de su Dios resucitado"; 62). He then states that God wished the observance of the Sabbath to sanctify "not a dead man, but a living God who knew how to and did create the heavens when he wished ... [which] in their hatred of Judaism Gentiles do not admit." ("no a un hombre muerto, sino a un Dios vivo que supo y pudo criar los cielos cuando quiso ... que en el odio del judaísmo no admiten las gentes"; 63). Likewise, Orobio criticized Christianity for appropriating circumcision as a symbol of baptism, even though Genesis 17 states clearly that this ritual represents an everlasting covenant between God and the Jewish people whose purpose is to "differentiate Israel from Gentiles" ("para diferenciar a Israel de todas ellas [las gentes]"; 65).

A third means by which Orobio distinguishes Judaism from Christianity is to contend that Judaism may preserve itself due not only to its actions but also its separate identity. Thus, he claims in chapter 19 that the "hatred" ("odio") and "universal disdain" ("universal desprecio") of the Jewish people maintain their distinction and safeguard their rites (120). Orobio reasons that this disdain is understandable, given that non-Jews regard Jews as practicing a religion that consists in "doing everything possible to be detested" ("hacer todo cuanto basta para ser aborrecidos"; 120), such as accusing both the Messiah and Muhammad of being "false prophets and seducers of the nations" ("falsos profetas y seductores de las naciones"; 120). He further affirms in chapter 26 that such opprobrium and outright persecution have the benefit of shining a light on the centuries-long "constant perseverance" ("perseverar constante") of the Jewish people, "loving more to be loathsome to Gentiles than to stop being worthy of God's love" ("amando más ser abominable a las gentes que dejar de ser amable al Señor Dios"; 164). The polemicist states that were this disdain of Jews not to exist, they would intermingle with Gentiles and hence, "we would not be persecuted more, nor [be] the people of God, separate and chosen" ("ya no seríamos más perseguidos, ni pueblo de Dios, separado y elegido"; 164). He also emphasizes that despite "this ill-fated calamity ... that Israel has suffered and suffers ... [for worshipping] idols of stick and rock" ("esta infausta calamidad que padeció y padece Israel ... [por adorar] dioses de palo y piedra"; 166), God has stood by the Jewish people, as evidenced by the "eternal love and the unending right of Israel to call itself God's people" ("su eterno amor y el derecho perpetuo de Israel a llamarse suyo"; 166).[28]

---

28  In the same place Orobio also appears to refer to secret Jews among Iberian New Christians who "continue that wretched state [of idolatry] in outward

This message of divine favor of Israel carries over to the end of the first part of *Prevenciones divinas*, where the polemicist asserts that God will reciprocate human love, "which is the greatest reward to which our merit could aspire" ("que es el mayor premio a que podía aspirar nuestro merecimiento"; 186). Rather than loving God for the sake of attaining eternal glory, which Orobio calls a love of expedience, "we [should feel] rewarded only for having pleased God, without hope or wish of a greater reward" ("quedando nosotros premiados con solo haberle agradado, sin pasar a la esperanza ni deseo de mejor premio"; 195). In turn, he suggests that the greatest sign of God's love for humanity is the implicit expectation that Israel trust in the existence of such love, despite the invisibility of the divine (197). Thus, Orobio leaves no doubt that love for God must be unconditional, without ulterior motive, and rooted in the Hebrew Bible.

## Conclusion: The Unimpeachable Orthodoxy of Orobio—and the Dawn of Another Way

Orobio's letters to Prado as well as his longer polemics illumine the worldview of a former New Christian who established a Jewish identity by believing that the religion he could now practice openly was "all true, all holy, [and] all divine" (Révah, *Spinoza* 90). These works testify to Orobio's intense faith at a time when the Iberian Jewish community of Amsterdam had reached its apogee during the second half of the seventeenth century. At the same time, the letters contrast the orthodoxy of this community with the views of another New Christian who, unlike Orobio, found that the strict interpretation of Judaism there did not liberate, but rather marginalized him. Yet such marginalization achieved an unanticipated result, as Prado "unwittingly confronted his people with an issue they were unprepared to grapple with—namely, the possibility of nonorthodox Judaism" (Yovel, *Spinoza and Other Heretics* 70).

Not surprisingly, then, in response to this threat as well as those that his other adversaries represented, Orobio evinced a faith unimpeachable for its foundation in Jewish law. Ironically, the roots of this orthodoxy lay in Iberia, where Orobio's upbringing as a reluctant Catholic and secret Jew planted within him a hunger for an authentic and open Jewish life. Likewise, the fact that he spent more than half his life in Catholic lands imbued Orobio with a

---

acts" ("siguen ese miserable estado en los actos exteriores") and who, "purged [in the sense of punished] with the severity of the Inquisition, look for the center of divine Law through their punishment" ("los rigores de la Inquisición, buscan el centro de la divina Ley a fuerza del castigo"; 166), presumably at the hands of the Inquisition.

knowledge of the tenets of his opponents that would not have been possible had he grown up in a setting tolerant of Judaism. A further irony is the extent to which his history as a threat to a dominant ideology earlier in life directly affected how Orobio interacted with Prado in Amsterdam, but in reverse. Just as Inquisitorial Spain was unable to tolerate Orobio's crypto-Judaism, so the community he spoke for in Amsterdam could not reconcile the deism of Prado to its traditional, Torah-based understanding of Judaism. Finally, this idea of history reversed is visible in the way in which Orobio defended Judaism in the longer polemics by depicting a faith that in Iberia was heretical as one that, in Holland, brought its followers closer to God than he believed Christianity was able to do.

# 2
# "May Your Holy Inspiration Call Me in the Desert": New Jewish and Baroque Identity in the Poetry of João Pinto Delgado

THE POETRY OF JOÃO Pinto Delgado adopted conventions of Baroque Spanish literature to express an otherwise marginalized viewpoint: that of a Portuguese New Christian demonstrating in Spanish a Jewish identity, albeit outside the Iberian Peninsula. This chapter studies the influence of the Spanish Golden Age of the Renaissance and Baroque eras on the collection of poems that he published in Rouen, France, in 1627 to show how these works create a space in Spanish poetics for a "New Jewish," or heretofore hidden, Jewish voice. By analyzing the two longest of these texts, *Poema de la Reina Ester* (*Poem of Queen Esther*) and *Lamentaciones del Profeta Jeremías* (*Lamentations of the Prophet Jeremiah*) as well as the shorter *Canción, aplicando misericordias divinas y defetos proprios a la salida de Egipto hasta la Tierra Santa* (*Song Applying Divine Compassion and Its Own Imperfections to the Flight from Egypt to the Holy Land*), this chapter explores how Pinto Delgado communicated a Jewish perspective, regardless of his ability to live openly as a Jew. Additionally, by comparing his poetry with works of Jorge Manrique, Fray Luis de León, and Luis de Góngora, the chapter proposes that this Jewish perspective did not prevent Pinto Delgado from expressing a recognizably Spanish literary one. This ability of the poet to bridge the Jewish and Spanish-Portuguese elements of his background, despite the expulsion and forced conversion of Iberian Jewry in the late 1400s, testifies to what David Wacks has called "double diaspora" (3), by which Sephardic

Jews traced their roots to a first diaspora from the Holy Land in biblical and Roman times, and after the 1490s to a diaspora from Spain and Portugal.[1]

## A Return to Judaism among Portuguese Former New Christians beyond Portugal

Born in the early 1580s in Vila Nova de Portimão, a small town in the Algarve region of southern Portugal, João Pinto Delgado belonged to a family of descendants of Jews whom King Manoel had forcibly converted in 1497. He bore the same name as his paternal grandfather, who likewise was a poet, although never of the same renown. The younger João was the eldest of three sons born to Gonçalo Delgado and Agnes Munez, New Christians whose travel to and from northern Europe in some ways typified the living patterns of Sephardim post-1492. Thus, after marrying in Antwerp, in the Catholic Spanish Netherlands, Gonçalo and Agnes came back to Vila Nova de Portimão, where they had their children; they then moved to Lisbon with the younger two children, Diego Pinto and Gonçalo Delgado II. From Lisbon they returned to Antwerp before settling in Rouen in approximately 1609. After completing his intellectual formation in Lisbon, João traveled to Rouen in 1624–26, where, like other Portuguese New Christians, he worked in commerce. It was also in Rouen where João and his father became leaders of the small but visible community of crypto-Jews.

This community was one branch of a diaspora of Portuguese conversos that established itself throughout Western Europe in the two centuries post-1492. In port cities of this region, *converso* families such as that of Pinto Delgado demonstrated varying levels of a hybrid religious identity, depending on the extent of tolerance that the host Christian culture afforded them. Due to a crisis, in which one group of presumed sincere New Christians in Rouen—converts who were faithful to Catholicism—accused another group of living as secret Jews, which brought scrutiny from Inquisition officials in Spain, the Delgado-Munez family moved again, this time to Antwerp. João remained there after obtaining a certificate of Catholic orthodoxy from a priest in Rouen, perhaps through a bribe. Investigation of this orthodoxy by an ecclesiastical tribunal in Rouen continued despite the poet's absence, which most likely prompted his final move, to Amsterdam, in 1634. In the robust community of Iberian New Christians turned New Jews in that city,

---

[1] Wacks does not mention Pinto Delgado in his case studies of Sephardic authors from the 1200s to the 1500s. However, I believe that the conditions in which Pinto Delgado lived and wrote exemplify many of the criteria that situate these writers within a "double diaspora."

João joined other *conversos* in a complete rejudaization by changing his name to Mosseh and evidently serving as a *parnas*, or communal leader, before his death in 1653. Such a process of return existed in large part due to Saul Levi Morteira (1590s-1660), a Venetian Jew of Ashkenazic and possible Sephardic origin who, as chief rabbi of Talmud Torah, the community that joined the three formerly distinct Sephardic communities of Amsterdam, "regularly expressed in his sermons his zeal for the rejudaization of his congregants" (G. Kaplan, *Arguments against the Christian Religion* 31).[2]

*Poema de la Reina Ester*
*Poema de la Reina Ester*, the first of the poems in the collection published at Rouen in 1627, shows the influence of Spanish Baroque literary style as well as the perspective of Pinto Delgado as a convert of Jewish origin on a text that closely follows its biblical antecedent. The poem represents Esther as a secret Jew who, urged by her foster father Mordecai, heroically saves the Jews of Persia by revealing to her husband, King Ahasuerus, a plot by his minister, Haman, to have them all murdered. Despite being fictitious as a work of history, the Esther story resonated deeply with Iberian New Christians after 1492 by exalting a symbolic forebear in the Hebrew Bible who at great risk to herself defended Jewish identity. In his treatment of this story, Pinto Delgado situates himself firmly within the Spanish literary Golden Age of the 1600s by ennobling Esther using the idealized code of female beauty of that time. He also describes both Esther and Haman using language similar to that in works of his more famous contemporaries: Fray Luis de León, Garcilaso de la Vega, and Luis de Góngora. Likewise, Pinto Delgado's choice to write *Ester* and the other works in the collection in Spanish despite being a Portuguese living in France testifies to the esteem of this language during the Renaissance and Baroque eras, also perhaps indicating pride in his Iberian New Christian origin.[3]

---

2   The sources of this biographical description are Révah, "Autiobiographie d'un Marrane"; Roth, "João Pinto Delgado: A Literary Disentanglement"; and Oelman 49–52. Miguel de Barrios confirmed the presence of Pinto Delgado in Amsterdam by mentioning in his *Relación de los poetas* of 1683 Mosseh Pinto Delgado, author of poems treating Esther and the Lamentations of Jeremiah. Oelman claims that Pinto Delgado was a *parnas* (51). See G. Kaplan, *Arguments against the Christian Religion* 17–35, for a biography of Morteira and further discussion of how he participated in the rejudaization of Iberian conversos in Amsterdam.

3   Describing the case of Morteira in Venice and Amsterdam, Gregory Kaplan provides further context regarding the use of Spanish as a language of commerce and culture outside Spain and Portugal during the 1500s–1600s (*Arguments against*

As a New Christian whose family was prosecuted for Jewish heresy by the Portuguese Inquisition, Pinto Delgado also expresses through *Ester* the divine redemption of biblical Jews that validates the crypto-Jewish identity of conversos. If one sees Pinto Delgado viewing the world through the lens of double diaspora that Wacks describes, it is possible that in *Ester* the poet, a Portuguese converso sympathizing in Spanish with a Jewish heroine, "gives voice to a diasporic imaginary, a way of interpreting the world that is conditioned by [his] experiences of living in diaspora and by rabbinic, poetic, historiographical traditions of *galut* [exile] and *ge'ulah* [redemption; both Hebrew terms]" (Wacks 31). Themes of exile and redemption also underlie the messages of the other poems this chapter studies, showing the extent to which Pinto Delgado recurs to the presence of these themes in the Hebrew Bible as a way of understanding his geographic and literary displacement.

The Book of Esther is one of five *Megillot* (Scrolls) found in *Kethuvim* (Writings), the last broad section of the Hebrew Bible after the Torah and Prophets; the others are Song of Songs, Ruth, Lamentations, and Ecclesiastes. A short text consisting of ten chapters likely written in 400–300 BCE, Esther forms the basis of the celebratory holiday of Purim, the festival of lots, on which it is read twice. As Adele Berlin notes in her introduction to Esther in *The Jewish Study Bible*, Purim is the only biblical festival not alluded to in the Torah; likewise, it does not mention God or traditional Jewish religious customs such as prayer and culinary customs (1619–20). Despite or perhaps due in part to these anomalies, as well as its themes of hidden identity, existential threat, and ultimate redemption, Esther recounts a story that resonated strongly with Iberian New Christians of Jewish origin post-1492, in Spain, Portugal, and beyond. Given that Pinto Delgado's text follows closely the biblical antecedent, a summary of its main events is a useful starting point for an analysis of the innovations in his poem.

The book opens with the banishment of Queen Vashti, wife of Ahasuerus (perhaps a comical representation of Xerxes), king of Persia, for disobeying him by refusing to appear at a royal banquet and display her beauty in front of other guests. Lest Ahasuerus revoke this order, his attendants hastily scour the kingdom for "beautiful young virgins" so that the most appealing

---

*the Christian Religion* 22). Likewise, the tendency of Sephardim in Amsterdam to produce literary works in Spanish, in no small way a language of oppression, should not surprise us, given that "living in Calvinist Amsterdam, they [the emigres] were more conspicuously Iberian than ever before. This was a source of pride and an important component of their developing sense of collective self" (Bodian, *Hebrews of the Portuguese Nation* 18).

one may become his new queen. (2.1–4). The chosen maiden is of course Esther, an orphan and apparently assimilated Jew, whom her relative Mordecai—a palace guard of known Jewish identity in the service of the king—has adopted. Meanwhile, Haman, Ahasuerus's ambitious minister, is promoted by the king to chief minister. When Mordecai refuses Haman's order that all courtiers bow before him, Haman schemes to murder the Jews in Persia. Haman even offers the king a large payment as a bribe in order to obtain permission for the nefarious act he has planned. Accepting these terms rather passively, Ahasuerus authorizes the decree of destruction, to happen on a date that Haman determines by the casting of lots: the thirteenth day of the month of Adar (hence the name *Purim* in Hebrew, or "lots").

Mordecai impresses upon Esther that she must tell her husband of the impending doom of the Jews. The feckless Ahasuerus is unaware that not only does the edict that he just authorized include his own wife, but also that recently Mordecai has saved him from an assassination plot. Esther gains entry to the inner court of her husband in a series of banquets with Haman and reveals her Jewish identity by beseeching Ahasuerus to save her and her people from his evil minister. Livid with anger, the king executes Haman and displays his body on the very structure that Haman had constructed for murdering Mordecai. Esther again appears before her husband, imploring him to overturn Haman's order; although an edict once promulgated cannot be overturned, the king grants authority to Mordecai to communicate to Jews throughout the realm their right to attack those who would have killed them. The positive outcome of this story, in which "the Jews enjoyed light and gladness, happiness and honor" (8.16), served as a beacon to New Christians of the 1600s, who, throughout their diaspora, faced societal resentment and, in some cases, Inquisitorial investigation of their Catholic sincerity.

Written in hendecasyllabic verse common to the Baroque era, *Poema de la Reina Ester* consists of nine cantos of approximately 200 lines each, organized in sextets with an ABABCC rhyme scheme, and representative of corresponding chapters in the biblical text. The following analysis situates the work within the Spanish Golden Age literary tradition through three examples that show how it praises a life free from the encumbrance of power, idealizes female beauty, and censures imperiousness and pride in ways similar to those of canonical authors of the time. In the first such example, Pinto Delgado contrasts Ahasuerus's power and the ornamentation of his life at court with praise for the free will of humble subjects that indirectly harkens to the "Vida retirada" ("Solitary Life") ode in which Fray Luis de Leon celebrates the simplicity of country life in opposition to courtly vanity.

Despite obvious differences in the respective contexts of these two works, both describe the limits of power as a means of fulfillment. Thus, in the second canto, suddenly feeling alone after impetuously banishing Vashti and before his courtiers scour the kingdom for a replacement, the king laments, "What does subjecting the world low to my strength / matter (he says), [and] accumulating gold, / if I feel sad and, wounded, shed tears for / the deep sorrow of my profound love?" ("¿Qué importa [dice], acumulando el oro, / rendir humilde a mi valor el mundo, / si triste siento y lastimado lloro / la pena grave de mi amor profundo?"; 16).[4] While Pinto Delgado may mock Ahasuerus by ascribing to him words of a more reflective individual, this rare moment of awareness on the part of the king shows how an otherwise ignorant ruler recognizes the hollowness of amassing wealth and subduing others.

In contrast to the vanity of a powerful but self-pitying ruler, Pinto Delgado, speaking through the voice of Ahasuerus, praises an individual of modest means not bound by strictures of court, but rather as fully in possession of free will:

> Fortunate he who, humble in a free condition,
> does not suffer oppression of violent control.
> His execution itself is his care,
> and desire is subject to his free will,
> nor stops him, among his glory, the restraint
> of fierce stubbornness of another's pleasure.
>
> Dichoso aquél que, humilde en libre estado,
> no le oprime violento señorío,
> su misma ejecución es su cuidado,
> y el deseo sujeto a su albedrío,
> ni le detiene, entre su gloria, el freno
> de fiera obstinación de gusto ajeno. (17)[5]

---

4  All citations of poems by Pinto Delgado in this chapter are from the edition by Révah, which in most instances modernizes the spelling from the work of 1627. I also consulted a facsimile edition of the original text contained in a subsequently inaccessible Nabu Public Domain Reprint. See Slavitt for a lyrical but nonliteral translation of *Poema de la Reina Ester*, and Oelman for translations of fragments of this and other works of Pinto Delgado.

5  Zepp writes that this strophe is particularly important because its expression of free will is a principal theme of Pinto Delgado's representation of the book of Esther (123).

This lament for a freedom to act of one's own volition that eludes the all-powerful king shows how Ahasuerus recognizes, at least in this moment, the inability of royal power to grant personal contentment that he has forsaken by ousting Vashti. Additionally, perhaps this rare moment of introspection leads the king to consider the comparative good fortune of his humble subjects in terms of their free will, thus leading him to respond to the subsequent entreaties of Mordecai and Esther. Praise of the exercise of free will in an unadorned setting links the words of Ahasuerus with those of the first-person speaker of the first ode of Fray Luis, "Vida retirada," who describes a joyful flight from the ostentation of court to a *locus amoenus* free of the distracting company of others:

> What a restful life,
> that of the one who flees worldly noise,
> and follows the hidden
> path, on which have gone
> the few wise men who have been in the world.
> . . . . . . . . . . . . . . . . .
> I want to live by myself;
> I want to enjoy the good things that I owe to heaven,
> alone, without witness,
> free from love, from jealousy,
> from hatred, from hopes, from suspicion.
>
> ¡Qué descansada vida
> la del que huye el mundanal ruido,
> y sigue la escondida
> senda, por donde han ido
> los pocos sabios que en el mundo han sido.
> . . . . . . . . . . . . . . . . .
> Vivir quiero conmigo;
> gozar quiero del bien que debo al cielo,
> a solas, sin testigo,
> libre de amor, de celo,
> de odio, de esperanzas, de recelo.
>                     (McCaw and Thornton Spinnenweber 64, 66)[6]

---

6   For this and other translations of Golden Age poets, I consulted the prose translations of corresponding poems by Rivers and the notes by McCaw and Thornton Spinnenweber. For example, I translated "conmigo" as "by myself," following Rivers; and "bien" as "good things," following McCaw and Thornton Spinnenweber.

In a setting of admittedly idealized beauty, the narrator disdains wealth, false appearances, gossip, and preoccupations about lineage that contribute to a shallow and soulless existence. Instead, life in the country is infinitely richer due to unpretentiousness, purity, and immersion in the wealth of the natural world.

Regardless of possible familiarity with the works of Fray Luis—circulating in manuscript at the time he was writing—Pinto Delgado shows in the *Ester* poem the importance of individual choice that "Vida retirada" also celebrates, especially when such choice resists ills of court, such as false appearances, self-aggrandizement, and unbridled ambition. Thus, if Haman personifies a courtier whom the excesses of his surroundings have corrupted, Mordecai and Esther stand, literally, as symbols of free will and decency. Mordecai refuses to bow to Haman (31), while Esther, appearing before her husband, compares the evil minister with biblical Egyptians and begs God to hinder his murderous conspiracy against the Jews, just as God thwarted Pharaoh (81).[7]

In the second example linking *Poema de la Reina Ester* with contemporaneous works, Pinto Delgado describes Esther when she first enters Ahasuerus's court in the second canto, using the idealized code of feminine beauty characteristic of Spanish Golden Age poetry. In so doing, he follows a tradition dating to Petrarch and evident in, among others, Garcilaso de la Vega and Luis de Góngora—in whose poems teeth are pearls, lips are rubies, hair is golden threads of sunlight, the neck is alabaster, and hands are snow—as the following sonnet of the latter poet shows:

Now kissing crystalline hands,
now joining myself to a white and smooth neck,
now spreading over it [the neck] that hair
which Love extracted from the gold of his mines,
now breaking into those smooth pearls
sweet words without deserving it,

---

7 Their respective experiences with the Iberian Inquisition suggest that both writers valued individual will and free choice. Fray Luis de León spent nearly five years in an Inquisitorial jail for heresies he supposedly shared with students at the University of Salamanca, although in his ode 23, "A la salida de la cárcel" ("On Leaving Prison"), he blamed the ordeal on "envy and lies" ("la envidia y mentira"; McCaw and Thornton Spinnenweber 77). João Pinto Delgado left Rouen for Antwerp when an inquisitor arrived in the French city to investigate the Catholic sincerity of the Portuguese New Christian community there.

now picking from each beautiful lip
purple roses without fear of thorns,
was I, oh transparent jealous sun,
when your light, wounding my eyes,
killed my glory and finished off my luck.
If heaven now is not less powerful,
so that your rays do not produce more anger,
may they cause your death, like your son's.

    Ya besando unas manos cristalinas,
ya anudándome a un blanco y liso cuello,
ya esparciendo por él aquel cabello
que Amor sacó entre el oro de sus minas,
    ya quebrando en aquellas perlas finas
palabras dulces sin merecello,
ya cogiendo de cada labio bello
purpúreas rosas sin temor de espinas,
    estaba, oh claro sol invidioso,
cuando tu luz, hiriéndome los ojos,
mató mi gloria y acabó mi suerte.
    Si el cielo ya no es menos poderoso,
porque no den los tuyos más enojos,
rayos, como a tu hijo, te den muerte. (Blecua 2: 46–47)[8]

Likewise, Pinto Delgado uses similar imagery, stretched over a series of strophes that describe Esther while the courtiers of Ahasuerus prepare her for presentation to the king. The poet starts by comparing Esther to heavenly bodies, saying her soul is the sun and her beauty a star, and then notes that her eyes, "divine signal of inner piety" ("de piedad interior divino indicio"), are turned towards heaven "in fervent prayer" ("en ardiente oración"; 19). Next, he compares her lips to a sweet rose by saying they represent the flower's vivid color, and that in turn through their smile they show her teeth as pearls. Pinto Delgado continues the panegyric by describing Esther's cheeks and the wave-

---

    8    The "son of the sun" refers to Phaethon, who in Greek mythology loses control of the chariot of his father, Helios, the god of the sun, prompting fires in the heavens and on Earth and leading Zeus to strike him with a thunderbolt (see Ovid, *Metamorphoses* 47–63, bk. 2, lines 19–329). For an additional example of feminine beauty described according to Golden Age poetics, see sonnet 23 of Garcilaso de la Vega, "En tanto que de rosa y azucena" ("As long as rose and lily").

like gold of her braided hair (20), going so far as to suggest a divine role in the creation of such beauty: "[her hair] is an ornament of a singular miracle, / where the supreme painter of the world and heaven / made clear for us a model of her power" ("es ornamento del milagro estraño, / donde el sumo pintor del mundo y cielo / de su poder nos decifró un modelo"; 20). While the biblical Esther was "shapely and beautiful" (2.7) and even more attractive after a year spent applying oil of myrrh, perfumes, and cosmetics in preparation for her night with Ahasuerus, little else is known of her appearance. Those tantalizing details, however, provided Pinto Delgado sufficient license with which to embellish her beauty according to contemporary literary standards.

From the moment she appears in his court, an idealized virtue of character complements the beauty of Esther as a prerequisite for the privileged position to which Ahasuerus elevates her. Pinto Delgado creates images of serenity and equanimity to communicate the virtuous character of the queen-to-be: "No cruel envy, which afflicts her master, / spreads its poison in her breast" ("No la envidia cruel, que al dueño aflige, / dentro en su pecho esparce su veneno"; 24); "Neither ambition, nor unjust pride / change the high intent" ("No la ambición, ni la soberbia injusta, / en su mudanza, muda el alto intento"; 25); and "A calm sea, where the winds do not stir up / the smallest wave in their furor, / is her interior" ("Un mar tranquilo, donde no conmueven / la menor onda en su furor los vientos, / es su interior"; 25). In contrast to this description of Esther stands the self-importance of Haman, described in canto 3. An insecure social climber, Haman accumulates great power and a false sense of invincibility as the king's second-in-command, in part due to the passivity of the monarch. Haman rises quickly because he experiences little impediment from those around him, as the following description of his new power confirms:

Servants of the king, obeying, bend
(fierce command) their knee to the ground,
who, blind in their deceit, do not imagine
that they give to the man [Haman] what they owe to heaven:
and if that which is apparent forces desire,
time is a staff that punishes their error.

Siervos del rey, obedeciendo, inclinan
(fiero precepto) su rodilla al suelo,
que entre su engaño, ciegos, no imaginan
que al hombre dan lo que se debe al cielo:

y si el deseo lo aparente lo obliga,
el tiempo es vara, que su error castiga. (30)

The only individual who refuses to offer subservience is Ahasuerus's guard Mordecai, a fact that establishes a dichotomy between a Jewish servant loyal to God and king and an evil courtier who would salve his wounded pride by destroying the Jews in the kingdom.

The censure of prideful conduct on the part of Haman that *Poema de la Reina Ester* narrates serves as a third example positioning it within concurrent trends in Golden Age literature. More than half a century ago, Edward Wilson claimed a parallel between Haman in the Esther poem of Pinto Delgado and Polyphemus in the *Fábula de Polifemo y Galatea* of Góngora but did not explain his reason for doing so ("The Poetry of João Pinto Delgado" 133). Further investigation of the two antagonists in the respective poems demonstrates the rationale behind Wilson's assertion of this parallel. Góngora develops a myth from the *Metamorphoses* of Ovid, in which the jealous one-eyed cyclops Polyphemus interrupts with fatal consequences the love of the sea-nymph Galatea and Acis because he himself wants the young woman for a bride. Pinto Delgado quite possibly knew the work of Góngora, especially given that his own intellectual coming of age in Portugal occurred when the works of the latter circulated in manuscript, including *Fábula de Polifemo y Galatea*, a poem completed in 1612–13.

A comparison between Pinto Delgado's Haman and Góngora's Polyphemus shows similarities in the ways each poet treats pride and fear. After the love of Galatea and Acis is clear, Polyphemus, who is a shepherd, attempts to impress the nymph with his flocks, hives, and, as the following citation suggests, physical attributes:

When I'm seated, my strong arm can collect
the sweet fruit from the lofty palm's high head;
standing, my body shields from summer's heat
innumerable goats with its ample shade.
It's vain, trust me, for a mountain to compete
by seeking for itself a crown of cloud:
standing on this rock, I reach so high
I can write my woes with my finger in the sky.

(Dent-Young 203, strophe 52)[9]

---

9   The bilingual edition of Dent-Young is the source of this and the following translation of quotations from the *Fábula de Polifemo y Galatea*.

> Sentado a la alta palma no perdona
> su dulce fruto mi robusta mano;
> en pie, sombra capaz es mi persona
> de innumerables cabras el verano.
> ¿Qué mucho, si de nubes se corona
> por igualarme la montaña en vano,
> y en los cielos, desde esta roca, puedo
> escribir mis desdichas con el dedo? (Dent-Young 202, strophe 52)

As Góngora does in the case of Polyphemus, Pinto Delgado depicts Haman as an individual whose self-worth is rooted in an exaggerated sense of importance and prowess. This prideful attitude is particularly present during the early parts of the poem, when the king bequeaths undeservedly high esteem on his minister. The following lines comparing Haman with a reckless ship communicate the danger that such unearned esteem represents:

> The ship proud of her boastfulness
> rushes confidently among the waves,
> in a frenzy the wind blows the sail,
> light in its error and heavy in arrogance
> and that well-being [of the ship], which invites damage [that Haman causes],
> with common disdain incites his glory.
>
> Entre las ondas confiada vuela
> de su jactancia la soberbia nave,
> el viento mueve con furor la vela,
> de error ligera y de arrogancia grave,
> y aquel bien, que el agravio solicita,
> con desprecio común su gloria incita. (29)

Yet in both cases, pride impedes the very end it has sought to achieve. Once Ahasuerus realizes the greed motivating the anti-Jewish crusade of his minister, Haman sees his glory and triumph reduced to shame. Upon discovering the amorous liaison between Galata and Acis, violent jealousy corresponding to his disproportionate size and strength compels Polyphemus to unearth a large boulder and hurl it at Acis, causing the death of his rival. However, just as Haman's effort to destroy the Jews of Persia brings about his own demise, so this murderous act of Polyphemus makes Acis immortal when, thanks to divine intervention, his remains become the source of an ever-flowing river that bears his name:

> Scarcely had the fateful boulder settled
> over his shattered, mutilated limbs,
> then the feet of all the biggest trees were clothed
> in precious liquid gushing from his veins.
> His white bones now to flowing silver turned,
> kissing the flowers and silvering the sand,
> he comes to the sea, and pityingly by her
> is recognized as son, annointed river. (Dent-Young 207–09, strophe 63)

> Sus miembros lastimosamente opresos
> del escollo fatal fueron apenas,
> que los pies de los árboles más gruesos
> calzó el líquido aljófar de sus venas.
> Corriente plata al fin sus blancos huesos,
> lamiendo flores y argentando arenas,
> a Doris llega, que, con llanto pío,
> yerno lo saludó, lo aclamó río. (Dent-Young 206–08, strophe 63)

The plot of each poem punishes its antagonist for trying to impose his will on others through force and fear. Polyphemus and Haman thus achieve an infamous renown that shows the limits of their power and contrasts directly with the marital conquest and the destruction of a people, respectively, that they sought to bring about.

Concomitant with traits it shares with other Golden Age texts, *Poema de la Reina Ester* expresses a worldview indicative of both Pinto Delgado's place as a New Christian "in and out" of mainstream Iberian society as well as a type of wish fulfillment resulting from this marginalization. In this perspective, Inquisitorial Iberia functions as a poetic subtext linking the rescue of biblical Persian Jews with the suppression of truly held faith, dislocation of exile, and reinvention as New Jews that many seventeenth-century conversos experienced. Thus, the queen, herself a secret Jew and hence *ex illis*, saves the Jewish people of her realm from a fate even worse than that of their brethren in Spain and Portugal in the late 1400s, although both were condemned for reasons as much political and economic as religious. In this situation, Esther is a heaven-sent miracle whose presence alone awakens the king's romantic interest:

If I look at heaven, a heaven in you I gaze upon,
that with its turning moves its harmony,
of whose lights, of modest example,
the day shines in my darkness;
forming in your beauty an argument,
that seen, I am unaware of, and, not understood, I feel.

Si el cielo miro un cielo en ti contemplo,
que con su giro mueve su armonía,
de cuyas luces, de modesto ejemplo,
en mi tiniebla resplandece el día;
formando en tu hermosura un argumento,
que visto ignoro, y, no entendido, siento. (55)

The beauty of Esther that Ahasuerus exalts here, and that permits the subsequent awakening of his conscience, parallels her exaltation among New Christians. Moreover, she privileges people over self when beseeching God and king to spare the Jews of Persia. Thus she implores God, "look not at my life, but rather look at that of your people, / let live for you he who yearns for you" ("mi vida no, la de tu pueblo mira, / viva por ti el que por ti suspira"; 78), and entreats her husband, "look at the blow of the raging sword / against my people, in unjust punishment ("el golpe mira de furiosa espada / contra mi pueblo, en el castigo injusto"; 90). The quiet yet firm advocacy that Esther undertakes before these authority figures at potential risk to herself explains why crypto-Jews post-1492 regarded her as a saint.[10]

Despite contributing to Muslim and Christian societies in medieval Spain in roles that ranged from working as artisanal laborers to advising caliphs and kings, by 1492 Jews had become expendable due to the perceived threat they represented to the Catholicism of recent converts. In fact, the Inquisition helped convince Fernando and Isabel to issue their edict of expulsion in 1492 by insisting that Jews were contributing to the recidivism of recent converts to Catholicism, as the following words from that document attest:

---

10   Attribution by crypto-Jews of sainthood to Esther, as well as to Moses and David, demonstrated the syncretism of their beliefs. The three-day fast dedicated to "Saint Esther," the *Pascua del cordero* later in the spring (Passover), the *días desgraciados* in midsummer that marked the destruction of the First and Second Temples as well as other calamities, and the *Día del perdón* in the fall (Yom Kippur) were all sacred holidays in this religion.

According to which, we are informed by the Inquisitors and by many other religious persons, ecclesiastical and secular, it is evident and apparent that the great damage to the [New] Christians has resulted from and does result from the participation, conversation, and communication that they have had with the Jews, who try to always achieve by whatever ways and means possible to subvert and to draw away faithful Christians from our holy Catholic faith and to separate them from it, and to attract and pervert them to their injurious belief and opinion, instructing them in their ceremonies and observances of the Law, holding gatherings where they read unto them and teach them what they ought to believe and observe according to their Law . . . (qtd. in Gerber, *The Jews of Spain* 286)

Segun somos ynformados de los ynquisidores e de otras muchas personas religiosas, eclesiasticas y seglares, consta e parece el gran daño que a los christianos se a seguido de la participaçion, conbersaçion, comunicaçion que han tenido y tienen con los judios, los quales se prueban que procuran siempre por quantas bias e maneras pueden subvertir e subtraer de nuestra santa fee catolica a los fieles christianos e los apartar della e atraer e perbertir a su dañada crençia e opinion, ynstruyendolos en las çeremonias e obserbançias de su ley, haziendo ayuntamientos donde les leen e enseñan lo que han de creer y guardar segun su ley . . . (qtd. in Suárez Fernández 392)[11]

In *Poema de la Reina Ester*, Mordecai expresses this age-old expendability when, upon learning of Haman's decree, he warns his adoptive niece, "do not think, no, that your crown can / flee the destruction now in wide-reaching effect, / because it [the crown] does not pardon betrayal of the [royal] scepter" ("no pienses, no, que puede tu corona / huir el daño en general efecto, / que la traición al cetro no perdona"; 49). Mordecai also represents a Jew—or, in the time of Pinto Delgado, a secretly Jewish New Christian—esteemed for recognizing this treachery and refusing to bow before it. At the same time, his voice, portraying a biblical speaker, laments the recent history of Iberian Jews in a way that recognizes the guilt of conversos for abandoning Judaism while also seeking divine compassion for their forced conversion. Thus, upon learning of Haman's decree in canto 4, Mordecai laments to his people:

---

11   Gerber cites the translation of the edict in *The Expulsion 1492 Chronicles*, edited by David Raphael, Carmi House Press, 1992.

> Ah, punished children of Jacob,
> who in the anguish of ancient pain;
> sins bound up in your harm,
> you bow your neck to oppression;
> . . . . . . . . . . . . . . . . . . . .
> since you lost the great benefit of Zion,
> prepare your necks for the knife.
>
> Ah, de Jacob los hijos castigados,
> que en los tormentos del antiguo daño;
> en vuestro mal envueltos los pecados,
> la cerviz humilláis a yugo extraño;
> . . . . . . . . . . . . . . . . . . . .
> pues de Sion el alto bien perdisteis,
> preparad al cuchillo vuestros cuellos. (43)

A converso reading of these lines somewhat conflates the predicament of Persian Jews and Iberian New Christian: their own sins, including, perhaps, conversion, conspire against the Jews, forcing them to submit to an intolerant religion; having lost the privileged position of their faith, they then must prepare to die. Later in the same passage, Mordecai casts aside guilt in order to lament Persia's Jews through a rhetorical question that could well describe the fate of their Iberian brethren:

> What heart will be able to endure the suffering
> that memory conceives in speech,
> seeing in the theater of a foreign city
> dishonor alive and our glory dead:
> punishment if not equal to guilt,
> [at least equal to] death, finally, after so many sufferings?
>
> ¿Cuál corazón podrá sufrir la pena
> que en el discurso engendra la memoria,
> viendo en teatro de ciudad ajena
> viva la infamia y muerta nuestra gloria:
> si no castigos a la culpa iguales,
> la muerte, al fin, después de tantos males? (44)

By the end of the poem, Mordecai, who "with a pious staff / liberates his people and humiliates his adversary" ("con piadosa vara, / su pueblo libra y el contrario ofende"; 103), and his coreligionists have replaced guilt and suffering with divine justice, as Pinto Delgado celebrates agency on the part of Jews whose denial he must have felt as a New Christian.

While Mordecai remains loyal to both his people and king despite religious and ethnic otherness, Haman is the cruel inquisitor feigning loyalty, whose "ambitious fury / ... / opposes heaven in shameless outrage" ("ambiciosa furia / ... / se opone al cielo en atrevida injuria"; 30). Pinto Delgado uses the biblical story to emphasize how the power-hungry courtier, attempting to create a nonexistent threat regarding the insubordination of Jews in Ahasuerus' kingdom, provokes his own downfall.[12] The clearest example of this hubris is Haman's assumption that Ahasuerus is thinking of him when soliciting advice regarding appropriate recognition for someone who has done a great service to the king, when in fact Ahasuerus wants to honor Mordecai for uncovering a plot against the monarchy. Losing power as quickly as he had obtained it, Haman laments, "Now my enemy equals me in power, / now I am the deep hell of his heaven" ("Ya mi enemigo en el poder me iguala, / ya de su cielo soy profundo abismo"; 75). Besides serving as a triumph for those whom he would have victimized, his downfall expresses hope for divine and royal favor of New Christians in an era of persecution.

Reading *Poema de la Reina Ester* from a converso perspective suggests that the text would have inspired New Christians who secretly identified with the religion of their Jewish forebears. To fulfill this end, the poem effectuates a role reversal, as the oft-victimized Jewish people, like a long-dormant snake waking in summer, "Goes up to the rock, on it shines / the lightning bolt, and a lightning bolt seems their fury" ("Sube a la peña, en ella resplandece / el rayo, y rayo su furor parece"); such that "the disconsolate children of Zion / ... / if vanquished yesterday, are victorious today, / having become, formerly offended, your offenders" ("tal de Sion los hijos afligidos / ... / si vencidos ayer, hoy vencedores, / son, de ofendidos, vueltos ofensores"; 102). Pinto Delgado provides a model for conversos of his day wishing to rededicate themselves to Judaism by noting of the Jews of Persia after their salvation, "in sweet subjugation, humble, the grateful people / bends its neck to God

---

12   Despite the comic representation of Haman in Esther, Pinto Delgado describes the antagonist of the Jews with great seriousness, recognizing the danger he represents and thus corroborating the subsequent observation of Berlin that "Haman's false claim about the Jews is a prototype of anti-Judaism" (Introduction to Esther 1620).

on high" ("en dulce yugo, humilde, el cuello inclina / al alto Ser el pueblo agradecido" (107).

As well, the poet refers to Exodus in ways not found in the book of Esther in order to emphasize divine favor of Jews, and by extension, New Christians wanting to live as Jews. Thus, his Esther describes the miracle of the sea parting for the fleeing Hebrews, while Haman is a hard-hearted pursuer whose plan of destruction, like that of Pharaoh's Egyptians, drowns in a wall of water (80–81). When Esther compares Haman with the Egyptians and then seeks that God prohibit the minister from carrying out his plot (81), Pinto Delgado speaks to the condition of Iberian conversos living in fear of the Inquisition and perhaps feeling bereft of any protection from the tribunal except that of God. Finally, asserting that a compassionate God redeems the just, whose "glory is born from their very sufferings" ("gloria nace de sus mismas penas"; 109), Pinto Delgado implies divine recognition of sadness that some New Christians felt for not being able to live as Jews.

*LAMENTACIONES DEL PROFETA JEREMÍAS*
The second work of Pinto Delgado that this chapter considers, *Lamentaciones del Profeta Jeremías*, glosses and expands upon the first two chapters of the Book of Lamentations, which like Esther is a scroll in *Kethuvim*. With great feeling, the biblical work describes the siege and loss of Jerusalem in 586 BCE and subsequent Babylonian captivity as divine justice for the idolatry, vanity, and inconstancy of the Israelites. Each of the book's five chapters is a poem consisting of twenty-two verses, a number corresponding to the number of letters in the Hebrew alphabet. Additionally, the first four chapters are acrostics, in which successive verses begin with the next letter of the alphabet. This organization "gives expression to the enormity... of the destruction (extending 'from A to Z')" that the book catalogs (Berlin, Introduction to Lam. 1582). Written from the perspective of witnesses and participants, Lamentations clearly resonated with Pinto Delgado due to the marginalization and conflict that informed his life and writings as a New Christian.

A brief summary of Lamentations contextualizes Pinto Delgado's paraphrase of the work while also establishing a basis for recognizing the role of his New Christian perspective on the variations he introduces. In the first chapter, Jerusalem herself grieves her ruin while admitting, "The Lord is in the right, / For I have disobeyed him" (Lam. 1.18). Chapter 2 presents an apparently merciless God who calls down on the Israelites an unending rain of travails including anthropophagy; while in Chapter 3, a first-person speaker bewails the sufferings that God has imposed on him as an exile. Chapter 4 repeats images of degradation in Jerusalem due to the Babylonian siege, and in the final chapter, a collective speaker implores divine mercy in light of such abasement: "Remember, O Lord, what has befallen us; / Behold, and see our disgrace! / . . . / Take us back, O Lord, to Yourself, / And let us come back; / Renew our days as of old!" (Lam. 5.1, 21). Yet even as its speakers catalog this woe, Lamentations also expresses individual responsibility as well as hope for and belief in divine forgiveness. Thus, soon after describing his afflicted state as an exile, the speaker of Chapter 3 declares:

> Let us search and examine our ways,
> And turn back to the Lord;
> . . . . . . . . . . . .
> I have called on Your name, O Lord,
> From the depths of the Pit.
> Hear my plea;
> Do not shut Your ear
> To my groan, to my cry!
> You have ever drawn nigh when I called You;
> You have said, "Do not fear!" (Lam. 3.40, 55–57).

Through its concomitant narration of woe and aspiration, the work reaffirms the belief of the Israelites in the innate goodness of God, recognition of their spiritual wrongdoings, and commitment to the divine covenant.

Measuring more than 3,700 lines, *Lamentaciones del Profeta Jeremías* consists of forty-four sections of thirteen to twenty-five *quintillas* each that paraphrase the forty-four verses of the first two chapters of Lamentations. Pinto Delgado introduces each of these sections, or laments, with a prose translation of the corresponding Hebrew verse based closely on the Judeo-Spanish (Ladino) translation of the Bible produced in Ferrara, Italy, in 1553, as well as, less frequently, those of the Vulgate and the *Biblia del Oso* (Oso Bible) of the Spanish Protestant Casiodoro Reyna of 1559.[13] Through its discussion of culpability, enslavement, and trust that the crying of the speaker "will be as dew / that makes the earth fertile" ("será como el rocío / que fer-

---

13   Oelman attributes to Pinto Delgado's Jewish identity the use of the Ferrara Bible in the introductory prose translations, and the explanations from the Vulgate in the poem itself to his Christian upbringing (133). Such reasoning testifies to the tendency of secret Jews to incorporate elements of both faiths into their theological worldview. The Oso Bible owes its [nick]name to its title page, which contains the image of a bear reaching for honey in a tree.

tiliza la tierra"; 113), the poem represents a New Christian worldview rooted in displacement and guilt on the one hand and hope for divine redemption on the other. Rather than summarize the entirety of Pinto Delgado's text, the following analysis examines the presence and effect of these characteristics in three themes that appear throughout the forty-four glosses. These themes include the natural world, especially in references to the sea and the *locus amoenus* (a pleasing place of idealized natural beauty); time, as seen in the contrast between previous grandeur and current desolation; and hope for divine faithfulness in the presence of despair.[14] The analysis of the poem concludes with a comparison between its language and that in the Judeo-Spanish translation of the Ferrara Bible and the Vulgate in order to show the hybridizing effect of these texts on Pinto Delgado's work.

Regarding the natural world, allusions to the fathomlessness and unrestrained power of the sea that occur throughout the work represent the depth of suffering of the Israelites as well as the abandonment of God that has precipitated such ruin. Thus, the speaker in the first lament of the poem, identifying the sins of the Jerusalemites as the cause of their destruction, asks their city somewhat rhetorically:

> Who will be able to look at you,
> seeing your lost glory,
> who does not wish that his life
> be a sea of tears,
> in order to be able to mourn you?

> ¿Quién te podrá contemplar,
> Viendo tu gloria perdida,
> que no desee que un mar
> de llanto sea su vida,
> para poderte llorar? (114)

Alongside this image of a sea of tears inadequate to lament Jerusalem, Pinto Delgado depicts Zion, as he and the Bible also refer to the city and the Jewish people, as a space of disorder. He does so to contrast loss that forsaking divine law causes with salvation resulting from adhering to it. For turning

---

14  For another paraphrase of Lamentations, see *Lágrimas de Hieremías castellanas*, a work of Francisco de Quevedo of 1613 that consists of a translation and commentary on the twenty-two verses of the first chapter of the biblical text. Reasons of space and scope preclude an analysis of this work in the present chapter.

away from God, Jerusalem has become rudderless and solitary, deserving of the Babylonian siege; not even friends stand by her:

> And seeing you sail
> without a pilot, and without a rudder,
> in this deep sea,
> with reason drowned,
> [they] allowed you to drown.

> Y viéndote navegar,
> sin piloto, y sin timón,
> en este profundo mar,
> anegada la razón,
> te dejaron anegar. (121)

Concomitantly, by describing the great potential of the sea to harm those who traverse it, Pinto Delgado adapts a well-worn storm/port dichotomy to his purpose of commenting upon the idolatry of biblical Jews.[15] Thus, the omniscient witness of Lament 2.19, addressing Jerusalem directly in the second person, implies that the ruin of the city is like the devastation of a raging sea:

> Today, that the fiercest rigor,
> if I compare it
> to the rigor of your storm, is less.
> What grief can there be,
> that equals my emotion?
> Only in a raging storm
> have I compared you to the sea.

---

15    Another example of the juxtaposition of port and potentially stormy sea is found in the aforementioned "Vida retirada" ode of Fray Luis de León, whose speaker, praising a contemplative life in nature, waxes enthusiastically, "Oh, mountain, oh spring, oh river! / Oh secret, safe [and] delightful! / Almost wrecked the ship, / to your sacred rest / I flee from this stormy sea!! ("¡Oh monte, oh fuente, oh río! / ¡Oh secreto seguro, deleitoso! / Roto casi el navío, / a vuestro almo reposo / huyo de aqueste mar tempestuoso!"; McCaw and Thornton Spinnenweber 65; I also used their translation for the last three lines of this strophe). The editors note that "navío" describes the soul of the speaker and that "almo" is a poetic term that can mean "sacred" in addition to "nourishing" or "venerable" (65n10).

> Hoy, que el más fiero rigor,
> al rigor de tu tormento
> si lo comparo, es menor;
> ¿Cuál puede ser el dolor,
> que iguale a mi sentimiento?
> Sólo en furiosa tormenta
> te he comparado a la mar. (275–76)

In a complementary example of storm/port polarity, the first-person speaker embodying Jerusalem in Lament 1.9 represents the sea as a site of transgression against God and the idea of port as one of deliverance:

> That in this deep sea
> of sin, in which I see myself,
> only in you am I able to find
> the refuge of my desire,
> where I ponder myself saved.
>
> Que en este profundo mar
> del pecado, en que me veo,
> en ti sólo puedo hallar
> el puerto de mi deseo,
> donde me pienso salvar. (157)

The contrast between sin and salvation and the recognition by the Israelites that God alone may grant them salvation despite their misdeeds connect Pinto Delgado's poem with its biblical forebear by showing that belief in divine redemption and mercy still exists.[16]

In addition to adapting images of storm and port common to the Spanish Golden Age for his purpose of representing the immorality and potential salvation of biblical Jews, Pinto Delgado adheres to literary norms of his day through images of Jerusalem that recall a lost *locus amoenus*. He does so in

---

16 Emily Colbert Cairns shows the importance of the sea in *Poema de la Reina Ester*, where, unlike in *Lamentaciones*, Pinto Delgado uses the sea as "the primary metaphor for freedom and opportunity for the Portuguese nation [of *conversos*] ... a space where identity is negotiated and where economic opportunity through trade occurs in the Diaspora" (192). According to this argument, the sea facilitates geographic mobility and, through its surface calm and submerged turbidity, represents the conflict of identity formation of so-called port Jews such as Pinto Delgado (193).

*Lamentaciones del Profeta Jeremías* by contrasting the destruction of Jerusalem with images of the city prior to its destruction that stand out for their idealization of natural beauty and that recall nature as a harmonious setting in the aforementioned "Vida retirada" ode of Fray Luis. Thus, for example, in Lament 1.4, the shade-giving trees, flower-covered meadow giving off delightful scents, whispering springs, and chirping birds that once characterized Jerusalem are now a shade of their former selves in a city "so abandoned" ("tan desierta"), where "the paths of Zion / mourn their solitude" ("los caminos de Sion / lamentan su soledad"): the trees and the meadow personify sadness, while the once-pleasing sounds of fountains and springs resemble tears (128–29). Fray Luis describes an orchard using similar imagery; although his *locus amoenus* does not evoke loss, as occurs with Pinto Delgado, it instead fulfills a more Christian-focused objective as "an evocation of Paradise [where] the *vida retirada* is the ideal setting for a dialogue with the Divine" ("una evocación del Paraíso [donde] la vida retirada es el lugar ideal para el diálogo con la Divinidad"; Alonso 27). Consequently, like Pinto Delgado, Fray Luis depicts a meadow of full of birds whose sweet sounds he implores to awaken him, flowers that perfume the air, a life-giving spring, and trees whose branches gently sway in the breeze (McCaw and Thornton Spinnenweber 65–67). However, Fray Luis's speaker seeks to enjoy this natural bliss alone, perhaps as a means of finding God without distraction, whereas the speaker in *Lamentaciones* connects the present solitude of the erstwhile *locus amoenus* with God's punishment of the Israelites for their blasphemy and idolatry.[17]

Seen in the contrast between the previous grandeur of the Israelites and their current desolation, the concept of time serves as a second lens through which to view the New Christian worldview of Pinto Delgado against the background of Golden Age Spanish literature. During much of the poem, various speakers introduce a temporal element when reflecting on how the Israelites have squandered their privileged position in the eyes of God, thus precipitating the destruction of Jerusalem. For example, a lament (1.11) describing the present tribulations of a mother, a child who while short of

---

17  I should like to acknowledge the commentary of Álvaro Alonso for helping me see "the double aspect—human and religious—of the ['Vida retirada'] ode" ("la doble vertiente—humana y religiosa—de la oda"; 27), so that I better understand this poem not only as praise of life in the countryside free from the vanity of court but also as a means by which Fray Luis creates an ideal natural world that facilitates the speaker's journey to God. See also 49n5.

breath drinks his own tears, and an elder, leads to an observation rooted in the concept of *desengaño*:

> Since, from the day we are born,
> we move towards our end,
> between diverse extremes,
> and that which we most strive to achieve,
> is what we leave behind most quickly.

> Que, del día que nacemos,
> a nuestro fin caminamos,
> entre diversos extremos,
> y lo que más pretendemos,
> eso, más presto dejamos. (169)

In Spanish Golden Age literature, such *desengaño* describes a process not strictly of disillusionment, but rather of enlightenment that, among other characteristics, consists of a "waking to true awareness . . . to see things as they are and hence to arrive at 'wisdom'" (Green 4: 44).[18] The conclusion of Pinto Delgado's lament, indicative of disillusionment as awareness, suggests that, despite Israel having to shoulder responsibility for its apparent abandonment by God, death is an implacable force against human hopes, especially the most ardently felt ones.

This notion of life as a journey leading ineluctably to death recalls *Coplas por la muerte de su padre* of Jorge Manrique. Not surprisingly, *Lamentaciones* shares other characteristics with the fifteenth-century poem, including a variation on its famous verses—"Our lives are the rivers / that lead to the sea, / which is death" ("Nuestras vidas son los ríos / que van a dar en la mar, / que es el morir"; Cash and Murray 371)—and several instances of the *Ubi sunt?* ("Where are they now?") theme. In the first instance, Jerusalem compares itself to "the plentiful river" ("el abundante río") whose waters are tears flowing to God: "I offer my tribute / to my divine ocean" ("Ofrezco el tributo mío / a mi divino océano"; 187). In the second, *Ubi sunt?*, a device that poeticizes the fleetingness of life regardless of station, Pinto Delgado dramatizes the extent of Zion's fall by describing the heights of its exuberant,

---

18   Explaining *desengaño* in the works of Gracián, Quevedo, Calderón, and Cervantes, Green also describes this concept as "*caer en la cuenta*—to come to oneself" (4: 49, 52, 60).

albeit romanticized, past. Thus, after indicating the direction of this contrast in the first quintet of Lamentation 1.6,

> Now the beauty of Zion,
> and the proud architecture
> of royal palaces,
> do not offer fleeting signs
> of their former form,
>
> Ya de Sion la hermosura,
> y de palacios reales,
> la soberbia arquitectura,
> ni de su antigua figura
> ofrecen breves señales (139),

the speaker catalogs a state of ruin that has brought low individuals at every level of society: "the servant, up to the lord, / the chief, down to the peasant" ("el criado, hasta el señor, / el príncipe, hasta el villano"; 142). The bitterness of captivity exempts no one, as all share in its cause, be they the powerful who yesterday measured wealth in gold and silver and today barely do so using tears, or the poor man to whom God will deny compassion (141).

An important difference between the laments of Manrique and Pinto Delgado is that for the first poet, death equalizes all implacably, at least to a certain extent, regardless of social and material status, while for the second, an offended God wreaks havoc on the Israelites for their idolatry.[19] In a poem exalting his father for his exploits fighting Muslims in the 1400s, Manrique recognizes this equalizing power, as in the following example:

> thus, there is no impervious being,
> because Death treats popes and emperors
> and prelates

---

19  I include the qualifier "to a certain extent" in describing the equalizing power of death in the *Coplas* because later in the poem, the voice of death speaks directly to Rodrigo Manrique, father of the poet, promising renewed life "much better / than the other [one] fleeting / [and] impermanent" ("muy mejor / que la otra temporal / perecedera"; Cash and Murray 383). The poem suggests that, just as he was exalted in life for his virtue and valor, Rodrigo will continue to stand apart from the majority of humanity in the life to come.

just as she does poor shepherds
of cattle.

así que no hay cosa fuerte,
que a papas y emperadores
y prelados,
así los trata la Muerte
como a los pobres pastores
de ganados. (Cash and Murray 375)[20]

On the other hand, despite the *desengaño* that runs through *Lamentaciones* as a means of explaining the situation of the Israelites, Pinto Delgado more often emphasizes the role of agency as a cause of suffering. Thus, in place of the inevitability of fate to which Manrique ascribes human mortality, the Baroque poet has his collective speaker in Lament 1.2 identify Jerusalem, that is, the Jewish people, as responsible for their own abandonment:

Hearing that your wickedness
opposed, in a thousand ways,
divine justice,
everyone distanced themselves from you,
by leaving you in your filth.

Oyendo que tu malicia
se oponía, por mil modos,
a la divina justicia,
por dejarte en tu inmundicia,
de ti se apartaron todos (120).

This witness and member of the fallen city subsequently admits to God, "our stubbornness was / the just cause, that denies / forgiveness in your eyes" ("fue nuestra obstinación / la justa causa, que niega / en tus ojos el perdón";

---

20   The death-as-equalizer trope in Spanish literature became common enough that Cervantes mocked it in the prologue to book 1 of *Don Quixote*, when the friend of the fictional narrator suggests the inclusion of a quotation from Horace referring to this theme as a way to help the narrator complete the prologue and lend it authority: "pale Death knocks with the same foot at the hovels of the poor as the towers of the rich" ("pallida Mors aequo pulsat pede pauperum tabernas / regumque turris"; Ode 1.4, lines 13–14; Horace 6).

304), and then bewails the consequences of such intransigence, including the sight of mothers killing children due to their own hunger (305). These and other moments in which the poet draws attention to the shortcomings of Israel in its relationship with God demonstrate a New Christian perspective in several ways: they reflect an awareness of inherent, collective New Christian guilt for conversion to Christianity; and they connect the privations of Jerusalem to the reality of Inquisitorial persecution of conversos deemed inauthentic Christians.

In addition to nature and time, the expression of hope amid overwhelming despair functions as a third theme that sheds light on the New Christian perspective of *Lamentaciones*, especially toward the end of the work. It is here that, as A. D. H. Fishlock noted more than sixty-five years ago, Pinto Delgado states the inherent meaning of the poem: "Trusting in the power of penitent tears to mitigate the wrath of God, Zion must return to her Lord" ("The *Lamentaciones* of João Pinto Delgado" 60). Conscientiously or not, Pinto Delgado expounds steps of this return in Laments 2.18 and 2.19 in ways that show hope for divine redemption in light of tribulations he experienced as a New Christian. One such step consists of a reordering of values so that the soul, previously tormented by pain and vanity, achieves a place of contentment, in opposition to Zion's current perdition. In such a state the heart weeps no more and the thirst for gold is nourished "by another liquor" ("de otro licor") where "content, the soul calms down" ("alegre el alma respira"; 295–96). As Fishlock further observed, six words of the poem distill how Pinto Delgado understood the history of the Israelites according to biblical prophets in a way showing divine faith in Zion: "[A people] although rebellious, chosen / loved, although punished" ("[pueblo] Aunque rebelde, escogido / querido, aunque castigado"; 298; Fishlock, "The *Lamentaciones*" 60–61). According to a *converso* perspective on these words, God still esteems New Christians despite their "rebel" status for occupying a space between Judaism and Christianity and suffering "punishment," whether from Old Christians who deem them insincere converts; or from themselves, especially those who identify as secret Jews, for the guilt of conversion.

A second step of the return of Jerusalem to God includes a command that the Israelites recognize their prior wrongs and embrace humility. Within several pages, the omniscient speaker tells Jerusalem, "lift your thought," "lift your heart," and "humble, lift your hands" ("levanta tu pensamiento," "levanta tu corazón," and "levanta, humilde, tus manos"; 298–301). These imperatives bespeak a faith in the willingness of God to absolve the Israelites of their hard-heartedness should they show repentance. Several times throughout the poem, Pinto Delgado describes the relationship between God and the Israelites as akin to that between a gardener and a vine. The gardener planted and protected the vine, which produced fine fruit, but then, as the narrator says to God, "And, at the end, their powerful error, / you crushed, with your power" ("Y, al fin, su error poderoso, / con tu poder, vendimiaste"; 303).[21] Now, however, the poet affirms the elect status of the Israelites, contrasting divine punishment in various forms, from the image of a wine press to that of desperate mothers forced to abandon their children, with divine love for Israel rooted in the everlasting promise of redemption. The following stanza confirms the commitment of God to a repentant Israel, regardless of its misdeeds:

> Although his excessive guilt,
> in this perilous moment, dismays him,
> your love, which rekindles his faith,
> does not desire that man die,
> but rather that, repentant, he live.
>
> Aunque su culpa excesiva,
> en este paso, le asombre,
> tu amor, que su fe le aviva,
> no quiere que muera el hombre,
> mas que, arrepentido, viva. (309)

These lines emphasize the *converso* perspective of Pinto Delgado by lending themselves to a Catholic reading that might evoke absolution and renewed life, and a Jewish one that might see parallels in the relationship of the Jewish people with God throughout the Hebrew Bible.[22]

---

21   Although *vendimiar* principally means to harvest or pick, Pinto Delgado seems to broaden the meaning of the verb to include a subsequent part of viniculture, during which a *lagar* (press) crushes the grapes. For example, in Lament 1.12, the poet uses this more forceful image in order to illustrate how God crushes humanity for its idolatry: "And seeing that my sin / was the fruit of my pleasure, / the Lord, angered with justified reason, / as is right, / with anger has crushed me" ("Y viendo que mi pecado / el fruto era de mi gusto, / con justa razón airado / el señor, como es tan justo, / con ira me ha vendimiado"; 172).

22   Examples abound in the Hebrew Bible of a loving God offering deliverance to a repentant humanity. In Exodus 32, Moses convinces God not to punish the Israelites for having made the Golden Calf. In Psalm 89, God warns the people of

A brief comparison of language in *Lamentaciones*, the Judeo-Spanish translation of the Ferrara Bible, and the Vulgate testifies to the hybridity that informed Pinto Delgado's text, perhaps not unlike his own worldview formed by Jewish and Christian influences. As Oelman (133) and Fishlock ("The *Lamentaciones*" 53) noted, Pinto Delgado follows the Ferrara Bible in his prose translation of individual verses from Lamentations at the start of each lament, whereas the Christian versions—the Vulgate and the Oso Bible of Casiodoro Reyna—influence more closely the poet's subsequent paraphrases. Thus, for example, Lament 2.18 nearly duplicates the corresponding verses in the Ladino translation: "Exclamó su corazón al Señor, o muro de hija de Sion, haz descender como arroyo lágrimas de día y de noche, no des reposo a ti, no calle niña de tu ojo" (294); "Esclamó su coraçon a *Adonay*; O muro de compaña de Zion, faz descender como arroyo lagrima de dia y de noche, no des reposo a ti, no calle niñeta de tu ojo" (*Ladino Biblia* 661, italics in original).[23] Not unexpectedly, given the setting of the work's publication, Pinto Delgado changes "Adonai" to "Señor"; equally to be expected, the Vulgate's translation of this word is "Dominum" (596). On the other hand, the intensity of tears running through the lament more closely approximates the description of this phenomenon in the Vulgate, "torrentem," than does the "arroyo" of the Ladino translation, as the following *quintilla* shows:

> Oh people, you who are seeing
> that your old estate
> is like a river that flows upstream,
> may your tears be a river,
> may they never cease.

> O pueblo, que viendo estás
> que tu antiguo señorío
> es río, que vuelve atrás,
> sean tus lágrimas río,
> que no se vuelvan jamás. (297)

---

David of punishment for wrongdoing but promises them abiding love even during such difficult moments.

23   My translation of the first two verses of Lam. 2.18 as rendered by Pinto Delgado is as follows: "Their heart exclaimed to the Lord, o wall of the daughter of Zion, make your tears fall like a river both day and night, don't give yourself rest, may the pupil of your eye not be silent."

Once again Pinto Delgado uses the natural world to represent the volume of Israel's suffering; if previously a sea of tears was hardly equal to her weeping, so now the poet implores such tears to run like a river.

*CANCIÓN, APLICANDO MISERICORDIAS DIVINAS Y DEFETOS PROPRIOS A LA SALIDA DE EGIPTO HASTA LA TIERRA SANTA*

Another narrative poem, *Historia de Rut moabita*, follows *Lamentaciones*, and then the collection finishes with three shorter poems. The first of these, *Canción, aplicando misericordias divinas y defetos proprios a la salida de Egipto hasta la Tierra Santa*, demonstrates how, within the lens of Spanish Golden Age poetics, Pinto Delgado uses a central event of biblical Judaism—the Exodus from Egypt and its aftermath—as an allegory to describe the progress of the soul towards salvation. Across 111 lines divided into seven fifteen-line stanzas followed by a six-line conclusion, a first-person speaker establishes a confessional relationship with God and seeks divine remedy for the personal shortcomings he describes. The work represents Egypt as the origin of the soul's sinful condition and then describes steps and challenges in its journey towards God against the backdrop of biblical events such as the crossing of the Red Sea (stanza 3) and the Golden Calf (stanza 4). Rather than address the *Canción* in its entirety, the following analysis shows its affiliation with Spanish Golden Age literature by exploring the presence within it of *desengaño* and imagery such as that which Fray Luis de León uses to describe the journey of the soul towards God.[24]

The first lines of the poem establish a dichotomy between light and dark that in turn foregrounds the relationship the speaker yearns for with God. Thus, the speaker implores the Almighty not only to shine a light on his soul in its metaphorical Egyptian captivity, but also that "May your holy inspiration be my guide / that, in the glow of the loving fire, / calls me in the desert" ("Sea tu santa inspiración mi guía / que, entre la luz del amoroso fuego, / me llame en el desierto; 349).[25] Two subsequent antitheses bring the narrator on a path closer to God in ways that suggest the familiarity of Pinto Delgado with Spanish Baroque poetic tendencies. The first, occurring

---

24  I would like to acknowledge Fishlock, "The Shorter Poems of João Pinto Delgado" 136, as the source of the comparison with Fray Luis de León, while also proposing to describe it in greater depth, particularly with regard to Ode III, "A Francisco de Salinas," by the latter poet. Likewise, Fishlock's stanza-by-stanza explanation of *Canción . . . hasta la Tierra Santa* in this article has greatly aided my understanding of the poem.

25  These words are the source of the first part of the title of this chapter.

within the space of several lines in the second stanza, involves a transition from *engaño* to *desengaño*, that is, from ignorance to awareness. In this instance, the "hard-hearted desire" ("obstinado deseo"; 350) of the soul is Pharaoh, who keeps free will from making a sacrifice to God and disdains the exalted position of the latter. The speaker then solicits divine assistance freeing him from deceits that led his soul into error, comparing such conduct with overseers who inflicted punishment on the backs of Israelite slaves in Egypt:

> May I feel your arm, untying mine
> from the fierce prison of my deceit
> that, humiliating my back under its weight,
> made me a slave of false judgment.

> Sienta tu brazo, desatando el mío
> de la fiera prisión de mis engaños
> que, mis espaldas humillando al peso,
> siervo de error me hicieron. (350)

The comparisons continue as the speaker juxtaposes his own senses with spells that the magicians of Pharaoh tried to conjure in response to the plagues that God rained down on the Egyptians. However, just as God triumphed over these magicians in Exodus 7–8, so God triumphs over the previously untrustworthy senses of the speaker. This change leads the soul from a state of error to one of enlightenment, a feat that the speaker recognizes by declaring to God, "Then may extraordinary awakenings / form the process against their transgressions; / they became great for your praise" ("Entonces prodigiosos desengaños / contra sus culpas formen el proceso, / para tu loor se engrandecieron"; 350).

A second antithesis that brings the speaker closer to God involves the motif of *vivir muriendo* in the fourth stanza in a way that calls to mind "A Francisco de Salinas," the third ode of Fray Luis de León. This poem describes how the musical compositions of Salinas, a blind organist who taught at the University of Salamanca and a friend of Fray Luis, guide the soul through the heavens towards spiritual union with God. In this journey, the soul moves from the earthly world of materialism and transient beauty to the highest sphere of the universe, where, in the presence of divinely composed music, it achieves new life through a figurative death:

> Here the soul navigates
> through a sea of sweetness, and finally
> so sinks in it,
> that no accident
> strange or foreign does it hear or feel.
> Oh, fortunate fainting!
> Oh, death, you who give life! Oh, sweet forgetfulness!
>
> Aquí la alma navega
> por un mar de dulzura, y finalmente
> en él ansí se anega
> que ningún accidente
> extraño y peregrino oye y siente.
> ¡Oh, desmayo dichoso!
> ¡Oh, muerte que das vida! ¡Oh, dulce olvido!
> (McCaw and Thornton Spinnenweber 70)[26]

Likewise, in the *Canción* of Pinto Delgado, the speaker enthuses how his soul following a path towards God will reach a place "where that divine sound / of your admirable song / will teach me the way in which, dying, I live" ("donde aquel son divino / de tu admirable canto / me enseñe el paso en que, muriendo, viva"; 352). To reach this place, however, the speaker reflects that he must tame "my thoughts, which, worshipping gold, always disdain / your preeminent glory" ("mis pensamientos, que tu gloria altiva / desprecian siempre, idolatrando el oro"; 352). Concomitantly, perhaps referring to Exodus 32.20 when Moses burns the Golden Calf, he implores his own tears to achieve divine mercy so that this latter virtue "may forget my sins, turned into ash" ("vueltos ceniza, olvide mis pecados"; 352).[27] In sum, these instances of achieving unity with God by disdaining material wealth and by weeping

---

26 The notes of McCaw and Thornton Spinnenweber to these lines were especially helpful for my translation. Their observation that "the word 'accidente' is a musical term referring to sharp or flat notes" that, in this context, can suggest "discordant notes" (70n25) affirms the message of Fray Luis that the perfectly harmonious music of Francisco de Salinas accompanies the soul on its ascent to idealized divine union.

27 See Fishlock, "The Shorter Poems" 135–36, for an explanation of the Golden Calf episode of Exodus 32 as a possible subtext to the fourth stanza of Pinto Delgado's *Canción*.

unending tears of repentance highlight the importance the speaker places on distancing himself from gold, which is represented as base and idolatrous.

## Conclusion: Despair Yielding to Hope

The antisemitism that Jews in Iberia had endured since at least the end of the 1300s, when a widespread pogrom ushered in the last century of their existence there, expressed itself in societal contempt for or at least suspicion of New Christians during the time of João Pinto Delgado. This reality of being a New Christian whom Old Christians regarded as a Jew—a religious and ethnic other—contributed to the bifurcated treatment of God and biblical Jews by Pinto Delgado in his poetry, where God was by turns merciful and vengeful; and the latter faithful and idolatrous, victim and cause of their suffering. At the same time, the lingering stigma of having been socially in and out of favor as a New Christian in Iberia helps explain the extent to which Pinto Delgado infused the texts studied here with varying degrees of a similarly split message of despair and hope. Thus, in *Poema de la Reina Ester*, the poet juxtaposed the imminent danger confronting Esther and the Jews of Persia with her ability to bring about their salvation. In *Lamentaciones del Profeta Jeremías*, he contrasted the desolation of Jerusalem and its people for blasphemy, idolatry, and other sins with a desire that through humility and tears Israel might beseech divine forgiveness. Finally, the *Canción* proposed that just as in the Exodus the biblical Jews escaped captivity from Egypt, so the soul may achieve greater proximity to God through a metaphorical journey of *desengaño* that leads to greater awareness of its formerly sinful conduct. Pinto Delgado wrote these poems using imagery and language that call to mind more canonical Spanish authors while also expressing a recognizably converso perspective.

# 3
## "There Is No Greater Nobility than Sublime Virtue": Converso Identity in the Poetry of Antonio Enríquez Gómez

ANTONIO ENRÍQUEZ GÓMEZ STANDS out from the other writers whom this book studies for being the only one who returned to the Iberian Peninsula to live permanently. This reverse migration shows the fluidity of the converso diaspora during the 1600s and the pull that Spain, especially, exerted professionally and psychologically on New Christians who forsook the hard-won opportunity to live freely as Jews elsewhere through such a journey. Testifying to the complexity and protean nature of New Christian identity, the return of Enríquez Gómez to Spain did not necessarily suggest an intention to live as a crypto-Jew in the shadow of the Inquisition. At the same time, however, converso status exerted a profound influence on his life and writing, especially the poetry published outside Spain that the present chapter will discuss.

Born in Cuenca, Spain, in 1600 or 1601, Enríquez Gómez worked as a merchant of cloth and other goods while also writing prolifically as a poet, playwright, and essayist; married an Old Christian; witnessed the detention of his father Diego Enríquez Villanueva by the Inquisition for Judaizing heresy and the confiscation of Diego's material possessions as a consequence of the latter's trial; lived in France for approximately fourteen years, although not necessarily for religious reasons; returned to Spain, where he lived in Seville under various pseudonyms; and in 1660 was detained by the Inquisition, in whose prison he died in 1663.[1] The instability and restlessness that

---

1   The bibliography of Enríquez Gómez is vast. For information about the author, especially as it pertains to his works addressed in this chapter, see publications

characterized these and other experiences explain why his texts are filled in some cases with wanderers who travel from place to place lamenting the vices of allegorical settings, and in others by historical and biblical characters who personify virtue and faithfulness to personal conscience against intolerance and injustice.

Both the autobiographical aspect and the breadth of Enríquez Gómez's writing illumine the worldview of a writer who was figuratively in and out as he strove to create a space for himself in Spanish literature of the mid-1600s. This chapter addresses the converso perspective that informs three texts of his exile in France, not to look for signs that their author was a crypto-Jew, but to show how he advocated a world of greater transparency, tolerance, and individual free will. Along with the poem *El triunfo lusitano* (*The Lusitanian Triumph*, 1641), Enríquez Gómez began the period of his French work with the first of these works, *Academias morales de las musas* (*Moral Academies of the Muses*), published in Bordeaux in 1642.[2] The sadness of exile expressed in *Academias morales* contrasts with the more openly religious themes of the other two works that will be studied here.[3] The "Romance al martirio y felicísimo tránsito de don Lope de Vera y Alarcón" ("*Romance* to the Martyrdom and Most Blessed Death of Don Lope de Vera y Alarcón"), circulated as a manuscript in 1644 or 1645, eulogizes an Old Christian who declared himself a Jew while a student at the University of Salamanca.[4] Calling himself Judá Creyente ("Judah the Believer"), he refused all efforts of the Inquisition compelling him to renounce his newfound faith and was burned for what the tribunal called "heretical wickedness" ("herética pravedad"). Enríquez Gómez celebrates the Jewish identity of Lope de Vera, whose poetic voice welcomes his death at the stake:

---

cited in the bibliography by Brown; Dille; McGaha; Oelman; Révah; Rose; and Warshawsky.

2   Enríquez Gómez wrote *Triumpho lusitano*, a pamphlet in verse, at the invitation of Portuguese ambassadors to Cardinal Richelieu, from whom they hoped to receive recognition as well as financial and military support of Portuguese independence from Spain in 1640. Intended to be given to the new Portuguese king, João IV, the propagandistic work extolled the mission of the ambassadors, which, unfortunately for the Portuguese, did not yield financial support from Richelieu (McGaha, Introduction, *The Perfect King* xxiii-xxiv).

3   McGaha asserts that Enríquez Gómez had completed much of *Academias morales* before leaving Spain in 1635 (Introduction, *The Perfect King*, xxiv–xxv).

4   Brown, *De la cárcel* 64–65.

and so that it may be known to the world,
nations, I am a Hebrew.
*I am a Castilian Jew,*
the Law of Moses I profess,
given on Mount Sinai
by the creator of the heavens.

y porque le conste al mundo,
naciones, yo soy hebreo.
*Judío soy castellano,*
la Ley de Moséh confieso,
dada en el monte Sinaí
por el Autor de los cielos.
            (Brown, *De la cárcel* 168, lines 299–304; italics in original)

Regardless of Enríquez Gómez's own possible crypto-Judaism, the "Romance" praises Lope de Vera for beliefs that the martyr, and perhaps the poet, considered virtuous and divinely favored. The third text that the chapter studies for its converso perspective, *Sansón Nazareno* (*Samson the Nazarene*), is an epic poem written almost entirely before Enríquez Gómez returned to Spain, but not published in its entirety until 1656. This work acclaims Samson as a hero appropriate for a New Christian readership, given the betrayal he suffers and the spiritual vindication and moral triumph of his death, by which time he has overcome his own defects of character and the injustices of his oppressors.

## A Poetry Rooted in Exile

As exile is omnipresent in his poetry, one must ask why Enríquez Gómez decided to travel to Bordeaux, in the southwest of France, in 1635, accompanied by his wife Isabel Basurto and two of their three children. By that time, he had already witnessed the tribulations of his father and uncle at the hands of the Inquisition; lived in Cuenca, Seville, and Madrid; and, working as a merchant, principally of wool, silk, and finished cloth, witnessed financial greed. These experiences help explain the praise of virtue and justice, the restlessness of narrators, and the strong criticism of avarice and similar vices, especially in the *Academias morales*. Enríquez Gómez left Spain not so much for religious reasons, but for economic and/or political ones. In his declaration to inquisitors in 1661, after his own arrest, the poet said he owed money to various people in Seville and admitted "that in Segovia he owes more than 500,000 *reales* to different merchants of cloth and wool who lent to him on credit when he was living in Madrid in the year [16]35" ("que en Segovia debe más de quinientos mil reales a diferentes personas de paños y lana que le fiaban viviendo en Madrid el año de treinta y cinco"; McGaha, "Biographical Data" 136).⁵ Nevertheless, given the emphasis on moral integrity in his writings, it seems out of character that Enríquez Gómez would have completely evaded paying his debts, especially when such a decision would cause him to leave his cherished homeland.

The political standing of Enríquez Gómez seemed as unstable as his precarious financial situation. Perhaps the author was worried about the consequences of having referred impertinently to the king, Felipe IV, and his *valido*, the Count-Duke of Olivares, in plays such as *La soberbia de Nembrot, Engañar para reinar* y *El gran cardenal de España* (McGaha, "El prólogo" 313). The first of these works even attacks the divine right of monarchs to rule (McGaha, "Antonio Enríquez Gómez" 65–66). Using a language of concealment common to many of his texts, the poet alludes to the political cause of his departure from Spain in the prologue of *Academias morales* when explaining to the reader why the book was published in France:

> You will wonder (and rightly so) about the publication of this book in a foreign land. Let my reply be the "Elegy" that I wrote about my wandering, if not voluntary, forced, and if not forced, caused by some who, corrupting the republic, mutually deceptive, sell the poison as an antidote to those who serve under the throne.
>
> Extrañaras (y con razón) haber dado a la imprenta este libro en extranjera patria. Respóndate la "Elegía" que escribí sobre mi peregrinación, si no voluntaria, forzosa, y si no forzosa, ocasionada por algunos, que infeccionando la República, recíprocamente falsos, venden por antídoto el veneno a los que militan debajo del solio. (9v)⁶

---

5    In this publication, McGaha cites a copy of the dossier of 1661 (leg. 2067, exp. 25) that the Inquisition of Seville sent to the Supreme Council of the Inquisition (*Consejo de la Suprema y General Inquisición*, or *Suprema*, for short) in Madrid. Both the original version of this testimony of Enríquez Gómez and the record of his trial (*proceso*) compiled by the Inquisition of Seville during the years 1661–63 have been lost. "Leg." is short for *legajo*, or file containing a bundle of documents; "exp." is short for *expediente*, or specific case within the file.

6    All citations to *Academias morales* in this chapter are from the edition of 1642 published in Bordeaux by Pedro de la Court.

Someone had apparently defamed Enríquez Gómez to the count-duke and his retinue around Felipe IV, a fact which explains the reference to "some deceptive people" ("algunos falsos"), "poison" ("veneno") and "those who serve under the throne" ("los que militan debajo del solio"). In the following lines, the poet compares himself with Seneca to exempt himself from guilt by association and mentions "Neros" ("Nerones") and "Sauls ("Saúles") to make a comment on the lack of morality at court. By associating himself with Seneca, Enríquez Gómez boasts of his own virtue, and by referring to Nero, who ordered Seneca to complete suicide, he alludes to the count-duke, who, according to popular legend, was born in the palace of Nero in Rome. Mentioning "Sauls without a scepter" ("Saúles sin cetro") permits the poet to criticize Olivares and his advisers—contemptuously called "the synagogue" ("la sinagoga"), due to the converso roots of some of them, including Olivares—for their excessive influence over Felipe IV (McGaha, "El prólogo" 313–14; Introduction, *The Perfect King* xix–xxii). The comparison was apt, because just as the biblical Saul lost his reign over Israel due to greed and his jealousy of David, so Olivares would fall from power shortly after the publication of *Academias morales*.[7]

## *ACADEMIAS MORALES DE LAS MUSAS*

Once settled in Bordeaux, where his uncle Antonio Enríquez de Mora was living,[8] Enríquez Gómez discovered that unhappiness, restlessness, and melancholy replaced his prior fears about personal safety. The texts of *Academias morales de las musas* express these and other emotions across nearly five hundred pages, distributed in four books called academies, all of which adhere to a similar structure, as the poet explains in his prologue (8v). Each section begins with an introduction in a setting of idealized natural beauty

---

7   For the history of Saul, see 1 Sam. 9-31. For the downfall of Olivares, see Elliott 640–51.

8   Antonio Enríquez de Mora left Spain after the Inquisition judged him and his brother, Diego Enríquez Villanueva, the poet's father, guilty of wearing clothes prohibited to the children of a condemned Judaizer (the grandfather of Antonio Enríquez Gómez). Enríquez de Mora subsequently left Bordeaux for Livorno, where he was circumcised and lived openly as a Jew. Enríquez Villanueva remained in Spain for several years after his trial, but left for Nantes, a port town along the Loire River, after the Inquisition punished him for heresies related to culinary preparation. Following the death of his first wife, Isabel Gómez, an Old Christian and the mother of Antonio, Diego married Catalina Fonseca, a Jewish woman from Antwerp, once he took up residence in Nantes (Rose, "The Marranos of the Seventeenth Century" 58–62).

(*locus amoenus*), in which four pairs of speakers dressed as shepherds and other rustic characters recite poems about love and its complications and then listen to the chivalric tale of another individual who has entered the scene. During the academy itself, these same individuals discuss and debate themes of *desengaño*, and whether to respond to them with laughter or tears. These themes include, among others, *vanitas vanitatum*, the pain of exile, the guilt of humanity for its condition in life, and *beatus ille*, or idealization of nature and rustic living. Finally, a comedy concludes each academy.[9] Although Enríquez Gómez writes in the prologue that the purpose of the collection is "to persuade souls, not to the entertainment of the love poetry, but to the pleasure of the moral poetry" ("inclinar los ánimos, no a la recreación de los versos amorosos, sino a la delectación de los versos morales"), he recognizes that "variety is the spice of understanding" ("la variedad es la sal del entendimiento"; 8v). The individuals who speak in the introductions and the academies themselves are more spokespersons of the poet than characters of much depth, and even those who participate the most, Albano and Danteo, differ from each other not so much for their actions as for the points of view that they represent. While their perspectives voice the disillusionment and anxiety of Enríquez Gómez, they also show that his melancholy does not lessen his passionate belief in the importance of justice and virtue.

Albano establishes this connection between a lament for individual and collective ills and insistence on moral uprightness in "El pasajero" ("The Voyager"), the first significant poem of the first academy.[10] This lengthy and repetitive poem uses the image well-worn in Latin and Spanish poetry of a ship in a stormy sea that seeks the safety of port to symbolize the journey of someone searching for refuge from dangers of the world.[11] Although the didactic message of the poem is not particularly inventive, several passages embody the converso perspective of Enríquez Gómez: "Don't trust your secret

---

9   For analysis of these comedies, see Dille, *Antonio Enríquez Gómez* 21–43; and "Antonio Enríquez Gómez's Honor Tragedy *A lo que obliga el honor.*" For more information about literary academies as a genre, see Sánchez 10–25; this work refers to Enríquez Gómez on 187–92.

10   I use Dille's translation of "el pasajero" as "the voyager" (*Antonio Enríquez Gómez* 47–48).

11   For example, see Ode 1.14 of Horace, which begins, "O navis, referent in mare te novi / fluctus" ("Oh ship, new waves will bring you again into the sea"; Horace 13–14); and the fourteenth ode of Fray Luis de León, "¡O ya seguro puerto" ("Oh Now a Safe Port"; Blecua 1: 200–02).

to anyone / if you wish to esteem yourself a wise man" ("No fíes de ninguno tu secreto / si te quieres preciar de hombre discreto"; 19–20);

> Don't boast about lineage
> boast about virtue, as there is no offense
> more loathsome and ugly
> than making a costly show of another undertaking.

> No blasones de sangre
> blasona de Virtud, que no hay delito
> más detestable y feo
> que hacer gala costosa de otro empleo (20);

and "don't live with a *malsín* (informer), and if you see one / be silent in his presence while you listen to him" ("no vivas con malsín, y si le vieres / calla delante de él mientras le oyeres"; 22).

In the first of these quotations, the poet may refer to crypto-Judaism when he writes of keeping secrets, but it is equally possible that he describes the stigma of being a converso. Indeed, to avoid this stigma, many post-1492 New Christian families invented false genealogies. Regardless of intent, the advice of Albano makes clear the author's converso anxiety with regard to social position. In the second citation, Enríquez Gómez repeats his oft-stated belief in the virtue of actions over that of birth, while concomitantly disdaining the privilege accorded to so-called purity of blood (*limpieza de sangre*) in 1600s Spain. The warning in the third citation to avoid the *malsín*, or Inquisitorial informant, testifies to the obsessive preoccupation of Enríquez Gómez with this figure.[12] Such spies could include conversos who informed upon family members and neighbors from within New Christian communities, often for reasons not entirely spiritual. This fear of Enríquez Gómez concerning the potentially harmful motives of people around him explains why he infuses the entire poem with a lament about deceitful appearances, as in the following lines:

> Imagine that the world is a palace,

---

12  In *El siglo pitagórico y vida de don Gregorio Guadaña* (*The Pythagorean Century and Life of Don Gregorio Guadaña*), another work of Enríquez Gómez from his time in France, the wandering soul that is the principal character of the work transmigrates into the body of a *malsín*. See this episode in the editions of Amiel 23–33 and Santos 85–96; and Shepard 72–76 for information about the word *malsín*.

> a bewitched labyrinth,
> before entering, a tomb already fashioned,
> . . . . . . . . . . . . . . . . .
> no aspect [of this palace] is what you see, because its center
> is all vanity; if within,
> deceived voyager, you were to look at it,
> you would remain frightened of seeing it.
>
> Imagina que el mundo es un palacio,
> laberinto encantado,
> antes de entrar, sepulcro moldeado,
> . . . . . . . . . . . . . . . . .
> ninguno es lo que ves, porque su centro
> es todo vanidad, si por de dentro
> pasajero engañado le miraras
> espantado de verle te quedaras. (24–25)

Through these words of Albano, Enríquez Gómez affirms that nothing is as it appears, thus reflecting a worldview of marginalization through which the poet considers society.

The poet complements "El pasajero" with another address of Albano that sheds light on the pain of exile. Although the tercet that begins this text, "When I consider my past glory, / and I see myself without me, my condition doubts / if my memory will die with me" ("Cuando contemplo mi pasada gloria, / y me veo sin mí, duda mi estado / si ha de morir conmigo mi memoria"; 59), differs little from the first verse of the sonnet of Garcilaso de la Vega, "When I stop to consider my condition" ("Cuando paro a contemplar mi estado"; McCaw and Thornton Spinnenweber 40), the autobiographical element of Enríquez Gómez's text contributes to its originality. The poetic speaker blames his birth for his exile, laments the subsequent loss of freedom, and compares the frustration of not being understood in a new land with being in Babylon. The lines "I weep for my homeland, and from her I am absent, / misfortune of birth must have caused it, / original burden of he who does not realize it" ("Lloro mi patria, y de ella estoy ausente, / desgracia del nacer lo habrá causado, / pensión original del que no siente"; 59) show how the lineage of which the poet was proud contributed to his exile from his beloved homeland.

In 1634, Enríquez Gómez had testified in the Inquisitorial trial of Bartolomé Febos, a Portuguese converso who represented the commercial interests in Madrid of his merchant father, Rodrigues Lamego, who lived in Rouen (McGaha, "Antonio Enríquez Gómez" 64). This trial grew out of Inquisitorial scrutiny of the New Christian community in the French city mentioned in chapter two, in which one group of conversos accused another of crypto-Judaism. Participation in the trial might have led Enríquez Gómez to fear that the Holy Office would open a trial against him as well. It certainly contributed to the poet's decision to leave Spain shortly thereafter, especially when added to political reasons arising from his aforementioned criticism of Felipe IV and the Count-Duke of Olivares in several comedies of the 1630s. Regardless of possible motives for these verses in *Academias morales*, Enríquez Gómez frequently describes New Christian origin as an indelible misfortune or shortcoming (here, *desgracia*), perhaps because he saw it as an event beyond an individual's control.[13]

The second academy addresses questions without easy answers; fittingly, its most important component consists of three "Epístolas de Job" ("Epistles of Job"), poems written in tercets that, despite being spoken by Danteo and Anfriso, are clearly autobiographical. It seems logical that Enríquez Gómez identifies with his biblical forebear because the conflict between past goodness and present adversity that Job experiences helps explain the situation of the poet himself (Rauchwarger 73). Due to exile, possible political misfortune, financial difficulties, and the anxiety of being a converso, Enríquez Gómez in the first epistle envisions Job as a character who associates birth with sin. Job feels isolated because "Without any doubt, I committed first / a profound transgression, when I entered / in this world to be a prisoner" ("Sin duda alguna, cometí primero / algún delito grande, cuando entraba / a ser en este mundo prisionero"; 162). Job does not explain the contents of this sin, but perhaps for Enríquez Gómez it symbolizes the stain of his converso lineage.

Additionally, by calling attention to the hopelessness and dejection that Job represents, Enríquez Gómez personalizes his own disillusionment, as the following questions make clear:

Who is man, or who will make him be
worthy of being [a man], his life being
a temporary life that is directed towards dying?
. . . . . . . . . . . . . . . . . . . . . . . . .

---

13    Constance Rose believed that his participation as a witness in the trial of Febos made Enríquez Gómez "a marked man" in the eyes of the Inquisition ("The Marranos of the Seventeenth Century" 61).

> What is to be of me, I who was born conceited about
> the days, vanity, and absurdity
> from the same dust that is awaiting me?
>
> ¿Quién es el hombre, o quién le hará que sea
> merecedor del ser, siendo su vida
> vida prestada que en morir se emplea?
> . . . . . . . . . . . . . . . . . . . . . . . . . .
> ¿Ay de mí, que nací lisonjeando
> los días, vanidad, y devaneo
> del mismo polvo que me está aguardando? (160).

Job laments his fate using the theme common to the Spanish Baroque of life as a melancholy journey towards inevitable death (*vivir muriendo*). As he states in the following tercets, even a tree is more fortunate, because "when [its branches have been] cut / . . . / it returns," ("cuando destroncado / [...] él vuelve"; 160), while he will become dust.[14] Nevertheless, towards the end of the first epistle, Job permits himself to yearn for a less chaotic world: "Oh, if so much absurdity were to die! / Oh, if so much lack of judgement were to end! / Oh, if man were to be born without desire!" ("¡O si muriera tanto devaneo! / ¡O si acabara tanto desatino! / ¡O si naciera el hombre sin deseo!"; 164). Just as the biblical Job longs for times, now lost, when he felt the presence of God and was respected by others (Job 29), so the Job of Enríquez Gómez longs for a just world without anguish caused by the inherited sin of converso lineage.

Speaking in the second epistle with less circumspection regarding potentially compromising biographical details, Enríquez Gómez depicts Job blaming himself for the anguish of the first letter. The feeling of betrayal by those who should have supported the author, including his parents, other relatives, and friends, sharpens the lament of Job: "My honor, my vanity, and my adornment / I lost, my lost fame scattering / in the swiftest paths of the wind" ("Mi honor, mi vanidad, y mi ornamento / perdí, volando mi perdida fama / en los rumbos más rápidos del viento"; 166). Although the poet does not explain the circumstances of his abandonment by those whom he trusted, the resultant isolation explains the melancholy of the text. Most certainly representing Enríquez Gómez, Job blames himself for his predicament: "In the palace my fantasy was seen, / [and] also I saw myself covered in vanity, / but woe betide the fool who trusts palaces" ("En palacio se vio

---

14  See Job 14.7–12 for the same comparison.

mi fantasía, / también de vanidad me vi adornado, / ¡mas ay del loco que en palacios fía!"; 165). Enríquez Gómez uses the word *palacio* to represent the royal court, symbolic of deceitful appearances, pride, and avarice.¹⁵ Through this self-criticism for allowing the court to beguile him, Job also censures the court itself, perhaps because the poet for whom he speaks never felt truly welcome there.

Although in the third epistle Job affirms again that the sin of birth and the betrayal of others have caused his suffering, he begins and ends the text with a plan for improvement. Thus, at the start he proclaims, "I plan to grab onto the sacred tribunal / seeking my justice and my right / from he who gave the order / for me to leave" ("Del tribunal sagrado pienso asirme, / pidiendo mi justicia y mi derecho, / a quien orden me dio, para partirme"; 168) and promises to be his own witness before the court. Glen Dille noted a clear reference to the Inquisition in these lines (*Antonio Enríquez Gómez* 52), and it is certain that Enríquez Gómez confronted the Holy Office in life as in literature. For example, in 1624 he sued the Inquisition to recover his family's property sequestered and then confiscated during the trial of his father, Diego Enríquez Villanueva, for secret Judaism.¹⁶ Additionally, he prepared a detailed, documented plan for reforming the Holy Office in *La política angélica* (*Angelic Politics*; Rouen, 1647) and satirized the court in *La Inquisición de Lucifer y visita de todos los diablos* (*The Inquisition of Lucifer and Visit of All the Devils*), a manuscript of the 1640s written in the genre of dream fiction.¹⁷ The same determination with which Enríquez Gómez stood up to the Inquisition helps him formulate a plan for Job to address God during the final

---

15   Another example of the court as a locus of these vices occurs in the poem "El peregrino" ("The Wanderer") found in the third academy, as part of the narrator's description of "the first city that I saw in the world" ("la primera ciudad que vi en el mundo"; 245; see 243–48 for the entire poem).

16   See McGaha, "Biographical Data" 130–34, for a thorough summary of how, through this suit, Enríquez Gómez and his wife, Isabel Basurto, recovered some of their property. The assets for which they sought payment included the value of a quantity of silk entrusted to the merchant Miguel Fernández de Fonseca to sell in Lisbon; the dowries of Isabel Gómez (Antonio's late mother) and Isabel Basurto; and five hundred ducats as compensation for Isabel Basurto and her maidservant for their "work and investments ... in the family business" (132).

17   For the *Política angélica*, see McGaha, Introduction, *The Perfect King*; and "'Divine' Absolutism." For *La inquisición de Lucifer y visita de todos los diablos*, see the edition of Rose and Kerkhof; and Warshawsky, "A Spanish *Converso's* Quest for Justice."

tercets of the third epistle. Here Job tries to lessen his abandonment through an intense belief in God:

> I await in divine omnipotence
> sublime favors without limit,
> trusting in the pardons of its essence.
> I still wait with faith, with a new life,
> to see in other delicate material
> the greatness of God illuminated.
> Then my trusting hope,
> singing psalms to his divine name,
> will rejoice in the delightful sight of him.
>
> Yo aguardo en la divina omnipotencia
> mercedes soberanas sin medida,
> fiado en los perdones de su esencia.
> Aun espero con fe, con nueva vida,
> ver en otra materia delicada,
> la grandeza de Dios esclarecida.
> Entonces mi esperanza confiada,
> psalmos cantando a su divino nombre,
> gozará de su vista regalada. (174)

Just as Job at the end of the biblical text recognizes the preeminence of God, so the speaker in the poem recognizes in God a solution to "a horde of insolent suffering" ("un tropel de penas atrevidas"; 172) and to a feeling of isolation "without life and without belongings" ("sin vida y sin hacienda"; 173). This declaration of the power of divine redemption contrasts with the previous pessimism of the epistles, as Job comes to trust God to lessen his inherited suffering.

The third academy explores in greater depth the restlessness that characterizes Enríquez Gómez as a converso, an exile, and an observer of societal hypocrisy. In "El peregrino" ("The Wanderer"), the speaker Pacor describes a journey through allegorical sites including a palace, a meeting of a group of fools, and a madhouse in which the defects of a world upside down triumph over virtue, justice, and reason. The title of this poem conveys how, in the converso worldview of Enríquez Gómez, the word *peregrino* generally does not describe a religious pilgrim but an exile in flight or at the very least a life of geographical and spiritual wandering.[18] A subsequent poem, "Al engaño de la naturaleza" ("On the Deceit of Nature"), interprets the observations of "El peregrino" using a tone of disillusionment that grows out of awareness by the speaker Albano of the vanity of ambition. Thinking that his life must involve the pursuit of wealth, Albano laments, "I boarded the ship of greed" (enbarquéme en la nao de la codicia"; 261). Nevertheless, this avarice only enriched the narrator at the expense of widows and the poor. Now aged, Albano counsels the reader, for whom there is still time to mend ways, "live to die [well], take in your hand / the path of the law, because with it [the law] / your adverse fortune will be kind" (vive para morir, toma el camino / de la ley en la mano, que con ella / será benigna tu contraria estrella"; 264). This advice situates the poem within the theme of Spanish Baroque literary *desengaño* and, at the same time, by directing the attention of the reader to justice ("el camino de la ley"), emphasizes a quest by Enríquez Gómez for moral integrity.

The fourth and final academy of *Academias morales* tries to make sense of the faults of the world lamented in the first three by juxtaposing the laughter of Democritus with the tears of Heraclitus. Danteo and Albano represent these philosophers in four complementary elegies that advocate for virtuous living in a world disdainful of virtue. Through these speakers, Enríquez Gómez laments the continual difficulties of his life, as, for example, when Danteo (Democritus) states resignedly, "if when I came into the world I entered dying, / it will be good to go out living now: / crying I came and laughing I shall leave" ("si cuando vine al mundo entré muriendo, / bueno será salir viviendo ahora: / llorando vine, y me saldré riendo"; 360). For his part, Albano (Heraclitus) recognizes that "laughing at the world is the surest knowledge" ("reír del mundo es ciencia más segura"; 373). However, lacking Danteo's capacity of reacting with humor in the face of moral corruption, he asks himself, "How must I not weep in this life, / if all of it is full of suffering, / being incurable its terrible wound?" ("¿Cómo no he de llorar en esta vida, / si ella toda está llena de dolores, / siendo incurable su terrible herida?"; 375). His only response is to appeal to justice, thus invoking a concept that for Enríquez Gómez always serves as a guide in an unjust world.

In the *romance* (narrative poem) that follows the elegies of Democritus and Heroclitus, Enríquez Gómez, speaking through Albano, summarizes his

---

18   Given the distinct meaning that Enríquez Gómez attaches to the word *peregrino*, I translate it as "wanderer" rather than pilgrim, here and throughout the book. See Rose, "Antonio Enríquez Gómez and the Literature of Exile" 65–66, for further explanation of this sense of *peregrino*.

worldview as a New Christian. To do so, the author underlines the restlessness that has pursued him since birth; juxtaposes laughter with tears; blames a tribunal, presumably Inquisitorial, that has made his life difficult; laments the condition of exile; and uses these experiences to share advice with the reader. The thread of a geographic and figurative journey winds through the text from its beginning, for example, when Albano describes himself as a "wanderer in grief / from the first cradle" ("peregrino en los dolores / desde la cuna primera"; 402). The poem also makes clear the identification of Enríquez Gómez with Heraclitus, the philosopher of tears, when Albano continues, "I was born mourning my offense / before I committed it" ("nací llorando el delito / antes que le cometiera"; 402). As José Guillermo García Valdecasas noted, these lines show that the anxiety of the poet sprang from his lineage, an "offense" ("delito") that cast a lifelong shadow (84). Proclaiming subsequently, "In the tribunal of the world / false witnesses damage me" ("En el tribunal del mundo / falsos testigos me alteran"; 403), Albano describes an informant, perhaps one who helped precipitate the hasty flight of the poet from Spain. The subtext of betrayal to the Inquisition present in these lines shows how, using "half words with double intentions" ("medias palabras con dobles intenciones"; García Valdecasas 84), Enríquez Gómez communicates his message without stating it openly.

Finally, no composition of the poet discussing a journey would be complete without a lament of exile, a circumstance that explains why Albano says of himself:

> Wanderer in misfortune
> wearing down foreign lands,
> the angel of experience
> opened my eyes to pain.
>
> Peregrino en las desdichas
> fatigando ajenas tierras,
> me abrió los ojos al daño
> el Ángel de la experiencia. (403)

This restlessness imbues the catalog of advice directed to a "voyager" ("pasajero") with which Albano concludes the poem. Advocating self-determination over lineage and social climbing, these commands could well serve as a creed for conversos of the 1600s, as in the following examples: "never boast of lineage, / because there is no greater nobility / than sublime virtue" ("jamás blasones de sangre, / porque no hay mejor nobleza / que la virtud soberana"; 404); and "from affiliations with informers / flee always, because these [affiliations] / always end up in mournful tragedies" ("de malsines compañías /.../ huye siempre, porque paran / en lamentables tragedias"; 405).[19]

## "Romance al martirio y felicísimo tránsito de don Lope de Vera y Alarcón"

The openly Jewish message of the first part of the "Romance al martirio y felicísimo tránsito de don Lope de Vera y Alarcón" and messianic fervor of the second make the poem anomalous in the corpus of Enríquez Gómez. Whether or not this work corroborates the possible Jewish identity of the poet at the time of its composition, as Brown has argued convincingly in his meticulous and well-reasoned study *De la cárcel inquisitorial a la Sinagoga de Amsterdam* (45–46), the "Romance" clearly expresses the admiration of Enríquez Gómez for the Jewish faith of Lope de Vera. As a result, throughout the "Romance," the voice that the poet assigns to Lope de Vera strongly articulates a belief in the ethical and spiritual superiority of Judaism to Christianity. Resisting efforts of priests and inquisitors to convince him of the immorality of this belief, the fictional Lope de Vera of Enríquez Gómez also criticizes what the poet regarded as the hypocrisy of the Inquisitorial tribunal.[20]

The preparation and circulation of the "Romance" testifies to the fluid and unpredictable conditions that impacted a diasporic converso author proud of his Spanish and Jewish roots. Enríquez Gómez produced multiple variants of the poem after having possibly read aloud an archetype in Rouen to "a literary group where conversos on the path of their reconversion to Judaism would have gathered" ("un cenáculo donde se reunieran conversos

---

19   The first of these quotations is the source of the title of this chapter. In part 2 of *Don Quixote*, just before Sancho Panza begins his governorship of the island of Barataria, Don Quixote offers his squire advice effectively identical to the first of these commands: "Consider, Sancho: if you take virtue as your means, and pride in performing virtuous deeds, there is no reason to envy the means of princes and lords, because blood is inherited and virtue is acquired, and virtue in and of itself has a value that blood does not" (2.42.730–31).

20   Oelman affirms that both sections of the "Romance" also demonstrate that Enríquez Gómez created a Jewish self-identity from various sources, despite not growing up within established Judaism (Enríquez Gómez, *Romance al divín mártir* 117). In the same work, Oelman also states his belief that Lope de Vera's words from the stake at the end of the first part of the poem are "in effect, a declaration of the poet's own Judaistic credo" (40).

en camino a su reconversión al judaísmo"; Brown, *De la cárcel* 66). The existence of these variants arises from the probability that listeners who heard Enríquez Gómez read the poem requested copies of it, which he then wrote up and sent, "but each time he prepared a copy, he would make small changes to the text" (Brown, email to author, 21 May 2009). Three manuscripts of these variants, directed to a Spanish-Portuguese Jewish audience, found their way to Amsterdam (A), Hamburg (H), and Oxford (O). A manuscript of a fourth variant (L), intended for a real or imagined Spanish-Portuguese Inquisitorial reader, was included in a miscellany containing documents defending Judaism later found in Livorno (Brown, *De la cárcel* 24–27, 105, 133).[21]

Although none of these four variants contains a signature of the author, Miguel de Barrios, writing in Amsterdam during the 1680s, asserts several times that Enríquez Gómez wrote the "Romance." For example, in a pamphlet entitled *Relación de los poetas y escritores españoles de la nación judaica amstelodama* (*Account of Spanish Poets and Writers of the Jewish Nation of Amsterdam*, 1682), he lists this text and *Sansón Nazareno* among "famous poems" by Spanish-Portuguese Jewish authors (célebres poesías"; Kayserling, "Une histoire de la littérature juive 285–86; also qtd. in Brown, *De la cárcel* 44). As well, in the "Memorial of Martyrs" of *Triumpho del govierno popular* (*Triumph of Popular Government*, 1683), Barrios cites Enríquez Gómez and Manuel de Pina for celebrating the "marvelous strength" ("maravillosa firmeza"; 505) of Lope de Vera in their respective poetry.[22] Brown has prepared a text of the poem identified as C1/C2 (C=Calgary) that accounts for the distinctions and textual omissions of all four manuscripts, with the purpose of "depicting the most logical and correct reading between them" ("representar las lecturas más lógicas y correctas de entre ellos"; *De la cárcel*

---

21   These four versions are held in the following libraries: the Ets Haim Library-Livraria Montezinos of the Portuguese Synagogue in Amsterdam; the University of Hamburg Library; the Bodleian Library, Oxford University; and the Talmud Torah Library of the Jewish Community of Livorno (Comunità ebraica di Livorno).

22   Brown, *De la cárcel* 44. Brown also affirms that Enríquez Gómez alludes to the "Romance" in his anti-Inquisitorial prose satire *La inquisición de Lucifer y visita de todos los diablos* (43–44). The reference occurs when a Lutheran heretic being interrogated declares to the Inquisition of the [current] era ("Inquisición del siglo," that is, the Holy Office), "and I was born more to produce autos de fe in verse, than to represent them in public" ("y más nací para hacer autos de fe en verso, que para representarlos en público"; Enríquez Gómez, *La Inquisición de Lucifer* 43). The exact date of publication of this work has not been established, but as Rose and Kerkhof wrote in their introduction, it could have been before or after 1649 (xviii–xix).

157).²³ Given these characteristics, citations to the "Romance" in the following analysis are to C1/C2. This analysis addresses lines 1–388, in which Lope de Vera insists upon the superiority of Judaism to Christianity, rather than lines 389–587, which consist of a messianic and kabbalistic prophecy, due to the apparently narrower connection of this latter section with the history of the protagonist as well as limitations of space.²⁴

A proud and challenging tone characterizes the poetic voice of Lope de Vera, who, in an introduction found only in the Livorno manuscript, demands that an Inquisitorial priest carefully read the following lines, "which boast about the Law that I follow / and the truth of its Lord" (que ostenta la Ley que sigo / y la verdad de su Dueño (160, lines i–iv). The following thirty verses, narrated in the third person, maintain this assertiveness as they dramatize the history that has led Lope de Vera to the stake, from where he addresses an invective towards the priest trying to obtain from him a last-minute repentance of Jewish heresy. These lines equate Lope de Vera with a biblical hero, first as another Judah Maccabee, due to the "tortures so great and excessive [that] he suffered" ("padeció tantos / y desiguales tormentos"; 161, lines 11–12), and also as Abraham, for having circumcised himself in prison. Indeed, the circumcision that Lope de Vera performed, using the bone of a chicken sharpened with a nail, was a defining characteristic of crypto-Jewish martyrs of the era (Bodian, *Dying in the Law of Moses* 169–70). Combined with his Old Christian lineage, this act contributed to his renown in the diaspora of former conversos returned to Judaism as well as among conversos of Iberian lands less willing or able to identify as secret Jews.²⁵

The narrative voice of these first thirty lines does not identify the Inquisition by name, but the phrase "the cruel dragons / of that haughty tribunal" ("los fieros dragones / de aquel tribunal soberbio"; Brown, *De la cárcel* 160,

---

23   Readers may compare this modern text with the four manuscript versions on which it is based in the synoptic edition of the "Romance" in Brown's edition (160–75). Also see Révah, *Antonio Enríquez Gómez* 336–61, for his edition of the poem "based principally" ("essentiellement fondée"; 336) on the manuscripts at Oxford and Amsterdam and to a lesser extent on the one at Livorno; and the Oxford manuscript in the edition prepared by Oelman (Enríquez Gómez, *Romance al divín mártir Judá Creyente* 133–70).

24   For explanations of this prophecy and interpretations of the "Romance" as a messianic and kabbalistic text, see Brown, *De la cárcel* 75–100, 139–40, and 180–83; and Oelman in Enríquez Gómez, *Romance al divín mártir Judá Creyente* 100–01, 105–17, and 175–78.

25   The testimony that Lope de Vera had a small amount of Jewish lineage "appears to have been mere rumor" (Bodian, *Dying in the Law of Moses* 242n1).

lines 1–2) alludes to the Holy Office with surprising directness. Equally bold is the metaphor in the following line that describes the Inquisition as a court "whose olive [branch] was the sword" ("cuya oliva fue la espada"; 160, line 3). This phrase refers to the shield of the Holy Office to emphasize the hypocrisy of the court, which for the poet consisted of Christian mercy offered under threat of coercion and violence.[26] Although in his published works Enríquez Gómez generally does not describe characters representative of Judaism as transparently as in the case of Lope de Vera, the passage is not completely anomalous.[27] For example, calling Lope "martyr [who was] the most [steadfast] wanderer" ( "el mártir más peregrino"; 160, v. 5), he reminds the reader of multiple images of wandering in the *Academias morales*; and the sincerity of the hero, in whose mouth "deceit was not found" ("no se halló engaño"; 161, v. 29), testifies to the importance of honesty for the poet. Enríquez Gómez shows admiration for Lope de Vera when his speaker proclaims, "Long live the name of Adonai, / holy creator of the universe!" ("¡Viva el nombre de Adonay, / Sacro Autor del universo!"; 161, lines 31-32), as these words show how the martyr derives strength confronting the tribunal through faith in a Jewish understanding of God.

During his soliloquy following these introductory lines, Lope de Vera refutes the arguments of the priest who tries to reconcile him with Christianity, up to and including at the beginning of his execution. However, not even by offering the relative mercy of death by garroting before the stake is lit can the priest sway Lope de Vera from his argument. To compose this argument, Enríquez Gómez must have read a letter written by a possibly apocryphal inquisitor that strove to show the compassion of the Inquisition as it tried to compel Lope de Vera to abjure his heresy and the stubborn refusal of the defendant to do so. Just as the "Romance" itself consists of four manuscript variants, so two variants of this letter exist, both addressed to a Marchioness

---

26   See McGaha, "Antonio Enríquez Gómez" 74, for additional examples of literary imagery juxtaposing the olive branch and the sword.

27   See instances of Jewish characters in Enríquez Gómez in his twenty-six "Sonetos sobre los antiguos patriarcas del Viejo Testamento" ("Sonnets about the Ancient Patriarchs of the Old Testament"), from a manuscript held at the Biblioteca di Brera in Milan that Brown has reprinted in *De la cárcel* 344–57. Three of these sonnets ("En alabanza de Adán," "En alabanza de Enoch," and "En alabanza de Noé") are also included in *Academias morales* 33–35 and five have women as their subject. In another publication, written with contributor Cyndi Valerio, Brown notes that Enríquez Gómez shows a more evident Jewish identity "in his unedited and manuscript work" ("su obra inedita y manuscrita"; "Nuevas calas" 54), a trend that the "Romance" further evinces.

(*marquesa*) of Monterey, as Brown has shown: in one, the author spells his name Bartolomeo Márquez Mirezo, and in the other, Bartolomé Márquez de Morquecho.[28] In the absence of documentation about the identity of this individual, Brown conjectures that the names of Bartolomé Márquez de Moscoso and Gerónimo Morquecho y Saoba, two Inquisitorial officials of Cuenca mentioned in the trial of the father of Lope de Vera y Alarcón, also called Lope de Vera, evolved to become those of the author of the letter and the *marquesa* to whom it was addressed (*De la cárcel* 361–63, 402, 413). With its partiality towards the Inquisition, this letter could have circulated through the Sephardic diaspora to try to counteract the propagandistic success of martyrdoms such as that of Lope de Vera.[29]

Enrolling at the University of Salamanca at the age of fourteen, Lope de Vera had studied Hebrew, Chaldean, Greek, Latin, and the Hebrew Bible there for five years when arrested in 1639. The letter of Márquez Mirezo (or Morquecho) would have appealed to Enríquez Gómez for describing this course of study as well as the Judaism of Lope de Vera and the young student's dramatic resistance to the Inquisition during the five years of his imprisonment and trial. For example, of the two individuals sentenced to the stake out of twenty-five punished for Jewish heresy at the auto de fe of July 25, 1644, in Valladolid, he was the only one burned alive (the other was burned in effigy). In the words of Márquez Mirezo, the letter also states how Lope de Vera showed himself to be "the greatest Judaizing heretic that I think there has been in the Church ... such resolve as this youth had has not been seen, nor has there been written nor are we aware of a similar case" ("el mayor judío hereje que pienso ha habido en la iglesia ... no se ha visto tal firmeza como este mozo tenía ni se ha escrito ni tenemos noticia de cosa semejante"; British Library copy qtd. in Brown, *De la cárcel* 364, 366). Enríquez Gómez communicates this resolve and affirmation of Judaism by Lope de Vera through questions by which the accused interrogates Catholicism. These questions

---

28   The variant of the letter by Bartolomeo Márquez Mirezo is held at the British Library, while that in which the author's name is spelled Bartolomé Márquez de Morquecho is at the University of Hamburg Library. Brown includes both letters in *De la cárcel* 364–66; Barnett also published and translated the version belonging to the British Library (235–39).

29   See Bodian, *Dying in the Law of Moses* 27–31, for analysis of the "extended drama" (27) between inquisitors who strove to the very last minute to compel those accused of heresy to recant, and individuals such as Lope de Vera who refused to abjure their beliefs.

emphasize to a 1600s Sephardic audience the elect status of Judaism and its superiority to Catholicism, as in the following examples:

> If on Mount Sinai
> voices of heaven have been heard,
> who will be so reckless
> that he rejects their [divine] echoes?
> . . . . . . . . . . . . . . . . .
> If God and man signed
> this holy covenant
> and it has been given to us in writing,
> how can there be another new one?
>
> Si en el monte de Sinaí
> se oyeron voces del cielo,
> ¿quién será tan atrevido
> que Le rechace los ecos?
> . . . . . . . . . . . . . . . . .
> Si Dios y el hombre firmaron
> este sacro testamento
> y se nos da por escrito,
> ¿cómo ha de haber otro nuevo? (162–63, lines 81–85, 105–08)

For Lope de Vera, another "holy covenant" does not exist, a belief that explains his subsequent declarations that no reason should impede people from continuing to keep it, especially since "the holy Law / that God wrote with his own hand" ("la Ley santa / que escribió Dios con Su dedo"; 163, lines 131–32) has not lost its sanctity. Through this belief, he justifies his refusal to abjure the Law. Lope de Vera proclaims these statements surely blasphemous to inquisitors because his impending martyrdom frees him from worrying about the safety of other crypto-Jews and "defend[ing] rabbinic Judaism," instead allowing him to focus on his own interpretation of the Hebrew Bible (Bodian, *Dying in the Law of Moses* 36).[30]

In the following section of the poem, Lope de Vera defines his Judaism as a rejection of many core beliefs of Catholic Christianity, including the Trinity, the visible representation of God, the Eucharist, and the redemption

---

30   See Bodian, *Dying in the Law of Moses* 36–37, for an explanation of how in their debates with inquisitors, impenitent crypto-Jews such as Lope de Vera held an advantage over medieval Iberian Jews who had engaged Christians in polemics.

of humanity by Christ (164–67, lines 153–272). The martyr uses his momentarily privileged position at the stake to rebuff the priest who has just given a sermon attempting one last time to reconcile him to Catholicism:

> Ridiculously daring,
> rhetorically foolish,
> you oppose the one who tells you
> I [am] the first and I [am] the last.

> Ridículamente osado,
> retóricamente necio,
> te opones a Quien te dice
> Yo el primero y Yo el postrero. (164, lines 165–68)[31]

Notwithstanding the question of whether he himself was "ridiculously daring" for choosing martyrdom, Lope de Vera then exalts the oneness and invisible presence of God, arguing that such Jewish beliefs show a greater faith in God than exists in Christianity. For example, he privileges the absence of divine imagery in Judaism as a sign of this presence: "Not seeing God and [still] to believe in God / is faith with mystery" ("No ver a Dios y crëerLo / es una fe con misterio"; 165, lines 193–94). Given the usual caution of Enríquez Gómez regarding faith and the fact that "almost all of his extant works are unimpeachably orthodox" (McGaha, "Antonio Enríquez Gómez" 68), one cannot claim with surety to what degree these affirmations of Judaism by Lope de Vera reflected the beliefs of the poet. Nevertheless, regardless of his own possibly varying religious identity throughout his life, in examples cited in this paragraph, including the following one, Enríquez Gómez shows how his converso worldview leads him to praise fundamental teachings of Judaism so eloquently:

> The holy Law, the pure Law,
> is that which the Hebrew keeps,
> as it knows one God alone
> by the light of understanding.

---

31   Brown described such a sermon as "antisemitic and condemnatory" ("antisemita y condenatorio"; *De la cárcel* 39). See 315–43 for examples of two such sermons, one given at the auto de fe of 1615 in Évora, Portugal, and the other at the auto de fe of 1649 in Mexico City.

> La Ley santa, la Ley pura,
> es la que guarda el hebreo,
> pues conoce un solo Dios
> por luz del entendimiento. (164, lines 209–12)

Lope de Vera personifies values that Enríquez Gómez most admired, such as resolve despite Inquisitorial prosecution and adherence to one's personal truth. Praising the Judaism of the martyr allows the poet a dramatic means of extolling this steadfastness.

Before entering into the messianic prophecy of the last part of the "Romance," Lope de Vera enthusiastically anticipates his imminent martyrdom by intensifying the ardor of his commitment to Judaism. The poet demonstrates his belief in the greater importance of deeds over lineage by means of the proud declaration of the martyr that testifies to this commitment:

> Wanderer in Israel
> will I be [as if] by birth,
> disdaining for the sake of the Law
> the lineage of my grandparents.

> Peregrino en Israel
> seré yo por nacimiento,
> despreciando por la Ley
> la sangre de mis abuelos. (167, lines 277–80)

Here *peregrino* does not evoke the wandering and insecurity of the term in the *Academias morales*, but rather the spiritual journey of Lope de Vera from the Christianity of his forebears to Judaism. To dramatize the sacrifice and the strength of this transformation, Enríquez Gómez equates his subject with biblical and deuterocanonical figures important to crypto-Jews for symbolizing divine redemption, often attained through fire (lines 272–93). For example, when Lope de Vera declares, "From the tribunal of Antioch / I go out to die in the fire" ("Del tribunal del Antíoco / salgo a morir en el fuego"; 167, lines 273–74), he emulates the seven unnamed Maccabee sons and their mother, often called Hannah, in 2 Maccabees 7, who prefer death at the hands of the Seleucid king Antiochus IV Epiphanes to eating pork. Through this image, Enríquez Gómez also reminds listeners and readers that the "Romance" introduced Lope de Vera as one "who revived the strength / of the strong Maccabees" ("que resucitó la fuerza / de los fuertes macabëos;

160, lines 14–15). The poet further glorifies the impenitent proselyte by having Lope de Vera liken himself to Elijah swept up to heaven in a chariot of flames in 2 Kings 2.11; and to Shadrach, Meshach, and Abednego, the three Jews who in Daniel 3 emerge unharmed from the furnace into which the Babylonian king Nebuchadnezzar has cast them for their refusal to pay homage to his golden statue.[32]

The martyrdom of Lope de Vera resists and criticizes what Enríquez Gómez regarded as the persecutory zeal of the Inquisition. The poet expresses this censure through the young defendant, who after calling his executioners "profane Antiochians" ("Antíocos profanos") exhorts them, "Carry out the decree / of the contemptible Inquisition, / *Tribunal of hell*" ("ejecutad el decreto / de la vil Inquisición, / *Tribunal de los infiernos*"; 168, lines 305–08; italics in original). Once again, Enríquez Gómez elevates his subject by equating Lope de Vera with the Maccabees and his Inquisitorial oppressor with Antiochus IV, proclaiming that in neither case can brute force compel these individuals to abjure their faith. The scene is literally weighted with tension, given that executioners have piled an amount of wood on the pyre likened to Mt. Etna, here called by an older name, "Mongibelo." Even as "his flesh began to crackle / and his bones were grinding" ("empezó a crujir la carne / y [estuvo] rechinando los huesos"; 168, lines 321–22), Lope de Vera achieves his greatest liberation, at least symbolically, when surrounded by flames, as he boasts, "that if I die for [the One for] whom I live, / I already live by that [for which] I die" ("que si muero por Quien vivo, / ya vivo de lo que muero"; 169, lines 347–48). He personifies this liberation from Inquisitorial reach by calling himself the phoenix, the mythological bird that regenerates itself from its own ashes: "but in the flames I will be / the simple bird that knows how / to die and live at the same time" ("pero yo seré en el fuego / el ave que simple sabe / morir y vivir a un tiempo"170; lines 374–76). By speaking of the ashes of Lope de Vera gaining life anew, Enríquez Gómez aligns the martyr with a tradition in diasporic Spanish-Portuguese Jewish poetry of the 1600s that regarded the phoenix as symbol of resistance to the Inquisition.[33]

---

32   Isaac Cardoso, the subject of chapter 4, praises the three courtiers from Daniel, as well as Hannah and her sons from 2 Maccabees, as examples of Jews willing to die for their beliefs. In a sonnet about Tomás Treviño de Sobremonte, Miguel de Barrios, the subject of chapter 5, exalts the martyrdom of this crypto-Jew of colonial Mexico in 1649 by likening him to Elijah ascending to heaven in a chariot of fire.

33   As Bodian, *Hebrews of the Portuguese Nation* 20, points out, Neve Shalom, one of the first Spanish-Portuguese congregations of Amsterdam, adopted the phoe-

The uncompromising Jewish faith of Lope de Vera that Enríquez Gómez celebrates in the "Romance" is all the more noteworthy given that summaries of his trial that the tribunal of Valladolid sent to the Suprema in Madrid indicate that the youth did not originally determine to be a martyr. For example, at an audience with inquisitors on June 13, 1640, nearly a year after his arrest, he justified his heterodox beliefs by saying that he enjoyed debate for the sake of debate and that, in the words of the scribe preparing one of the summaries, "he had been inclined to the Law of Moses ... but not with absolute determination, and that having this doubt was [due to] his own blindness and weakness" ("se había inclinado a la ley de Moisén... pero no con determinación absoluta y que fue ceg[u]edad y flaqueza suya el tener esta duda"; AHN, leg. 2135, exp. 16, 18v, qtd. in Brown, *De la cárcel* 374).[34] Later, he became famous throughout the Sephardic diaspora after unambiguously championing Judaism in the face of Inquisitorial attacks against this faith, rather than for his own specific knowledge of rabbinic Judaism (Bodian, *Dying in the Law of Moses* 177). Not surprisingly, given his own experience of injustice, Enríquez Gómez celebrates this defense of Judaism by his protagonist as a triumph of freedom of conscience over repression and intolerance.

### SANSÓN NAZARENO

In *Sansón Nazareno*, Enríquez Gómez strove to assert his skill as an epic poet, especially by imitating the five whom he most admired and whom he names in the prologue: Homer, Virgil, Torquato Tasso, Luis de Camoens, and Miguel de Silveira (56). Consisting of a prologue and 7,224 lines written in eight-line stanzas (octaves) of hendecasyllabic verse across fourteen books, his "heroic poem" ("poema heroico"; 56) employs ornate and Latinate language to achieve this goal.[35] As the printer of the poem, Laurent Maurry, explains in the prefatory "Al que leyere" ("To the Reader"), Enríquez Gómez had written thirteen books of *Sansón* at the time of his sudden departure from Rouen for Seville, but Maurry was unable to print the entire work until receiving its final book in 1656.[36] Using as a point of departure the story of Samson told in Judges 13–16, the poem analyzes, among other moments of the life of Samson, his prodigious efforts to free the Hebrews from oppres-

---

nix as its symbol, and the bird also appears in other literature exalting converso martyrs.

34  See Brown, *De la cárcel* 370–401, for transcriptions of five of these summaries.

35  Throughout the prologue, Enríquez Gómez uses this term for epic poem.

36  See Romero Muñoz for an edition of the prologue to *Sansón Nazareno* accompanied by detailed notes.

sive rule by the Philistines; his relationships with three Philistine women—Dalestina, a prostitute from Gaza, and Delilah—his blinding at the hands of the Philistines due to betrayal by Delilah; and the redemption that he attains not only for a renewed spiritual commitment to the God of the Hebrews, but also for causing the temple of the Philistines to collapse on them and him.

Despite the use of the title Nazarene (*nazareno*) to refer to Samson and Jesus, the term does not have the same meaning in each case. Samson was a Nazirite, or an Israelite who dedicated himself to the worship of God for a specific time through a series of vows including abstention from cutting his hair (Num. 6.1–21; Artigas, Introduction, Enríquez Gómez, *Sansón Nazareno* 26). He was not a Nazarene, or someone from the town of Nazareth in the Holy Land, unlike Jesus, who is called Nazarene at least in part because Joseph took him and Mary to this town upon their return from Egypt after the death of Herod (Matt. 2:19–23). As Oelman notes, Enríquez Gómez made a "linguistic error" by conflating the two terms; likewise, the overtly Jewish message of the end of the poem makes clear that his Samson is not "a prefiguration of Jesus" (*Marrano Poets* 209n1).[37] Samson himself explains his identity as Nazarene in the fateful moment of revealing to Delilah the secret of his strength:

> Nazarene of God is my command,
> never did a blade, of any kind,
> touch my hair because I would end up
> an ordinary man if my hair were to be cut.
>
> Nazareno de Dios es mi precepto,
> nunca el acero, de ninguna suerte,
> mi cabello tocó porque quedara
> hombre común si el pelo me cortara. (199, book 13, stanza 45)

Despite several similarities in the life stories of Samson and Jesus, including, for example, the "annunciation stories" of their birth and their redemptive

---

[37] Dille observed that the comedy *El valiente nazareno* (*The Valiant Nazarene*, 1638) by Juan Pérez de Montalbán might have influenced Enríquez Gómez to write about Samson (107). Indeed, in his prologue to *Sansón nazareno*, Enríquez Gómez includes Pérez de Montalbán in a list of "the most brilliant poets" in Spain ("lucidísimos poetas"; 60).

death for their respective religions, Samson's boast of his Nazirite vow confirms that Enríquez Gómez regards him a Jewish hero.[38]

Just as can be said of the "Romance al divín mártir," the identification by Enríquez Gómez with certain Jewish teachings throughout *Sansón Nazareno* may or may not testify to his religious beliefs when he wrote the poem.[39] What is certain is that this identification achieves two purposes that likewise characterize *Academias morales* and the "Romance": it challenges immorality, whether biblical or contemporaneous with the poet; and announces the triumph of divine justice, which in this work the poet associates with the God of Israel. Contrasting the actions and words of the Philistines with those of Samson, Enríquez Gómez adapts the story of the latter to his own converso perspective. Therefore, by the end of the poem, Samson rededicates himself to the God of Israel, even at the cost of his life, and recognizes that his prior conduct with the three women has contravened his vow as a Nazirite. In contrast, through the role of Delilah as a disingenuous talebearer who precipitates the mistreatment and death of Samson, the Philistines represent the ideology of Inquisitorial Spain that, at the very least, inflicted humiliation and impoverishment on New Christians accused of heresy.

The instability and anxiety common in other works of Enríquez Gómez instill the poem with a converso perspective in advance of its violent but redemptive dénouement. For example, when Samson confesses to his father his feelings for Dalestina, the first of the three Philistine women, Emanuel laments love as a debilitating force that has led the youth to wish to marry a Gentile:

Were calmer suns lacking in your noble Hebrew blood
where love might achieve

---

38   See Amit, footnote to 13.1–25, in *The Jewish Study Bible* 526 for the term "annunciation stories," in which a messenger of God appears unexpectedly to announce to a person or persons that a momentous event involving them will occur. Amit also mentions other such stories in the Hebrew Bible, such as the visit of three nameless men to Abraham and Sarah in which one of them tells her that she will conceive Isaac (Gen. 18.1–15). Likewise, in Christian Scriptures, the archangel Gabriel announces to Mary that she will conceive and give birth to Jesus (Luke 1.26–38).

39   In the detailed introduction to her edition of *Sansón Nazareno*, María del Carmen Artigas claims that Enríquez Gómez inhabited "a spiritual exile" ("un exilio spiritual"; 16) and that, through the voice of Samson, he expresses his own Jewish identity in the following lines near the end of the poem: "I die for Israel, and first / for your unutterable true Name ("Muero por Israel, y lo primero / por tu inefable Nombre verdadero" (30–31; 214, book 14, stanza 61).

sacred marriage owed to the Law
without a profane deity taking advantage of it?

¿Faltaban en tu sangre noble hebreo
soles templados donde amor lograse
el debido a la Ley, sagrado himeneo
sin que deidad profana le gozase? (80, book 2, stanza 17)[40]

The awareness of being a converso marked as belonging to a distinct lineage due to blood alone explains the preoccupation with relationships between groups that Enríquez Gómez expresses through Emanuel. As the son of one such mixed marriage and participant as spouse in another, the poet surely perceived the resistance of Emanuel to the romantic involvement of Samson with a Philistine woman. Through this complaint of Emanuel, Enríquez Gómez inverts an ideology that regarded conversos as indelibly tainted by suggesting that the Philistines are of impure lineage while the Israelites bear a divinely privileged status.

Enríquez Gómez emphasizes the unjust treatment of Samson and his subsequent redemption at the end of the poem because of his own awareness of injustice, learned, at least in part, while he lived under threat of denouncement to the Inquisition. He communicates this inequity and subsequent vindication by juxtaposing them with the appeal to avarice by Philistine leaders as they bribe Delilah to learn the source of Samson's strength:

If we worship money for the sake of God,
what universal cause do we obey?
What gilded salvation do we conquer
if with gold itself we lose it?
Help, God! Help, divine justice!,
that the world was ruined by greed.

Si al dinero por Dios idolatramos,
¿qué causa universal obedecemos?

---

40 The biblical account of the story does not identify this woman by name; instead, Samson tells his parents, "I noticed one of the Philistine women in Timnah" (Judg. 14.2). Likewise, in Judges, Samson's father is called Manoah. Enríquez Gómez appears to have altered the spelling of "hebreo" for the sake of assonant rhyme with "himeneo"; otherwise, the word would be written "hebrea" in order to agree with "sangre."

> ¿Qué salvación dorada conquistamos
> si con el oro mismo la perdemos?
> Aquí de Dios, aquí de su justicia,
> que el mundo se perdió por la codicia. (190, book 12, stanza 48)

Concomitantly, in his openly misogynistic representation of Delilah, Enríquez Gómez criticizes deceitfulness that accompanies this greed. Just as talebearing could ruin an entire New Christian family, even for nonreligious reasons, so in the poem Delilah betrays her promise to love Samson by compelling him to reveal his secret.[41] The poet thus scorns Delilah for her mendacity at the moment of Samson's indiscreet revelation:

> The cruel enemy, who joyfully heard
> the divine secret revealed,
> saw herself as queen, and wife of Balonte,
> and the brave Samson as a dead man.

> La enemiga cruel, que oyó gozosa
> el divino secreto descubierto,
> se dio por Reina, y de Balonte esposa,
> y el valiente Sansón por hombre muerto. (200, book 13, stanza 49)[42]

Notwithstanding the prejudicial tone of these lines,[43] the effort of the Philistines to deprive Samson of his strength as a consequence of this moment

---

41  Dille analyzed the symbolic parallels between an Inquisitorial informer (*malsín*) and Delilah on one hand, and a crypto-Jew and Samson on the other, noting how, "in an incautious moment," the secret Jew reveals his secret, suffers "degradation and humiliation," and resists the Inquisition through a "steadfast martyr's death" (*Antonio Enríquez Gómez* 114). At the same time, Dille carefully noted the difficulty of assuming a direct link between the message of the poem and the biography of its author due to "a religious ambiguity" in this and other works of Enríquez Gómez (*Antonio Enríquez Gómez* 121).

42  In the poem, but not the biblical account, Philistine leaders promise to Delilah the prince Balonte as a husband for her success prying from Samson the source of his strength, besides a payment of one thousand shekels (the amount in Judges is 5,500).

43  The negative representation of women occurs regularly throughout the poem. In an especially egregious example, when the Philistine youths consider using Dalestina to decipher Samson's riddle about honey that came out of the jaws of a lion that Samson previously killed, an elder, Dagon, says that ancient sages declared "woman

symbolizes their persecutory zeal, as well as, in a scarcely hidden comparison, that of the Spanish-Portuguese Inquisition.

At the end of the poem, Samson counters in a most dramatic way the symbols of greed and deceit that surround him. Praising God extensively and embracing a column of the temple with each arm, he summons the physical strength to make it collapse on the Philistines about to burn him at a spectacle akin to an auto de fe, causing the death of thirty thousand spectators (and his own).[44] Not only does Samson avenge the betrayal and cruelty of the Philistines, but he also expiates his previous relationships with multiple non-Jewish women:

> I offer up myself to death so that
> my people may be redeemed today
> from the harsh power of the Philistines,
> a judgement of tyranny itself.
> Let the Hebrew nation shake off its yoke,
> may it enjoy this triumph with my blood.
> Lord, save Israel. May my life be
> a holy sacrifice and a shining lamp.
>
> Yo me ofrezco a la muerte porque sea
> redimido mi pueblo en este día
> de la dura potencia filistea,
> arbitrio de la misma tiranía.
> Sacuda el yugo la nación hebrea,
> goce este triunfo con la sangre mía.
> Salva a Israel, Señor. Sea mi vida
> víctima santa y lámpara lúcida. (214, book 14, stanza 62)

In the telling of Enríquez Gómez, Samson washes away with his own blood the sufferings of the Israelites caused by the Philistines; liberated from captivity through his death, both he and the Israelites become symbols of divine

---

to be the most boastful hydra, / whose gossipy and harmful lips / ruin honor and deprive one of life" ("ser hidra la mujer más presumida, / cuyos parleros y nocivos labios / acaban el honor, quitan la vida"; 94, book 3, stanza 41).

44  Earlier in book 14 (206, stanza 10), the text says that three thousand men gathered in the Philistine temple to witness the death of Samson. Likewise, Judges 16.27 says that this same number of men and women had gathered on the roof of the temple to watch Samson dance.

justice triumphant. Like the defiance of Lope de Vera at his martyrdom in the "Romance," Samson's self-sacrifice as a means of redeeming the Israelites from intolerance represents the perspective of a converso author who turns an auto de fe into an affirmation of Judaism.

Additionally, at the same time that he exalts the Israelites, Enríquez Gómez also uses his perceptiveness of negative othering based on lineage to stigmatize the Philistines as a group, through the words of Samson declaring of his oppressors:

> What purpose, all-powerful Lord,
> does this nation of Philistine lineage serve?
> What glory will you derive from this contemptible people,
> scattered about in wickedness and immorality?
>
> ¿De qué sirve, Señor omnipotente,
> esta nación de sangre filistina?
> ¿Qué gloria sacarás desta vil gente
> en maldades y vicios peregrina? (214, book 14, stanza 64)

Here the poet inverts the stereotype of the wandering Jew to depict the Philistines as unmoored and removed from divine protection because of their "wickedness and immorality."

### Conclusion: Divine Redemption in Literature to Attain Vindication in Life

*Academias morales de las musas*, the "Romance a Lope de Vera" and *Sansón nazareno* illuminate the complex New Christian worldview of Antonio Enríquez Gómez by showing Jewish influences on his work without necessarily asserting his own possible crypto-Judaism. Written in a language that conforms to literary trends of Baroque Spain of the 1600s, these texts express the status of Enríquez Gómez as a converso both "in and out" by, among other examples, lamenting the solitude and melancholy of exile; prioritizing justice and criticizing false appearances; and identifying with Job, Lope de Vera y Alarcón, and Samson. Through the divine redemption that these protagonists attain after suffering unfairly, Enríquez Gómez juxtaposes pessimism occasioned by difficulties in his own life with a quest for vindication that he hoped to achieve at least partially as a writer. The poems discussed in this chapter argue for his inclusion in the first rank of seventeenth-century Spanish writers not only for their literary merits, but also because they have widened the parameters of Golden Age cultural production to include a worldview too often marginalized. Through this worldview, we see how Enríquez Gómez fulfills his own aspiration from the prologue of *Academias morales*, in which he writes, "I strive to assure that I live in the justification of my truth" ("pretendo asegurarme de que vivo en la justificación de mi verdad"; 10r). This success justifying his truth as a voice of morality and divine vindication becomes even more significant because Enríquez Gómez achieves it while personalizing his texts and attempting to minimize their potentially harmful effects to his own safety.

# 4
## "One God, One People, and One Law": *Las excelencias de los hebreos* of Isaac Cardoso as a Defense of Judaism through a Spanish-Portuguese Lens

THE LIFE AND WORKS of Isaac Cardoso open a window into the geographic and spiritual peregrinations of Iberian New Christians during the 1600s who became freely practicing Jews upon settling elsewhere in the Sephardic diaspora. This chapter studies his last such treatise, an encyclopedic defense of Judaism called *The Excellences of the Hebrews* (*Las excelencias de los hebreos*), as a text that shows the influence of Cardoso's Iberian origin and argues the merits of his recovered religion in ways that would have been impossible in Spain or Portugal. Specifically, the chapter examines how, through examples from Iberian Jewish history, the *Excelencias* validates Judaism as a religion and Jews as a people at a time when both were in eclipse on the Iberian Peninsula. In so doing, it shows the extent to which Cardoso demonstrates knowledge of Judaism despite living half his life deprived of this identity, as well as how awareness of the unjust treatment of Jews in Spain and Portugal contributed to his emergent Jewish sense of self. To achieve these aims, Cardoso first catalogs ten "excellences" of Jews and then refutes baseless but age-old slanders against Jews and New Christians, such as charges of perfidy against rulers, proselytizing, abuse of Christian icons, and blood libel. He supports these denials citing recent events from the Iberian world, including, for example, cases of baptized former Jews who refused to live as faithful Christians as well as of episodes in which Christians repeatedly and without evidence prosecuted Jews for crimes ranging from profaning the host to ritual murder. The Spanish-Portuguese lens through which Cardoso views and defends Judaism testifies to his dual identity as a

New Jew and former New Christian whose now openly held beliefs grew at least in part from the secrecy cloaking his formative years spent in lands of ingrained antisemitism.

### From Secret Judaism in Portugal to Rabbinic Judaism in Italy

A brief biographical summary can help contextualize the geographic and spiritual journey of Isaac Cardoso with respect to the always precarious place of converted Jews in the post-1492 Iberian world. He was born in Trancoso, Portugal, in 1603–04 and likely baptized Fernão or Fernam Cardoso. By royal decree his family had been New Christian since 1497, when the Portuguese king Manoel I changed the conditions of his own expulsion order and forced all Jews in the country to accept baptism. Given the fact that the designation of New Christian carried over through successive generations of a family's lineage, it came to refer increasingly to ethnicity rather than religious identity. While many such conversos throughout Spain, Portugal, and their overseas territories lived as faithful Catholics, others were crypto-Jews who to varying degrees practiced Jewish rites secretly. Not surprisingly, given Fernão's subsequent Jewish fervor, Trancoso is in an area of northeast Portugal that had become a locus of crypto-Jewish activity after Manoel's disastrous decree, despite efforts of Inquisition tribunals to eradicate this heresy.[1] Indeed, Fernão's brother Miguel, younger by some twenty years, wrote in an autobiographical text that his parents revealed their and his Jewish identity when he, Miguel, was six years old. The supposition of Fernão's biographer Yosef Hayim Yerushalmi that the older Cardoso heard a similar message during his own childhood suggests that "the parents were in some sense active Marranos [crypto-Jews], and that their 'Marranism,' whatever its form and content, was a family tradition transmitted from one generation to the next" (Yerushalmi 65).[2] Certainly the fact that later in life Cardoso embraced rab-

---

1   Isabel of Castile and Fernando of Aragon established, with papal approval, the Inquisition in 1478 to uncover, correct, and punish crypto-Jewish practices in their kingdoms. The tribunal subsequently came into existence in Portugal in 1536. For information about this court, see Kamen, *The Spanish Inquisition*. For crypto-Judaism, see Gitlitz, *The Lost Minyan* and *Secrecy and Deceit*.

2   Yerushalmi's masterful biography is the source of information about Cardoso's background in this chapter. Marrano is a generally pejorative word by which some Old Christians—and, later, sometimes converts and Jews—described crypto-Jews. Kamen states that, regardless of its unknown origin, no etymological evidence links this word to its commonly understood meaning of "pig"; instead, he writes that it may describe an individual who "mars" Christianity by being a hidden Jew (*The Spanish Inquisition* 402n13).

binic Judaism unequivocally and evinced a deep knowledge of it once he could live openly as a Jew in Italy supports the likelihood of a crypto-Jewish background.³

During the years 1604-10, the Cardoso family moved to Medina de Rioseco, near Valladolid, in central northwest Spain, as part of a wave of immigration of Portuguese New Christians to their ancestral homeland. Most likely they benefited from an offer of a special *finta*, or tribute, of nearly two million ducats from fellow converts to the Spanish monarchy that facilitated this emigration and with which the crown even obtained a papal pardon for former Judaizing practices of the new arrivals (Yerushalmi 66–67; Kamen, *The Spanish Inquisition* 289–90). Fernando, as he was now known, studied medicine at the University of Valladolid and quite possibly at Salamanca as well, earning his doctorate by the age of 21. A few years later, between 1627–30, Cardoso could be found at Madrid, where he became a physician in the court of Felipe IV, completing in reverse the journey of many Spanish Jews who, upon expulsion in 1492, had taken refuge in Portugal.

Several circumstances explain how a New Christian could hold such a privileged position in a society that continued to discriminate against the descendants of Jewish converts, nearly 150 years after the expulsion. First, Jews and conversos had served as physicians and courtiers to Christian and Muslim rulers in Spain and beyond since medieval times. Noteworthy examples from the medieval period included Hasdai ibn Shaprut, personal physician to Abd al-Rahman III, the first caliph of Córdoba, during the tenth century; and Moses Maimonides, who advised the Egyptian ruler Saladin during the

---

3   Regarding the historiographic debate about the Jewishness of the conversos, crypto-Judaism took stronger root in Portugal than Spain because the Jews who left the latter kingdom in 1492 were "stalwarts of Judaism by definition" due to their refusal to convert (Gerber, *The Jews of Spain* 143). Upon their forced conversion in Portugal in 1497, the substantial number of these sudden New Christians who tried to maintain their former Judaism over time formed "a new religion, neither wholly Jewish nor wholly Catholic . . . [that] combined secrecy with fear, partial memory with substantial loss" (Gerber, *The Jews of Spain* 143). Seeing the Cardoso brothers in this liminal space of Portuguese crypto-Judaism may explain the process of rejudaization in which they certainly participated in Italy, given that "all emigres from the Peninsula needed instruction in the basics of Jewish observance if they were to participate in the life of the community" (Bodian, *Hebrews of the Portuguese Nation* 96; while her observation refers to Amsterdam, it is relevant to Portuguese conversos elsewhere). Such rejudaization occurred amongst people who considered themselves a distinct "Nation," for many of whom "the ethnic dimension became more important than the strictly religious dimension" (Wachtel 13).

twelfth century after fleeing Córdoba with his family for Fez, Morocco, and Fustat, Egypt. More recently, Cardoso followed in the mold of Baltasar Alvares de Orobio, the subject of chapter one of this book.[4] A second factor explaining the privileged position of conversos in Spain despite societal disdain was their financial utility to the king. Thus, as mentioned in the introduction, during the mid-1620s, Gaspar de Guzmán, Count-Duke of Olivares, in his role as *valido*, or favorite, of Felipe IV, followed the Portuguese precedent from earlier in the century by inviting Portuguese converso bankers to Madrid to help lessen the monarchy's debt and by permitting the movement of conversos from Portugal in and out of Spain (Elliott 300–04). The visibility of some of these immigrants, the remnant presence of crypto-Judaism in Portugal, and "the probability ... that many if not most Luso-conversos retained a consciousness of belonging to an identifiable social group quite distinct from the Ibero-Christian mainstream" (Graizbord 53) led Old Christians in Spain and its colonies during the 1600s to conflate the terms "Portuguese," "Jew," and "New Christian." This conflation existed not just among popular parlance; the term "Portuguese" also appears in Inquisition trial records to describe followers of the Law of Moses.[5]

Perhaps with the fall of Olivares in 1643, Fernando and his brother Miguel, who had been born in 1627, at approximately the time when the elder sibling became a physician at court, no longer felt safe in the capital. So, following a route that Sephardic Jews and New Christians had taken for a century and a half, in 1648 they moved to the large Spanish-Portuguese Jewish community of Venice. There they shed the burden of living as crypto-Jews under the shadow of the Inquisition by undergoing circumcision and taking Hebrew names: Fernando became Isaac and Miguel, Abraham. However, within five years Isaac moved to Verona, where he married, earned a living as a physician, and wrote until his death in 1688. The brothers parted ways due at least in part to an irreconcilable conflict within the Jewish world that the messianism of the mid-1600s prompted. Abraham fell under the spell of Sabbatai Zevi and during the next four decades "became [the] most prolific and passionate spokesman" of the Sabbatean movement (Yerushalmi

---

4  For Shaprut and Maimonides, see Gerber, *The Jews of Spain* 46–52, 79–89.

5  For an example of the term "Portuguese" to describe a New Christian, see the Inquisition trial record of Manuel Bautista Pérez, the wealthiest converso merchant in Peru during the 1630s. A digitalized version of the trial record in the holdings of the Archivo Histórico Nacional in Madrid can be viewed at pares.mcu.es/Pares-Busquedas20/catalogo/description/1312214?nm.

304).⁶ In contrast, Isaac staunchly defended traditional rabbinic Judaism, a viewpoint that he championed in *Las excelencias de los hebreos*. This dissent between two brothers and former New Christians confirms "that the Marrano story draws most of its interest and significance from its *inherent dualities and ambiguities*," in this case the unquantifiable but ever-present influence of an Iberian Catholic formation on their distinct paths to Judaism (Yovel. *The Other Within* 400, italics in original; see also 324–26). Isaac revealed this formation in his writing at least in part by positing a Jewish identity in opposition to Catholicism, for example, through the oneness of God and crypto-Jewish martyrdom; whereas "in adopting Jewish mysticism in the unconventional way he did, Abraham was tacitly setting a Christian vision right and restoring it to authenticity" (Yovel, *The Other Within* 325).

## A Defense of Judaism through an Iberian Lens

*Las excelencias de los hebreos* was published in Amsterdam in 1679 by David de Castro Tartas, a converso of Portuguese origin born in France who subsequently obtained a position of leadership in the Iberian Jewish community of his adoptive city.⁷ A sprawling treatise more than four hundred pages long, the *Excelencias* praises ten "excellences" of Judaism occupying more than three-quarters of the work, and then refutes ten commonly held calumnies against the religion in the remaining pages.⁸ It corresponds to the genre of apologetic and polemical literature in defense of Judaism that New Chris-

---

6   See Gerber, *The Jews of Spain* 170–75, for a concise summary of messianism among 1600s Sephardim of the eastern Mediterranean.

7   For example, David de Castro Tartas wrote and gave a sermon to mark the opening of the Portuguese Jewish Synagogue in 1675. See Bodian, *Hebrews of the Portuguese Nation* 90–91.

8   The *excelencias* include "Chosen People of God" ("Pueblo escogido de Dios"), "One People" ("Gente una"), "Separated from All the Nations" ("Separados de todas las naciones"), "Three of Their Natural Traits" (Doing Justice, Loving Mercy, Proceeding Honestly; "Tres propiedades naturales suyas"), "Circumcision" ("La circuncisión"), "The Sabbath" ("El Sabath"), "The Divine Law" ("Ley divina"), "Prophecy" ("La profecía"), "Holy Land" ("Tierra Santa"), and "Witnesses to the Unity of God" ("Testigos de la Unidad de Dios"). The *calunias* (*calumnias* in modern Spanish) that the work contests are "False Adorations" ("Falsas adoraciones"), "Foul Odor" ("Mal olor"), "Tail and Blood" ("Cola y sangre"), "Praying Three Times Daily against Gentiles" ("Orar tres veces al día contra las gentes"), "Persuading Gentiles to [Convert to] Judaism" ("Persuadir a las gentes al Hebraísmo"), "Unfaithful to Princes" ("Infieles a los Príncipes"), "Merciless and Cruel" ("Impíos y crueles"), "Corruptors of the Holy Books" ("Corruptores de los libros sagrados"), "Profaners of Images" ("Di-

tians produced once they established themselves as New Jews in the Western Sephardic diaspora, principally Amsterdam. Claude Stuczynski regards the *Excelencias* not only as an apologia, as Yerushalmi described it (350–52, 366), but more "a major Jewish ex-converso theological-political manifesto" in which Cardoso argues for the differentiated status of the Jewish people in contrast to "the Iberian Catholic imperial idea of 'universal monarchy'" (221, 222). Likewise, Stuczynski asserts that *Excelencias de la monarquía y reino de España* (*Excellences of the Monarchy and Kingdom of Spain* [Valladolid 1597]) by the Spanish jurist Gregorio López Madera likely served as "probable inspiration" for Cardoso (222). He also understands López Madera as arguing that "Spanish kings were 'excellent' monarchs and thus . . . 'excellent' Catholics'" (223). This belief on the part of the jurist would have provided a framework for Cardoso to argue, in contrast, that Jews are a "republic apart" (Stuczynski 223 citing Cardoso 22, 374).

In this light, the work affirms the privileged and elect status of Jews, about whom Cardoso writes, "it is not a small wonder to see a scattered and separated people, exiled among the nations for so many centuries, keep their rites and ceremonies, and be as a republic apart, governed of themselves by the Law that God gave them" ("no es poca admiración ver una gente esparcida, y separada en medio de las naciones por tantos siglos desterrada, guardar sus ritos, y ceremonias, y ser como una república aparte gobernada de sí misma por la Ley que Dios le dio"; 22). Throughout the book, the author's experience of living a diasporic existence with circumspection, in and beyond Portugal and Spain, informs his sense of "wonder" ("admiración") at the ability of Jews to maintain their divine covenant meaningfully.

Cardoso dedicated the book to Jacob de Pinto, member of an influential family of Portuguese conversos in Amsterdam who likely paid to print the book. Apart from its wealth, the Pinto family was especially well known because Jacob's father and brother, Abraham and Isaac, had established the *Jesiba de los Pintos* in Rotterdam in 1650 and then brought it with them upon moving to Amsterdam in 1669. Jacob de Pinto also helped finance the yeshiva, which was not so much a school, as the name implies, "but a pious foundation to support needy young men" (Nahon 256).[9] Certainly the end of Cardoso's dedication contains the laudatory language common to such texts,

---

sipadores de imágenes") and "Killers of Christian Children to Use Their Blood in Their Rites" ("Matar niños cristianos para valerse de su sangre").

9   My thanks to Miriam Bodian for suggesting I consult this chapter by Nahon. For the supposition that Jacob de Pinto underwrote the publication of *Las excelencias*, see Yerushalmi 350.

as he writes of his benefactor, "common applause recognizes you [Pinto] as one of the most illustrious subjects of our Nation who with so much generosity and zeal for the Law supports a yeshiva" ("conociéndole el aplauso común por uno de los más ilustres sujetos de nuestra nación, que con tanta liberalidad, y celo de la Ley sustenta una jesibá"; Cardoso v–vi). These words help make clear the motive of Cardoso dedicating the book to Pinto, as the author recognizes his patron for maintaining a center of learning where young men study the historical imperative for defending Judaism upon which subsequent pages of the work expound.

One way to consider the *Excelencias* is by analyzing Cardoso's strident defense of Judaism and denial of long-held slanders against it, from biblical times to the Inquisition era, considering his worldview and experiences as a Spanish-Portuguese ex-converso. Such an approach builds on the work of Yerushalmi presenting Cardoso as an Iberian thinker by showing the extent to which Cardoso views Judaism through the lens of Iberian Jewish history. Through this Iberian-focused perspective, Cardoso resists the negative othering of Jews by exalting their relationship with God and the Holy Land itself, their distinct practices, and their fortitude against current persecution in the Iberian world. Examples of this positive otherness that Cardoso extols include the elect status of the Israelites as a chosen people, even in diaspora, as well as of the land of Israel; the centrality of their exodus from bondage in Egypt; their divinely mandated separation from other peoples; and the martyrdom of crypto-Jewish contemporaries who refuse to forswear their belief in the oneness of an invisible but omnipresent God.

In the dedication of the *Excelencias* to Jacob de Pinto, Cardoso frames the treatise as a means of resistance to centuries-long slanders and outright attacks against Jews and now former Jews, comparing such persecutions to lions and wolves that "long for their blood so much" ("tanto anhelan su sangre"; v). It is not difficult to imagine how someone aware of the persecution of Portuguese conversos in the case of the *Cristo de la Paciencia* ("The Patient Christ") in Madrid due to fabricated charges of whipping and burning a crucifix would feel that "it was necessary to relate frequently these slanders in view of other excellences . . . so that the truth might shine more . . . and so that Gentiles understand the falsehoods with which they accuse us and the impieties that they attribute to us" ("fue necesario contar por menudo estas calumnias . . . para que más luciese la verdad . . . y [para que] las gentes entendiesen las falsedades con que nos acusan, y las impiedades, que nos imputan"; v). Briefly, in this case the Inquisition asked leading questions of several young converso children as a way of further implicating their parents, who had already been detained as crypto-Jews. For example, Andrés ("Andresillo") Núñez and his sister Ana Rodríguez stated, without substantive and consistent evidence, that their parents and several other "Portuguese" abused a crucifix that, miraculously, wept, shed blood, and implored its assailants to explain their cruelty. Inquisitors knew that the testimony of Andresillo and Ana was flawed, but "the theme of the flagellated Christ . . . was seized upon as a perfect means to arouse the passions of Madrid, and transform an otherwise ordinary case of Judaizing into a shocking *cause célèbre*" (Yerushalmi 120). This evidence coaxed or compelled from frightened children helped condemn nine New Christians, six of whom the Inquisitorial court "relaxed" to secular authorities for burning at the stake as the centerpiece of the auto de fe of 1632 in Madrid, including the parents of Andresillo and Ana.

THE *EXCELENCIAS*: JUDAISM AS A SEPARATE AND SANCTIFIED RELIGION
In the first *excelencia*, "Chosen People of God," Cardoso juxtaposes the theme of exile with repeated claims of God's divine protection of Jews despite hardships they have endured to the present day due to their spiritual and geographic wandering. The subtext of such exile was a staple of the converso experience and of literature written by New Christians, regardless of whether they remained in the Iberian Peninsula or settled in places where they could become New Jews. Examples include the long narrative poems *Lamentaciones del Profeta Jeremías* of João Pinto Delgado and *Academias morales de las musas* of Antonio Enríquez Gómez discussed elsewhere in this book. Yet perhaps in part because he had lived as an openly practicing Jew for thirty years when he wrote the *Excelencias*, Cardoso did not regard exile with the same melancholy as these fellow New Christians of the 1600s. Instead, he notes that while Gentiles claim that proof of the non-elect status of Jews is their current state of wandering and misery, evidence of their continued election is the fact that God does not permit their destruction. Rather, Cardoso says somewhat sunnily, they live like a lamb among the seventy nations of wolves that do not tear them apart (13).

Throughout this first chapter, Cardoso lists various examples, principally biblical, in support of his claim that, though God may have punished Israel for worshipping idols and committing other sins, God has never ceased to esteem and shelter the Jewish people. Perhaps due to his medical background, the polemicist uses a physical image to convey divine punishment and protection: "[God] hardly gives the wound when God jointly gives the medicine and the cure" ("que apenas da la llaga, cuando juntamente da la medicina, y el remedio"; 12–13). As a way of further reconciling this apparent contrast,

Cardoso posits the Holy Land as both an idea and a place. Thus, while God may have scattered the Israelites so that they atone for their faults, through the promise of Israel as a land of repentance and redemption, God will never forget them (9–11). Cardoso then states that the current Jewish diaspora is not punishment for the death of Christ, which of course was a frequent disparagement of Christians against Jews in medieval Iberia, because the latter were "scattered throughout the world" ("esparcidos por el mundo"; 18) well before this event.

Further evidence of the privileged position of the Jewish people is the confluence between their oneness as a people and the oneness of God, a theme that Cardoso explores in the second *excelencia*, "One People." Making use of antitheses, as in the first chapter, the author states that the God of the Israelites is eternal, as are they, whereas other peoples and their respective gods, such as Baal and the pagan deities of Rome, are not (33). In the same way, wherever Jews live they are one nation, no matter that they increase their numbers, in contrast to the multiplicity of peoples in whose midst they have dwelled. For example, Cardoso notes, albeit perhaps not chronologically, how successive waves of Phoenicians, Chaldeans, Arabs, Goths, Iberians, Carthaginians, and Germans, among others, settled in Spain and Italy, and mixed to such an extent that their origins became indistinguishable. Stating how this unity as a people is "the greatest perfection and similarity [with] the creator" ("la unidad es la mayor perfección y semejanza del criador"; 25), he furthers the distinct connection between God and the Jews by emphasizing the oneness of the Law that God has given to them. This *excelencia* is also the source of the citation that forms the beginning of the title of this chapter, "one God, one People, and one Law" ("un Dios, un pueblo, y una Ley"; 33).

As its title suggests, the *Excelencias* turns the negative othering of Jews into positive recognition of their distinct practices, permitting Cardoso to celebrate the most sanctified rites of Judaism in contrast with foundational beliefs of other religions. One visible, literal marker of this difference is circumcision, which, as Genesis 17.10–14 states, God mandates of all Jewish males on the eighth day of life as a sign of the divine covenant with the Jewish people. In the fifth *excelencia*, "Circumcision," Cardoso goes beyond the differentiating aspect of this rite to suggest that it also creates greater intimacy between the Israelites and "the true shepherd of Israel" ("el verdadero pastor de Israel"; 88), because "by means of the sacrifice of the flesh we see the Lord" ("por medio del sacrificio de la carne vemos al Señor"; 91). Additionally, the polemicist argues, this act prepares the person undergoing it to sacrifice himself entirely for the sake of God later in life.

Cardoso continues to juxtapose separation of Jews due to disparagement from Gentiles with what he then claims are the ennobling characteristics of such separation. For example, the third *excelencia*, "Separated from All the Nations," states that those who wish to live among and like Gentiles are not able to be Jews, and that God has kept the two apart to maintain the purity of the Israelites and help them avoid sinful practices (49). Indeed, as Cardoso makes clear here and elsewhere, separation and the purity it is supposed to guarantee are intimately woven together in all aspects of Jewish life, including preparation and consumption of food, the sanctity of the Sabbath, sexual relations, and even the rite of burial. Cardoso further suggests in this chapter that Jews achieve an exalted position in the eyes of God not just by separating categories of food, but by doing so for reasons of morality. Thus, he uses his belief that "all the [impure] foods are called an abomination, for being loathsome and hateful to the clean and pure soul" ("todas las comidas [inmundas] se llaman abominación, por ser aborrecibles y odiosas al alma limpia y pura"; 42), to show why Jews must avoid animals associated with negative characteristics, such as raptors, regarded as ill-tempered and harsh, and instead consume herbivores, due to their "gentle" disposition (43, 44).[10] Later, in the seventh *excelencia*, "The Divine Law," the command to avoid the joint consumption of dairy and meat products (185), which comes from a passage that occurs three times in the Torah stating, "You shall not boil a kid in its mother's milk," symbolizes the elect and separate status of Israel (Exodus 23.19).[11] Cardoso then catalogs the many dietary restrictions of observant Jews, perhaps most notably that terrestrial animals for consumption be ruminates with completely split hooves, eloquently testifying to the importance of culinary rites as an expression of Jewish identity (186).

In the same way, just as rules governing food reaffirm the unassimilable character of Jewish identity crucial to its perpetuation, so the Sabbath testifies to the longstanding and distinguishing bond between the Israelites and God. Thus, in the sixth *excelencia*, Cardoso states that Jews must keep the Sabbath in part for its connection with the Exodus, since God alone both created the world in six days and brought about the rescue of the Israelites

---

10   Elsewhere in this passage Cardoso links "these prohibited foods" (i.e., non-Kosher items; "estas comidas inmundas") with "the impure spirit, which corrupts thoughts and deeds" (el espíritu inmundo, que contamina los pensamientos y obras"; 41).

11   The law forbidding the consumption of dairy and meat products together also occurs in Exodus 34.26 and Deuteronomy 14.21. For a brief commentary about this rule, see Tigay, *The Jewish Study Bible* 152.

enslaved in Egypt, as the first commandment proclaims: "I your God who took you out of Egypt . . ." ("yo el Señor tu Dios que te saqué de tierra de Egipto . . ."; 106). Throughout this chapter, Cardoso carefully notes how the Sabbath sanctifies the privileged status of Jews while also showing how observance of this day symbolizes an almost physical separation. Whereas the six days of the week represent the world as it is, or what he deems the body, the Sabbath is the world to come, the soul. Additionally, Cardoso parses the Hebrew letters forming the word Sabbath to show the preeminent position of this word as a symbol of divine privileging of Jewish identity. In his explanation, *shin* is the first letter of Shabbat itself; *bet* is the first letter in *berith*, the word for circumcision; and *tau* is the first letter of *tefillin*, which are the small boxes containing parchment scrolls of passages from the Torah with which men wrap their arm and head (108).[12] Cardoso then describes the physical nature of separation that the Sabbath represents by citing references from Josephus, Pliny, and 2 Kings to the mythical river Sambatyon, whose fast-flowing current reputedly ceased or even dried up on the Sabbath, hence originating the name of the seventh day (110).[13] Finally, after having sanctified this daylong observance with the prayer of *Kiddush* over wine, Jews mark its close with the ceremony of *Havdalah*, which literally means separation and serves as a way of marking this day from the six that are to follow.

One of the ways in which the *Excelencias* derives its relevance in Cardoso's time and ours is by commenting on the precariousness of Jewish existence and the repeated strength of Jews and subsequently conversos in the face of persecution. Thus, in the seventh *excelencia*, the author notes that wise men admire how Jews of the diaspora, "oppressed by all [nevertheless] persevere in their Law, preferring to spend their lives in extreme misery and shame to abandoning it [the Law]" ("oprimidos de todos, perseveren en su Ley, queriendo antes pasar la vida en una miseria y deshonra extrema, que dejar de seguirla"; 281). This commitment of Jews to maintain their faith regardless of poverty and second-class status to which Christian and Muslim

---

12    The commandment to wrap oneself in tefillin is part of the central prayer of Judaism, the *Shema* ("Hear, O Israel"), found in Deuteronomy 6, which states, "Bind them [God's commandments] as a sign on your hand and let them serve as a symbol on your forehead" (Deut. 6.8).

13    Gitlitz notes how mention of the legendary Sambatyon River in Inquisitorial testimony demonstrates the "eclectic . . . Sabbath lore" of crypto-Jews, including their belief that the lost tribes of Israel could not escape the Assyrian king Shalmaneser because they would not cross the river on the Sabbath, even though it was calm then (*Secrecy and Deceit* 340).

rulers subjected them likely inspired the perseverance of those conversos of Iberian lands who likewise tried to maintain a Jewish identity. In this context, the resolve of Jews to suffer oppression frames the choice of secretly Jewish conversos, or Judaizers in Inquisition parlance, whose false conversion led them to reject Christianity even at the cost of their lives.

Not surprisingly, then, the last of the *excelencias*, "Witnesses to the Unity of God," as well as the subsequent *calumnias* show the willingness of both biblical Jews and crypto-Jews contemporaneous with Cardoso to pay the ultimate personal cost rather than forsake their belief in the oneness of God. Starting with Abraham's near sacrifice of Isaac, Cardoso catalogs other biblical examples of selfless obedience to this central tenet of Judaism. One such case describes the miraculous salvation of Shadrach, Meshach, and Abednego, companions of the courtier Daniel during the Babylonian captivity. As Daniel 3 relates, faith in their God saves these three provincial administrators from a fiery death after their refusal to bow and worship a golden statue of Nebuchadnezzar prompts the enraged king to cast them into a furnace. Indeed, the sight of the three youths emerging unharmed from the fire so affects Nebuchadnezzar that he promotes them, blesses the God of the Israelites, and orders death for anyone who speaks ill of this God (Dan. 3.28–29).[14]

Another example that Cardoso cites, originally from the biblical book 2 Maccabees 7, describes the martyrdom of an unnamed Maccabee woman, subsequently often called Hannah. The Seleucid king Antiochus IV Epiphanes orders her killed after forcing her to watch the torture and execution of her seven sons for their refusal to profane God by eating pork. While less known than the archetypal crypto-Jewish heroine Esther, Hannah nevertheless resonated in the post-1492 Sephardic diaspora for her commitment to Judaism at the cost of her own life.[15] Conversos knew the books of Maccabees because of their inclusion in the Catholic Bible, and the declaration of one of the sons of Hannah at the start of their ordeal, "For we are ready to die

---

14   Cardoso refers to the three youths as Hananyá, Misael, and Hazaryá. While Cardoso accepts their story at face value, "the implausibility of the Babylonian king Nebuchadnezzar blessing the God of Israel and making a decree of protection argues for a humorous interpretation of this chapter" (Wills, notes to Daniel, *The Jewish Study Bible* 1643).

15   Goldstein argues that the terms apocryphal or deuterocanonical are not appropriate for describing the placement of 2 Maccabees outside the Hebrew Bible. Instead, in a statement entitled "The Apocrypha," he characterizes this as a book of "Jewish origins" that was not included in "the final Jewish Palestinian canon of Scripture." See ix and 289–317 for his translation of and commentary on 2 Macc. 7.1–42.

rather than transgress the laws of our ancestors" (2 Macc. 7), presages the steadfastness of crypto-Jewish martyrs of the Inquisition era. Indeed, Luis de Carvajal the Younger, the most famous victim of Inquisitorial prosecution in colonial Mexico, compared Spanish-Portuguese monarchs with Antiochus, perhaps as part of his identification with the Maccabees (Bodian, *Dying in the Law of Moses* 75).

Among other examples in his own time, Cardoso mentions various categories of individuals throughout the Iberian world, showing the transatlantic awareness of their fate. Thus, he praises Francisco Maldonado de Silva and Tomás Treviño de Sobremonte, two of the most infamous victims of the "Great Conspiracy" trials of the 1630 and 1640s in Lima and Mexico City, respectively (323). Another group includes several apparent old Christians who, having embraced Judaism, preferred death to renouncing their new faith, such as the Capuchin monk Diogo d'Asumpção, sentenced at the auto de fe of 1603 in Lisbon, and Lope de Vera y Alarcón, condemned at a similar spectacle in Valladolid in 1644 (363–64; see also chapter 3 of this book). Finally, in an example of a martyr who left the apparent safety of the Dutch orbit for lands under Inquisitorial jurisdiction, Cardoso praises Isaac de Castro Tartas, brother of the publisher of the *Excelencias*, detained in Portuguese-held Brazil in 1640s and burned after the auto de fe of 1647 in Lisbon (324–25).[16] The familiarity of Cardoso with these examples shows the influence of an Iberian worldview on his Judaism, especially given the importance of martyrdom to Spanish-Portuguese Jews and secret Jews as a means of exalting their faith against the backdrop of the Inquisition. This familiarity also shows the extent to which former conversos openly practicing Judaism beyond the Iberian sphere were aware of the fate of crypto-Jews in these "lands of idolatry."

## The *Calumnias*: Confronting Prejudice, Confirming Divine Privilege

The ten *calumnias* that Cardoso repudiates during the last quarter of his treatise serve as an unhappy consequence of the effort of Jews to assert and preserve their distinct identity that the ten preceding *excelencias* describe. In this portion of the work, he shows how societal ignorance and fear marginalize Jewish existence by placing it in a nearly untenable position: the very characteristics innate to the identity of Jews occasion baseless and scurrilous charges against them that threaten this identity. Some of the most unfounded ones include praying against Christians and proselytizing them,

---

16  For additional biography on d'Asumpção, see Bodian, *Dying in the Law of Moses* 79–116. For Isaac de Castro Tartas, see Bodian and François.

desecrating Christian images, and killing Christian children for the sake of using their blood in the preparation of matzah. By exposing the falseness of these slanders, Cardoso confronts the prejudices that doomed Iberian Jewry, showing the centuries-long reach of irrational fear and its consequences. Cataloging through his disproval of these calumnies many tribulations that Spanish-Portuguese Jews and New Christians endured before and after 1492, Cardoso testifies to the survival of Judaism despite continuous threats to its legitimacy and existence. In so doing, he shows how fear and resentment on the part of Christians on the Iberian Peninsula and beyond led them to hold unfounded beliefs about and commit unchristian actions against Jews and conversos.

Given the focus of this chapter on the Spanish-Portuguese perspective of Cardoso, the following section describes his refutation of calumnies using examples rooted in an Iberian context. These examples span events and attitudes of the 1400s in Spain that foregrounded the expulsion as well as the immediate results of this calamity there and in Portugal. Some of the most consequential of such examples include the anti-Jewish sermons of Friar Vicente Ferrer throughout the Peninsula during the early 1400s; the anti-Jewish treatise *Fortalitium fidei* (*Fortress of Faith*) of the 1460s by the Franciscan friar Alonso Espina; persecution of Jews for blood libel; the document of expulsion itself of 1492; and literature written in response to this edict. While Isabel and Fernando claimed not to harbor an anti-Jewish grudge—indeed, they were heirs to a tradition by which Spanish monarchs claimed that Jews "belonged" to them—Cardoso's catalog of slanders shows the even stronger tradition of ecclesiastical and popular animus towards Iberian Jews.

As two of the most consequential examples of such ecclesiastical hostility, Vicente Ferrer and Alonso Espina exploited canards rooted in folklore or outright lies to legitimate their anti-Jewish teachings. A Dominican from Valencia, Ferrer harangued Jews throughout Spain during the years after the widespread anti-Jewish violence of 1391 that the archdeacon of Écija, Ferrand Martínez, had instigated, pressuring those who had not converted to do so immediately. The success of Ferrer in this regard and establishing as churches former synagogues helped lay the groundwork for the anti-Jewish Laws of Valladolid of 1412–14. Among other restrictions, this legislation required city-dwelling Jews to live in separate neighborhoods, to wear markers on their clothes, and, among men, to grow beards and long hair, all as signifiers of difference. Additionally, the laws tried to limit contact between Jews and Christians by forbidding Jews to exercise commonly held professions in medicine, pharmacy, and administration of royal finances (López-Ibor 64–66).

Cardoso cites Ferrer and Espina for their respective libelous charges that Jews have tails and that the males among them menstruate, thus drawing attention to the role of false claims of physiological othering in the marginalization of Jews. Subsequently, the polemicist explicates the danger that fallacious teachings about Jews, including those of Ferrer and Espina, represent:

> The defects and imperfections that the adversaries of the Hebrews attribute to them are to be wondered at, without other motive than hatred . . . [and] to disparage and debase them [Jews] among Gentiles, even though experience and true inspection show them [Gentiles] the falseness and deceit of these charges, that malice invented.
>
> Es de admirar los defectos e imperfecciones que los adversarios de los hebreos les atribuyen, sin otro motivo que el odio . . . [y] para ponerlos en desestimación y vileza entre las gentes, aunque la experiencia y el verdadero examen les enseñe ser todo falsedad y engaño, que inventó la malicia. (346)

In these and other examples, Cardoso conveys the willful mendaciousness of authority figures who peddle lies about Jews in order to exploit popular sentiment against them.

Just as Ferrer and Espina perpetuate the lie of nonexistent, pejorative Jewish physical characteristics, Cardoso shows how the latter in *Fortalitium fidei* disingenuously represents Jews as a threat to Christians. Written in Latin, this sprawling work depicts the dangers that heretics, Jews, Muslims, and demons purportedly present to the "fortress" of Christianity, and then suggests remedies for the protection of the latter faith.[17] Not surprisingly, Espina saves his greatest vitriol in *Fortalitium fidei* for the Jews, a fact of ominous relevance given that his suggestion of their expulsion from Spain as a solution to the insincere Christianity of some conversos became royal policy a few decades later. One way in which he singles out Jews is by exploiting their role as perennial scapegoats, leading Cardoso to observe, "but as there is no malice that they [presumably Gentiles] do not stir up against the Jews, nor a crime that they don't attribute to them, [thus] all the evils that wolves perpetrate they impute to sheep" ("mas como no hay maldad que no levanten a los

---

17   See McMichael for an in-depth study of *Fortalitium fidei*, including translation of some of its components.

judíos, ni crimen que no les atribuyan, todos los males que cometen los lobos imputan a los corderos"; 404).

Subsequently, for evidence, in the ninth *calumnia* Cardoso cites an example from the *Fortalitium* that described how a Jewish pawnbroker in France, upon extending credit to a woman who had brought him a dress as security, offered to lend more money if she brought him a consecrated communion host. The banker threw the bread in boiling water, but when a child miraculously appeared swimming unharmed in the pot, authorities arrested the alleged culprit and his family and then burned him when he refused to confess his nonexistent crime (404). Continuing this image, standard throughout medieval Europe, of a Jew as greedy banker, Espina cleverly depicts the double bind of Jews in the financial sphere. On the one hand, banking was unpopular, given the Church's effort to keep Christians from usury and the subsequent characterization of Jews working in finance as "parasitic, benefiting from the constructive activities of others in society" (Chazan 188). On the other, Espina then disparages Jews precisely for filling a necessary societal role that Christians disdained.

In opposition to this depiction of Jews as an insidious other, Cardoso argues that across centuries they have been faithful subjects of the rulers at whose behest they have lived, both in Spain and elsewhere. Indeed, as he states in the sixth *calumnia*, "Unfaithful to Princes," the words of the edict of expulsion "did not impute to Jews any crime of lese majesty, nor of infidelity, nor of other large crimes" ("no les imputaron crimen alguno de lesa magestad, ni de infidelidad, ni de otros delitos enormes"; 372). Instead, the document claimed, anecdotally, that Jews influenced conversos to become recidivists; hence, the only way to protect the sincerity of New Christians was to remove their proximity to Jews. Various theories attempt to explain the rationale of Isabel and Fernando for authorizing this catastrophic decision, including, among others, the potential for financial gain from the possessions of the expelled; the outsized influence of the first inquisitor general, Tomás de Torquemada, especially over Isabel, whom he had served as confessor; and even perhaps the zeal of powerful New Christians themselves as apologists for their new faith. Regardless, as Jane Gerber has observed, the clearest reason lies in the document itself, whose words affirm the monarchs' belief in the deleterious influence of Jews on converts (*The Jews of Spain* 135–37). The proximity of recent converts and practicing Jews throughout Spain indeed enabled many New Christians to mix with their former brethren despite the presence of Inquisition tribunals from 1480 onward. Nevertheless, the sporadic persistence of Inquisitorial trials of alleged Judaizers in Spanish cities for two centuries after the expulsion of 1492 confirms that the tribunal prosecuted New Christians long after the departure of Jews who could directly influence them.

While the Catholic Monarchs believed that removing Jews from the midst of New Christians would ensure the purity of the new faith of the latter, Cardoso claims that Jews never had proselytized, saying that do so would have been a "grave sin ("pecado grave"; 372)." Instead, in the fifth *calumnia*, "Persuading Gentiles to [Convert to] Judaism," he emphasizes that, unlike other religions, Judaism has not grown through conquest and forced conversion. Citing examples from the Hebrew Bible, he claims that Jews urge Gentiles to follow natural, not Jewish law, "so that they [these non-Jews] be just, devout, [and] charitable" ("que sean justos, píos, caritativos"; 361). Several such examples of relationships not rooted in proselytizing that Cardoso mentions include David living as a vassal of the Philistine king Achish (2 Sam. 27) and the alliance between Solomon and Hiram, the king of Tyre who provided wood for the Temple (1 Kings 5).

Likewise, Gentiles from classical antiquity to Cardoso's own time who have become Jews have done so of their own accord, even in some cases at the cost of their lives, recognizing that "the divine Law is clear, perfect, [and] that it illumines one's eyes" ("la Ley divina es clara, perfecta, [y] que alumbra los ojos"; 362). Several cases from this catalog include Fulvia, the wife of Saturninus, advisor to the emperor Tiberius Caesar; Flavius Clemens, a Roman consul whom his cousin, the emperor Domitian, murdered due to Flavius's possible conversion to Judaism; and Old Christian converts to Judaism contemporaneous with Cardoso whom he celebrates here and elsewhere.[18] These instances of conversion to Judaism emphasize the individual nature and nearly uniform danger to the one undertaking this act, in contrast to the false charge that Jews attempt to proselytize Gentiles. Indeed, Cardoso shows the apparent hypocrisy of those who accuse Jews of trying to convert practitioners of different faiths, when in fact these others have made no secret of their own conversionary intent regarding Jews, particularly in the Spanish-Portuguese world.

Cardoso contrasts the title of the seventh *calumnia*, "Merciless and Cruel," with a declaration that this accusation against Jews is akin to call-

---

18   Tiberius ruled as emperor immediately after Octavian (14–37 CE). For a brief reference to Fulvia, see Gottheil and Krauss 528. For the apparent conversion to Judaism of Flavius Clemens, see Cassius Dio 349. Flavius was executed for atheism, "a charge on which many others who drifted into Jewish ways were condemned" (349).

ing snow black and fire cold, because they are in fact "pious, compassionate, and modest" ("piadosos, caritativos, y vergonzosos"; 378). Using this assertion as a frame, he shows that since biblical times Jews have suffered rather than perpetrated a litany of cruelties, citing on several occasions examples that Samuel Usque, a fellow Portuguese converso exile to Italy, described in *Consolation for the Tribulations of Israel*. A groundbreaking work at the time of its publication (1553), due to its language—Portuguese, instead of Castilian Spanish or Latin—and its message of optimism for the Jewish people despite suffering both self-inflicted and caused by others, the *Consolation* clearly informed Cardoso's own worldview. Written as a pastoral dialogue between the "shepherds" Ycabo, Numeo, and Zicareo, this chronicle foregrounds the tribulations of Spanish-Portuguese Jews and New Christians in Cardoso's time with similar afflictions in the past, yet concludes with a message that buttresses the latter's own recovered Judaism: "You have run the entire gauntlet of misfortunes... And since there is no further province for you to go to, your wandering will now end; you will begin to turn your face and your heart toward the ancient lands of your yearning... and there you will make penance for your sins" (Usque 236).[19]

Throughout this seventh *calumnia*, Cardoso cites Usque upon referring to some of the most egregious of these misfortunes. Examples include the expulsion of Jews from England in 1290 due to the libelous charge that they were the source of widespread plague, and the murder and conversion of Jews in medieval France and Germany due to the equally scurrilous claim that they had poisoned wells there (380, 381).[20] Likewise, of the various cruelties against Jews that Cardoso mentions, perhaps the one most seared into the minds of Sephardim of his era, as well as into ours today, was the separation of families by the Portuguese king João II, who in 1493 sent Jewish children to the recently colonized island of São Tomé, where the majority likely perished.

Conscientiously or not, Cardoso also imitates Usque at the end of this chapter by contrasting the ordeals to which Jews have been subject with their privileged position in the eyes of God, who despite their occasional short-

---

19 As Martin A. Cohen, translator of the *Consolation*, notes, a pastoral setting of idealized beauty where learned characters dressed as shepherds gathered to recite poetry and prose was a popular Renaissance [and Baroque] genre (10). In this citation, Numeo addresses Ycabo (Jacob), who personifies the Jewish people in the work.

20 Usque describes these events in *Consolation* 182–85 (England) and 191–92 (France and Germany). His account of the deportation of Jewish children to São Tomé is on 201–02.

comings never abandons them. While other nations have traded in, sacrificed, and even killed other human beings for sport, Jews have aspired to "peace and compassion" ("la paz y la piedad"; 389). As evidence of divine favor, here Cardoso cites Jeremiah 20.7, where the prophet states, "But the Lord is with me like a mighty warrior; / Therefore my persecutors will stumble; / They shall not prevail and shall not succeed." Considering the tragedies that have befallen the Jewish people, this claim to their divine privilege and accompanying ennoblement permits Cardoso to write with defiance and optimism for their survival.

Cardoso concludes the *Excelencias* addressing one of the most widespread and pernicious lies about Jews, the blood libel, by which they supposedly murdered Christian children to use the blood of the victims for ritual purposes. In the tenth and final *calumnia*, "Killers of Christian Children to Use Their Blood in Their Rites," he cites cases of this spurious crime throughout Europe as evidence of popular mistreatment of Jews "when hatred surpasses reason" to such an extent that judgement precedes a nonexistent crime ("cuando el odio domina sobre la razón"; 409). Of the various examples of such blood libels that Cardoso mentions, the one most impactful to Spanish-Portuguese Jewry was the case of the Holy Child of La Guardia, near Toledo, in 1490–91. In this show trial, the Inquisition tried and punished a group of Jews and conversos for supposedly crucifying a young Christian boy from La Guardia with the intent of using his heart and a stolen Eucharistic wafer as part of a spell that would kill inquisitors and other Christians (411, 416–17).[21] Despite the hearsay and contradictory nature of the accusations, the use of torture to extract confessions, and a complete lack of material evidence, the apocryphal violence that the Inquisition imputed to Jews and conversos in this trial contributed to popular anti-Judaism that helped facilitate the edict of expulsion decreed a few months later.

Cardoso defies the actual violence that Christians have justified in response to this fictitious violence of Jews, noting that "all these incidents and feigned histories are of hatred without other grounds than wishing to destroy and ruin a nation" ("todos estos sucesos y historias fingidas son del odio sin otro fundamento más que querer destruir y perder una nación"; 417) and quoting Jeremiah where God affirms the elect status of the Jewish people: "I will make an end of all the nations / Among which I have banished you, / But I will not make an end of you" (Jer. 46.28). These words could describe in part New Christians turned New Jews, such as Cardoso, as much as biblical

---

21   For a summary of this episode, see Gerber, *The Jews of Spain* 133. For a more detailed analysis, see Baer 398–423.

Jews, showing the extent to which the marginalized and often variable status of conversos framed his worldview long after he left the Iberian Peninsula.

## Conclusion: Confronting Antisemitism in Cardoso's Time and Today

Writing as a New Jew outside the censorious environment of 1600s Spain and Portugal, Cardoso, like many fellow conversos, fully claimed the religious inheritance previously denied him. However, the increased accessibility of this inheritance to Sephardim living beyond the Iberian Peninsula lessened the urgency of the *Excelencias* for contemporaries of the author and their descendants (Yerushalmi 476-77). At the same time, the trend towards assimilation among some Jews today and the persistence of the very loathing that Cardoso confronted in the *calumnias* testifies to the relevance and urgency of his work nearly three and a half centuries after its publication. More than eighty years ago, the Nazis unleashed the *Kristallnacht*, a coordinated pogrom against Jews and their property across Germany and Austria that left no doubt as to the willingness of the aggressors to merge violence in word and deed. In October 2018, an avowed anti-Semite allegedly shouting "all Jews must die" opened fire on Sabbath worshippers in the Tree of Life Synagogue in Pittsburgh, murdering eleven and wounding six, including four police officers, while in April 2019 a gunman attacked the Chabad of Poway, CA, synagogue, murdering a worshipper and wounding three, including the rabbi. Through these and other tragedies, we remember that, whether in Cardoso's time or ours, bigots throughout the world have recurred to images of Jews as contaminators, usurpers, and threats to some vague notion of Christian purity as justification for unpardonable antisemitic violence.

# 5
## "O Israel, If You Were to Return to God, How Quickly You Would Show Yourself Redeemed": The Literary and Spiritual Journey of Miguel (Daniel Levi) de Barrios

IN THE ALLEGORICAL PLAY *Contra la verdad no hay fuerza* (*Nothing Can Stand Up to The Truth*), Miguel (Daniel Levi) de Barrios, the most prolific author of the Spanish-Portuguese Jewish community of 1600s Amsterdam, uses Baroque Spanish poetics to represent the worldview of a converso returned to Judaism outside the Iberian Peninsula.[1] Published in Amsterdam sometime before 1672, *Contra la verdad* commemorates the deaths of Jorge Méndez de Castro (Abraham Atías, or Athias), Domingo (Yahacob, or Jacob) Rodríguez de Cáceres, and Beatriz (Raquel) Núñez Fernández, three conversos burned for crypto-Jewish heresy after the auto de fe of June 29, 1665, in Córdoba, Spain.[2] The work thus testifies to the fame that martyrs such as these gained throughout the Iberian Jewish diaspora of the mid-1600s for resisting pressure of Inquisition tribunals to live as faithful Catholics. By memorializing New Christian victims of the Inquisition, *Contra la verdad* also shows how a former converso returned to Judaism outside Spanish-Portuguese lands exalted these individuals as models of Jewish

---

1    This translation of the title *Contra la verdad no hay fuerza* is by Davidi (207). Swetschinski proposes "No Force Is a Match for the Truth" ("The Portuguese Jews" 64).

2    The names in parentheses represent the Hebrew aliases by which the three likely called themselves. Crypto-Jews of the late 1500s and 1600s who were committed to making known and dying for their beliefs frequently adopted a Hebrew name as an outward sign of their resolute faith. For more on this practice and examples of such individuals, see Bodian, *Dying in the Law of Moses* 36ff.

faith, albeit *in extremis*. This chapter discusses autobiographical references in the works of Barrios to show how his life story led him to extol the three for their faith; examines an eyewitness account of the auto de fe that made them (in)famous as well as poetry from the introductory pages of *Contra la verdad* reflecting on this fame; and then analyzes the play to show how Barrios inverts the format of an *auto sacramental* (sacramental act), a canonical genre of Spanish Catholicism, to assert a Jewish identity. The ability of Barrios to write a Judeocentric work in this genre shows his success adapting a Christian Baroque Spanish intellectual formation to a text whose publication would have been perilous in Spain.³

## Flight from Iberia and Return to Judaism in the Shadow of Adversity and Loss

His journey as a New Christian who subsequently became a leading voice of the Spanish-Portuguese Jewish community of Amsterdam informed the Jewish and Baroque Spanish identities that Barrios manifests in *Contra la verdad*. One way to understand this journey and how it influenced Barrios to adapt a literary genre of Spanish Catholicism to privilege Judaism is by studying several texts in which he sheds light on his own biography and Jewish spirituality. Perhaps because he wrote full-time for most of the last four decades of the 1600s, during most of which he lived in Amsterdam, the literary output of Barrios, especially that treating Jewish themes, exceeds that of the other authors studied in this work and is considerably more uneven. The present chapter acknowledges this reality by focusing on biographical references in his works, poetry from the introductory pages of *Contra la verdad*, and the allegorical play itself.⁴

In his background and geographical and spiritual journeys, Miguel de Barrios personified the fluidity of the Spanish-Portuguese converso diaspora of the seventeenth century. He was born in 1635 to a New Christian family in

---

3    This chapter builds, in part, upon research conducted in 2021 with University of Portland students Arielys Morffiz González and Fabi Zeller-Márquez through the Summer Undergraduate Research Experience (SURE) of the College of Arts and Sciences and published in *Reinvention: An International Journal of Undergraduate Research* (see Morffiz González, Zeller-Márquez, and Warshawsky). I wrote the present chapter subsequent to our SURE project while also expanding content I contributed to our jointly authored article.

4    For summaries of Barrios's life and works, see Lieberman, *El teatro alegórico* 19–33; and Scholberg, *La poesía religiosa de Miguel de Barrios* 3–80, and "Miguel de Barrios and the Amsterdam Sephardic Community."

the southern Spanish town of Montilla, near Córdoba, the same city where the Inquisition punished the crypto-Jewish subjects of *Contra la verdad* thirty years later. The more complete version of his elegy "Lamentación fúnebre en la muerte de mi padre Yahacob Leví de Barrios" ("Funeral Lamentation on the Death of My Father Jacob Levi de Barrios"), published in *Estrella de Jacob sobre flores de Lis* (*Star of Jacob above Flowers of Lis*; Amsterdam, 1686), includes six *décimas* (ten-line strophes) in which Barrios describes the secret Judaism of his progenitors and their Portuguese roots.[5] Thus, in the thirteenth strophe of the elegy, Barrios mentions his paternal and maternal grandfathers, Abraham Levi Caniso and Isaac Cohen de Sosa (Bartolomé-Pons 217), showing how Spanish-Portuguese New Christians, when possible, identified through their names with an exalted biblical past. Additionally, the same strophe indicates that Levi Caniso was from the town of Marialva in the Guarda region of northeast Portugal, an area where crypto-Judaism took root during the 1500s after the forced conversion of the country's Jews in 1497. Subsequently, some conversos in this region, many of whose families were originally Spanish, traveled to Spain in the early 1600s when permitted to do so.

Just as the father of Barrios, Jacob Levi de Barrios, had a Catholic name in which he had been baptized, Simón de Barrios, so his mother, whom the fourteenth strophe identifies as Sara Levi, had been baptized as Sebastiana del Valle (Bartolomé-Pons 217).[6] Conversos such as the parents of Barrios who took Hebrew first names and surnames did so at great risk, since doing so could call attention to their possible crypto-Judaism. After the expulsion of Spanish Jews in 1492, such naming practices usually occurred when con-

---

5   Barrios included a shorter version of "Lamentación fúnebre" in *Coro de las Musas*, published in Brussels in 1672. I agree with the claim of Esther Bartolomé-Pons (see 201–02) that Barrios wrote the entire poem by this earlier date but did not include six strophes (3 and 11–15) testifying to the Jewish roots and beliefs of his family that appear in the version published in Amsterdam fourteen years later. The poem also appears in the allegorical play *Maskil el Dal* (*Enlightener of the Poor*; see Lieberman, *El teatro alegórico* 155–61. The translation of the title *Maskil el Dal* is from Scholberg, "Miguel de Barrios" 136). The word "Lis" in the title of the collection containing "Lamentación fúnebre" (*Estrella de Jacob sobre flores de Lis*) refers to Francisco de Lis, who also called himself Abraham López Bernal.

6   See Scholberg, *La poesía religiosa* 3, for the identification of the parents of Miguel de Barrios in his baptismal record. In 3–4n2, Scholberg observes that one of the witnesses to the baptism, Alonso López Laguna, had the same last name as Daniel Israel López Laguna, the subject of chapter 6 of this book, but is unable to speculate on a possible connection between the two individuals.

versos left Iberian lands for places where they could live as Jews, or if they became martyrs for their crypto-Jewish faith while remaining in Spanish-Portuguese territories.[7] Simón and Sebastiana called themselves Jacob and Sara amongst family while living in Spain and then openly upon settling in Algiers in the mid-1650s.

Melancholy and misfortune cast their shadow over Barrios despite the good fortune that permitted much of his family to leave the "tierras de idolatría" ("lands of idolatry"), as escaped conversos referred to Spain, Portugal, and their American territories, for places where they could live openly as Jews. The impetus for their departure may have been the death at the stake of Barrios's cousin from Montilla, Marcos (Ishac) de Almeida Bernal, in the auto de fe of 1655 at Santiago de Compostela, Spain, for Jewish heresy. Barrios includes the name and a brief description of Ishac in a "Memoria de los mártires" ("Memorial of Martyrs") he wrote to mark the opening of the *Esnoga*, or Portuguese Synagogue of the Talmud Torah community of Amsterdam in 1675, in which he celebrates fellow conversos "burned alive ... for sanctifying the unbroken unity of the eternal Lawgiver" ("quemados vivos ... . por santificar la indivisa unidad del eterno Legislador"; *Triumpho del govierno popular* 504).[8] In this same "Memoria," Barrios also mentions Abraham Núñez Bernal, uncle of Ishac de Almeida Bernal and a martyr at the auto de

---

7   Gitlitz confirms the absence of surnames that would have identified the converso identity of their bearers: "I know of no surnames used exclusively or even preponderantly by conversos. The Inquisition, always vigilant to identify New Christians so as to scrutinize them for crypto-Judaism, never used surnames as a guide" (*Secrecy and Deceit* 211n11).

8   See *Triumpho del govierno popular y de la antigüedad holandesa* (*Triumph of Popular Government and of Dutch Antiquity*) 504–08 for the full list (hereafter abbreviated as *Triumpho*). Abraham was also an alias for Francisco de Lis, to whom Barrios refers in the title of the aforementioned *Estrella de Jacob sobre flores de Lis*. *Triumpho* is a miscellany consisting of poetry, allegorical plays (but not *Contra la verdad*), and descriptions of academies for religious studies and charitable works, the community's burial society, and the people who composed these groups, among other texts. My references to *Triumpho* are based on a digitized copy held at the Bibliotheca Rosenthaliana at the University of Amsterdam and accessible via Google Books. As far as I can tell, this version is copy 19G11, which has 696 pages (Scholberg, *La poesía religiosa* 353, indicates that 19G11 is of this length). The work also includes handwritten page numbers to which I have referred in my citations.

fe of 1655 in Córdoba; and the three from the auto de fe of 1665 in Córdoba whom he memorializes in *Contra la verdad*.[9]

The letter of 1682 to his brothers Isaac and Benjamin Levi de Barrios and Jacob López Puerto, husband of his sister Judith, that Barrios includes in the *epístola* (epistle) at the start of "Triumphal carro de la perfección por el camino de la salvación" ("Triumphal Carriage of Perfection by the Path of Salvation") describes the dispersion of the family after this trauma, confirming the geographic mobility of early modern Sephardim. For example, the parents of the poet, Sara and Jacob, died in Algiers within a few months of each other in 1670, while his siblings Francisco, Antonio, and Clara died in "my severe homeland" ("mi patria rigurosa"; *Triumpho* 582), that is, Spain. After likely passing through Nice, where a paternal aunt, Sara Levi de Torres, lived (Scholberg, *La poesía religiosa* 9n21), Barrios arrived in Livorno, in whose Spanish-Portuguese Jewish community he was circumcised as a visible sign of his identity: "I paid with my blood to love [the Law], / and today with her light there is not a shadow that frightens me" ("compré con mi sangre ser su amante, / y hoy con su luz no hay sombra que me espante"; *Triumpho* 581). Barrios credits his maternal aunt, Raquel Coen de Sosa, for guiding his return to Judaism in Livorno, writing that to her "I owe the first light of the pure Law" ("debo la primer[a] luz de la Ley pura"; *Triumpho* 582).[10] In Livorno Barrios married another former conversa, Débora Váez, but she died in 1660 on the Caribbean island of Tobago, then a Dutch colony, shortly after the couple arrived to start a new life there.

Barrios returned at once to Europe on the same ship, arriving in Amsterdam in 1662. Like Orobio and Pinto Delgado, Barrios undoubtedly chose to settle in this city because of the liberties of worship granted to Jews there. Additionally, he was "drawn [...] by the legacy of [Saul Levi] Morteira," whom he praises in *Triumpho del Gobierno Popular* (G. Kaplan, *The Origins of Democratic Zionism* 61). Besides founding the yeshiva Keter Torah, Morteira served as first rabbi of Talmud Torah, the Sephardic community formed by the joining together of three smaller ones, a position he held up to

---

9   See *Elogios que zelozos dedicaron* (*Praises That Zealous [Poets] Dedicated*) for a collection of poetry and prose in Spanish, Portuguese, and Latin that the Amsterdam Sephardic community wrote in memory of Abraham Núñez Bernal and his nephew Ishac de Almeida Bernal.

10  Barrios concludes the *epístola* through the inspired words he addresses to the Jewish people as a whole and which I have included in the title of this chapter: "¡O impelido Israel, si a Dios volvieras, / qué presto redimido te mostraras!" (*Triumpho* 583).

his death in 1660. During the next twelve years, Barrios traveled to Catholic Brussels an undetermined number of times to participate in the literary life of that city, then part of Spanish Habsburg dominions, while living within the observant community of Iberian Jewish immigrants to Amsterdam. In Brussels, he befriended successive governors as well as Spanish and Portuguese nobles, some of whom were apparently secret Jews, always with an eye to gaining their patronage. Such support permitted him to publish his first two collections of poetry there, *Flor de Apolo* (1665) and *Coro de las musas* (1672). Barrios also received a commission as a captain of cavalry in the Spanish army, although it is not in fact certain what duties, if any, he performed in this role (Lieberman, *El teatro alegórico* 25).[11] Meanwhile, in Amsterdam he married another former New Christian returned to Judaism, Abigail de Pina Fonseca Dias, and had three children with her.

Barrios might have split time between Brussels and Amsterdam, as Scholberg and Oelman claimed, or only made "quick trips" to Brussels under strict conditions that the Mahamad imposed, as Révah argued.[12] In either case, these early years of his literary career outside Spain presented financial, religious, and familial challenges that would continually beset him. Irregular income earned as a professional author compelled Barrios to write frequent encomia of potential and actual benefactors then and in many future texts. Additionally, despite the positive reception of his work in Brussels, Révah shows the unlikelihood that Barrios lived there, citing the penury of his life in Amsterdam and his apology of September 18, 1665, in the synagogue of the Talmud Torah community for having traveled to a "land of idolatry" (that is, Brussels) and not kept the Sabbath ("Les écrivains" 80, 82). Barrios himself conveys this contrition and acknowledges the decree of the Mahamad of 1644 that any Spanish-Portuguese Jew of Amsterdam who traveled to a Catholic land renounce this act from the pulpit of the synagogue and do penance before being readmitted to the community:

> and I also beg the pardon of the whole congregation, people of God, for the scandal I have caused, and of which I am very repentant, with all my heart; and the penitence that they [the Mahamad] have ordered, I will

---

11    Barrios tried to publish *Flor de Apolo* in Amsterdam, but the Mahamad forbade him from doing so (Lieberman, *El teatro alegórico* 25–26; see 25n27 for text [in Portuguese] of the Mahamad governing publication of works by community members). *Coro de las musas* was published there and in Brussels.

12    See Scholberg, *La poesía religiosa* 13–22; Oelman 219; and Révah, "Les écrivains" 82.

carry out, obeying completely, and beseeching God to pardon us, and that there be peace over Israel [as a people].

y a toda la congregación, pueblo del Dio, pido también perdón del escándalo que he dado, de que estoy muy arrepentido, de todo corazón; y la penitencia que me ordenaron, cumpliré obedeciendo en todo, y pidiendo al Dio nos perdone, y haya paz sobre Israel.

(Révah, "Les écrivains" 82)[13]

Although in his religious poetry Barrios always spells the singular *Dios* (God) with an -s, the omission of this letter here may symbolize an intent to demonstrate the sincerity of his apology. The shortened form suggests his awareness of a custom by which pre-expulsion-era Jews and subsequently conversos sometimes used the shorter spelling (*el Dio* or *Dio*) to denote the "unitary nature" of God rather than a plural, in this case tripartite, understanding of the divine, as in Catholicism (Gitlitz, *Secrecy and Deceit* 102).[14]

Nevertheless, given his military title, desire to remain connected to the Spanish-Catholic literary milieu of his earlier years, and continued appeals to patrons in Brussels, Barrios likely visited there after this pardon. Such visits necessitated separation from his family, a circumstance that, as Scholberg notes, Barrios laments in *Coro de las musas*, his collection of poems published in Amsterdam seven years after the pardon (*La poesía religiosa* 22).[15] In "Triumpho 53," the autobiographical speaker Mirtilo laments to Belisa (Abigail) his absence from her and their son Simón, whom he has earlier identified by name:

Without him, such are my sorrows,
without you (wife) such is my excess [of sorrows],
that I am more imprisoned by love
in the prison of my misfortunes.

---

13   See Révah, "Les écrivains" 81, for reference to the directive of 1644 from the Mahamad mandating public penitence by those Jews who traveled to Spanish-Portuguese lands. Lieberman, *El teatro alegórico* 25, also describes the public apology of 1665 that the Mahamad demanded of Barrios.

14   See Shepard 40–42 for examples of *Dio* in literature by Spanish Jews of the 1500s.

15   Scholberg directs readers to "Triumpho 53," the poem in *Coro* where this lament occurs, but does not cite an example from the text communicating the sadness that the poet feels.

Sin él, son mis penas tales,
sin ti (esposa) tal mi exceso,
que estoy de amores más preso
en la cárcel de mis amores. (280; 349 in PDF)

Despite his literary success in Brussels, hardship and tragedy did not loosen their grip over the poet. His second wife and their first two children, Simón and Raquel, predeceased him, and their surviving child, Ribca (Rebeca), was forced to care for him. The double sonnets Barrios published in memory of Abigail's passing, "La memoria renueva el dolor" ("Memory Rekindles Grief"), testifies to this sadness through antitheses typical of Spanish Golden Age poetry: "I in a sea of weeping, she in the heavenly summit, / the more [that] hope for her becomes clouded to me / the more [that] love gives her light to me" ("Yo en mar de llanto, ella en celestre cumbre, / cuanto más se me anubla su esperanza / tanto más el amor da en mí su lumbre"; Scholberg, *La poesía religiosa* 247).[16] Struggling to make ends meet on top of this grief, Barrios constantly needed to find literary patrons, a situation that helps explain the diffuse and uneven character of his writing.

By 1674 he renounced his military commission in Brussels where, ironically, he had enjoyed greater literary freedom than in the rigorous religious community of Sephardic Amsterdam. Confronting this change, his ever-present poverty, and the strictures of the Mahamad, Barrios turned to Judaism even more: "la [Ley divina] tengo en mis tormentas, por mi Norte" ("the divine Law I hold in my adversity, as my North Star"; *Triumpho* 582). Perhaps due to such adversity, during the 1660s Barrios had become a follower of Sabbatai Zevi and remained an adherent of Sabbateanism, at least for a time. His repentance of this belief by 1674 affected his mental health, causing him to experience visions periodically (Scholberg, *La poesía religiosa* 25; Lieberman, *El teatro alegórico* 27–28, 90–91). Throughout the last quarter of the 1600s, he never left Amsterdam again, and upon his death on March 2, 1701. was buried next to Abigail in the Portuguese-Jewish cemetery at Ouderkerk, the same resting place as that of Isaac Orobio de Castro.

---

16    This poem, part of *Estrella de Jacob sobre flores de Lis*, the same collection in which Barrios published "Lamentación fúnebre en la muerte de mi padre," consists of three groups of two consecutive sonnets, each followed by an additional quatrain. See Scholberg, *La poesía religiosa* 246–48.

## The *Auto Sacramental*: A Catholic Literary Genre in Celebration of the Eucharist

Using a canonical literary genre of Spanish Catholicism to privilege the Judaism of allegorical characters in *Contra la verdad*, Barrios adapts his literary formation from which this latter religion was officially absent to a setting of former New Christians in Amsterdam. According to the Dictionary of the Real Academia Española, an *auto sacramental* of the Middle Ages or Renaissance was a "short dramatic work based on religious or secular themes" ("pieza dramática de breves dimensiones basada en temas religiosos o profanos"; dle.rae.es/auto) that during the Baroque era, when Barrios was writing, came to focus especially on the Eucharist. As such, the plays were typically performed during Corpus Christi, the Roman Catholic feast that celebrates the Eucharist, or transubstantiation, "the supernatural transformation of the elements of bread and wine into the body and blood of Christ" (Thornton Spinnenweber 12). Even though most *autos sacramentales* were one-act plays, Barrios calls *Contra la verdad* a *comedia* (comedy), and indeed, as Davidi has observed (207), the play consists of three acts, consistent with Spanish plays of this latter genre.[17] Given their "catechetical and didactic purpose" (Thornton Spinnenweber 13), *autos sacramentales* were often presented on moveable *tablados* (stages) transported on *carros* (carts) in order to spread their message of divine grace to as many people as possible. The didactic purpose of Barrios, however, is to celebrate not the Eucharist but Judaism. He achieves this end by using the three martyrs of Córdoba as inspiration for affirming the Jewish faith of several allegorical figures in the play and, in the case of three of them, their willingness to die for it.

In Barrios's time, Pedro Calderón de la Barca (1600–1681) wrote more than seventy *autos sacramentales*, in several of which allegorical characters represent the triumph of Christianity over Judaism.[18] In other allegorical plays, Calderón adhered to a Spanish Golden Age literary tradition of using Greco-Roman mythology to foreground this triumph (Lieberman, "*Contra la verdad*" 186). For example, in *Los encantos de la culpa* (*The Enchantments of Sin*), a play that most likely was a source for Barrios, Calderón imbues the

---

17    Another example of an *auto sacramental* of more than one act and contemporaneous with Barrios is *El divino Narciso* by the colonial Mexican nun Sor Juana Inés de la Cruz, which contains five. Written in Mexico, likely in 1688, this play was first performed in Madrid the following year (Thornton Spinnenweber 12).

18    Lieberman notes that examples of *autos sacramentales* by Calderón in which Christianity and Judaism debate each other include *La vacante general*, *Llamados y escogidos* and *Psiquis y Cupido* (*El teatro alegórico* 66n30).

myth of Ulysses and the goddess and sorcerer Circe with a Christian message about humanity and temptation. In book 10 of the *Odyssey*, when they arrive to her island of Aeaea, Circe offers to Ulysses's men a concoction of cheese, barley, honey, and wine, to which she has added a potion that turns into pigs those who drink the mixture. Only Ulysses, who has remained on the boat, and his pilot Eurylochus, "who feared a snare" and hence has not consumed the drink, avoid this metamorphosis (172). Hermes provides Ulysses with a moly plant, whose magical properties confer immunity to the potion, and urges him to confront the goddess. Armed with this defense, Ulysses compels Circe to return his men to human form. Subsequently, the two sleep together, she befriends her visitors, and provides guidance for their continued journey.[19] Given that Barrios mentions Ulysses and Circe several times in *Contra la verdad*, a summary of *Los encantos* shows how this *auto sacramental* provides a structure through which, approximately a quarter century later, the converso poet inverts Calderon's privileging of Christianity to favor Judaism.[20]

Demonstrating how Spanish writers adapted works of classical mythology to a Christian context, Calderón transforms Ulysses into the allegorical figure Man (el Hombre), representative of humanity; Eurylochus into Understanding (el Entendimiento), the "judge and guide" of Man ("árbitro y guía"; 163n78); the crew of Ulysses into the five senses; and Circe into Sin (la Culpa). As humanity's conscience, Understanding foregrounds divine acceptance of sinners by telling the senses, "heaven, always open to human voices, / is a happy port to the shipwrecked pilot" ("el Cielo, a humildes voces siempre abierto, / al náufrago piloto es feliz puerto"; 160, lines 61–62), but then warns Man that by searching only for pleasures, "Sin you [and your senses] will find" ("la Culpa hallaréis"; 172, line 224). Indeed, emulating Circe in the myth, Sin changes each sense into a distinct animal when, self-indulgently, they imbibe a potion to which her vices Lust, Gluttony, Envy, Flattery, and Gossip have invited them (179–85). Understanding then orders Man to per-

---

19   Ovid also relates this story in book 14 of *Metamorphoses*.
20   For Calderón as the principal among several possible contemporary sources for *Contra la verdad*, see Wilson's review of Scholberg, *La poesía religiosa*; and Lieberman, "*Contra la verdad*" 185–86. In her introduction to *Los encantos*, Egido suggests that the work was first performed in Madrid in 1645 or possibly previously (52–53). As Lieberman notes ("*Contra la verdad*" 187), Calderón also adapted the myth of Ulysses and Circe to an allegorical comedy, *El mayor encanto, amor* (*Love, the Greatest Charm*). For commentary regarding this play, see Egido 23-35.

form three tasks to free his senses: seek pardon for encouraging them to sin, confess his own guilt in this sin, and repent of it (186–87).[21]

As soon as Man completes these tasks, Penitence (la Penitencia) appears on a rainbow, or *arco iris*, showing how Calderón conflates Iris, goddess of the rainbow in mythology, with God's promise of "my bow in the clouds" as a sign of the covenant with humanity after the flood (Gen. 9.13). Connecting the Greco-Roman world with Christianity, and, within the latter, humanity with God, Penitence becomes the key character in the play, as she communicates divine mercy to those who confess sin and repent of it. In this role as messenger, Penitence gives Man a bouquet of flowers tinged with blood representative of Christ's sacrifice that will make him immune to Sin's spell. Yet, reflecting Calderón's misogynistic representation of her as a seductress possessed of "forbidden knowledge" ("ciencias prohibidas"; 209, line 800), Sin nearly convinces Man to capitulate to her charms, and indeed, the flowers of the bouquet he has just received fall to the ground, symbolizing her apparent triumph. Penitence, however, retaining her faith in Man, retrieves the flowers, "keeping them for the time / when, repentant of his sin and his inflexibility, / Man seeks me out" ("guardándolas para el tiempo / que arrepentido me busque / de su culpa y de su hierro"; 219, lines 941–43).

The play reaches its dramatic climax during a dinner at Circe's palace when Sin instructs a musical chorus to convince Man to enjoy the pleasures of mortal life while at the same time Understanding directs him towards contemplation of death (227–28). Just when Sin declares her authority over Man, equating the scattered flowers of his bouquet with the loss of virtues, Penitence appears on a chariot, almost like a deus ex machina. She has gathered the flowers as signs of divine grace and humanity's ability to triumph over Sin.[22] Calderón deftly shows how, through the sacrament of the Eucharist, Penitence substitutes the gift of Christ for the rich foods with which Sin has tried to deceive Man: "this is not bread, / but a more noble substance; / it is flesh and blood" ("esto no es pan, / sino más noble sustancia; / carne y sangre es"; 235, lines 1228–30). Fortified so, Man happily obeys Penitence's order that he return to the ship of the Church (237), while Sin's palace collapses

---

21 In his notes to the text, Juan Manuel Escudero indicates that these instructions reflect the division of penitence into "contrition, confession, and works of repentance" ("contrición, confesión y satisfacción"; 187, notes to lines 450ff). Escudero cites the *Summa Theologica* of St. Thomas Aquinas as the source of this tripartition of penitence.

22 See 234–35, note to verses 1209ff, where Escudero indicates biblical sources of divine grace to which Calderón refers here.

in an earthquake as she admits her powerlessness "by virtue of that divine / sustenance that she [Penitence] gives as food" ("en virtud de aquel divino / manjar que da por vianda"; 242, lines 1352–53).

### The *Auto Sacramental*: Recovering Jewish Identity through Catholic Allegorical Theater

By reworking elements of the aforementioned plot into his own devotional play, Barrios uses Catholic allegorical theater to recover Jewish identity in the Iberian world and to create space for writing as a Spaniard and a Jew in the Inquisitional era. He dedicated *Contra la verdad* to Ishac Penso, father of his friend José (or Yosef) Penso de la Vega, with whom he later collaborated by submitting poetry to accompany prose works of the latter.[23] Ishac most likely aided Barrios financially, given that the latter, in his description of the Keter Torah religious academy, calls Ishac "most devout and a great giver of charity" ("religiosísimo y gran limosnero") and claims that Ishac "distributed to the poor more than 40,000 florins of tithing from his income" ("repartió más de cuarenta mil florines de los diezmos de sus ganancias entre pobres"; *Triumpho* 73, 78).[24] In another connection between the contents of Barrios's work and community members, the list of martyrs memorialized in *Contra la verdad* includes Isaac de Castro Tartas, older brother of David de Cas-

---

23  See Lieberman, *El teatro alegórico* 48–50; and Scholberg, "Miguel de Barrios" 148–49. The full title of the play is *Contra la verdad no hay fuerza, panegírico a los tres bienaventurados mártires Abraham Athías, Jahacob Rodríguez Cásares y Raquel Núñez Fernández, que fueron quemados vivos en Córdova, por santificar la unidad divina. En 16 de Tamuz. Año de 5425.* Scholberg based his edition on what he believed are the only three extant copies of the work, held at the Bibliotheca Rosenthaliana of the University of Amsterdam, the Ets Haim Library-Livraria Montezinos of the Portuguese Synagogue in Amsterdam, and the British Museum in London. All are missing pages that likely correspond to a *loa*, or short theatrical piece introducing an allegorical play, and the copy at the British Museum lacks fifteen pages from within the work itself (*La poesía religiosa* 110).

24  The International Institute of Social History, located in Amsterdam and affiliated with the Royal Netherlands Academy of Arts and Sciences, can compute the value of guilders from 1450 forward in euros in 2020. According to the online calculator of the Institute, 40,000 florins in 1683, the year when Barrios published *Triumpho*, would have had "a purchasing power" of 478,373 euros in 2020, or $545,345, using an average rate of exchange of $1.14 per euro for that year. See "Value of the Guilder versus Euro" and, for the average value of a dollar in euros in 2020, "Yearly Average Currency Exchange Rates." In the Netherlands, florins were also called guilders.

tro Tartas, who published the play.[25] It is not known if the play was staged in Amsterdam, especially considering the complex scenes involved, such as characters appearing in a pillar of fire, in a cloud, and mounted on a lion, or if Barrios wrote the play as he imagined its presentation (Lieberman, "*Contra la verdad*" 183; Den Boer 315). Likewise, the omission of the same pages in all three extant copies of the work suggest censure by the Mahamad of this content and perhaps of the play itself due to unease that its anti-Christian attitude might have caused (Roth, "An Elegy of João Pinto Delgado" 362–63; Lieberman, "*Contra la verdad*" 183n4).

The longest example of allegorical theater that Barrios wrote, *Contra la verdad* exemplifies Baroque complexity across nearly 3,400 lines in three acts. The work consists of a battle of wills between the allegorical figures Appetite (el Apetito), Error (el Error), Anger (el Enojo), Vice (el Vicio), and Lie (la Mentira) on one side, and Truth (la Verdad), Virtue (la Virtud), Zeal (el Celo), Understanding (el Entendimiento), and Free Will (el Albedrío) on the other. Against the backdrop of the three crypto-Jews who willingly die for their faith, members of the first group, especially Lie, try to convince Free Will to fall into the trap of temptation, that is, to abandon Jewish beliefs for Christian ones (249–50). Through a plot consisting of debates, competing choruses that attempt to sway Free Will, and even the shooting of an arrow by Lie at Free Will, they nearly succeed. However, by the end of the play, the latter group, simulating the example of Abraham Atías, Jacob Rodríguez de Cáceres, and Raquel Núñez Fernández, chooses death as a means to assert the triumph of the Law of Moses and the exalted celestial status that crypto-Jews believed such martyrdom achieved. A way to understand this diffuse play is through studying how its references to the three martyrs, despite their physical absence from the work's action, help communicate its privileging of Judaism, in other words, that, as the title proclaims, "nothing can stand up to the truth" ("contra la verdad no hay fuerza").

## THE AUTO DE FE OF CÓRDOBA (1655) AS INSPIRATION FOR *CONTRA LA VERDAD*

Given this absence, a brief study of Abraham, Jacob, and Raquel based on two firsthand *relaciones*, or accounts, of the auto de fe at Córdoba explains why Barrios uses their experience as the foundation of the sacramental play and glorifies them in poems included in the introductory pages of the orig-

---

25  See Scholberg, *La poesía religiosa* 333–34, for the reference to Isaac de Castro Tartas. His brother David de Castro Tartas also published *Excelencias de los hebreos* by Isaac Cardoso.

inal work. Certainly, these accounts, written by a Dominican friar, Pedro de Herrera, and a Franciscan, Pedro Mateo de Lara, evince the anti-Jewish biases of their authors; as such, they lack impartiality describing the public sentencing of June 1665 in the Plaza de Corredera and the events surrounding it. Nevertheless, their encyclopedic contents, including the names of all fifty-five defendants penanced and the respective heresies of which these individuals were accused, communicate the fame, or perhaps infamy, of Abraham, Jacob, and Raquel that might have appealed to Barrios. Herrera and Lara confirm both the focus of the Inquisition prosecuting New Christians during the 1600s and the Portuguese origin of most of them by noting that forty-nine of these fifty-five defendants were "Judaizers" ("judaizantes"), "Portuguese" ("portugueses"), and/or "descendants of Portuguese" ("descendientes de portugueses"; Gracia Boix 463–64, 493–94). As discussed elsewhere in this book, the term "Portuguese" frequently referred to conversos of Portuguese origin in Spanish territories of the seventeenth century; even New Christians themselves used the term to signify their Jewish lineage and self-identity as a distinct entity if they or their forebears were from Portugal.

Abraham, Jacob, and Raquel belonged to a group of seven conversos whom inquisitors "relaxed," or turned over, to secular authorities for burning at the stake as recidivist (*relapsos*) and/or unrepentant (*negativos*) Judaizers. Here as in other autos, the tribunal announced sentence according to categories of heresy, often reserving to the end of the ceremony the most severe, that of defendants to be relaxed (*relajados*). Besides all seven individuals in this last category at Córdoba being conversos, so too were six reconciled before their death (*reconciliados*) whose mortal remains, if found, were included in the proceedings; fifteen "absent fugitives" ("fugitivos ausentes") relaxed to the stake in absentia; and twenty-one people reconciled in person on whom the tribunal then imposed sentences of varying length that included having to wear penitential sackcloth (the *sambenito*), as well as imprisonment and exile. Given that defendants in the first two categories were not physically present, the tribunal paraded *estatuas*, or effigies of their likenesses, during the ceremony to show that Inquisitorial justice reached the dead and the escaped. The effigies of the twenty-one *relajados* were then consigned to the flames. Only six individuals punished at the auto were not New Christians: two convicted of bigamy and four of witchcraft (Gracia Boix 459–64, 489–94).

As the *relación* of Pedro Mateo de Lara describes with greater detail the seven condemned to the stake, especially the three among them who were to be burned alive for not recanting their heresy, the following comments cite this account rather than that of Pedro de Herrera. Even while the Inquisition assigned two *calificadores*, or theologians, to each of the condemned "to accommodate the content of their consciences and prepare them to die devoutly and as Catholics" ("para ajustar las materias de sus conciencias y disponerlos a morir católica y piadosamente"), the three "refused, stubbornly and foolishly, the generous hand of God, not wishing to accept the timely instruction" ("se negaron dura y neciamente, a la mano liberal de Dios, no queriendo admitir la oportuna receta"; Gracia Boix 479). Trying to show that Abraham, Jacob, and Raquel would be responsible for being consigned to the flames alive, the Franciscan friar narrates their last moments unsparingly, from preparations for the auto the night before to the scene at the *quemadero* (burning ground) in the field of Marrubial just outside the city walls. Thus, Jorge Méndez de Castro (Abraham Atías), whom Lara accuses of "incurable ignorance" ("incurable ignorancia") despite an ability to recite biblical verses by heart (479), "in a final, horrendous, and lamentable desperation embraced the flames" ("en última, horrorosa y lamentable desesperación las [llamas] abrazó"; Gracia Boix 479, 484). Domingo (Jacob) Rodríguez de Cáceres recanted his Jewish beliefs just as the flames were being lit, thus prompting secular authorities to garrote him first. Lara depicts this outcome as a triumph of the Inquisition and Catholicism, given that, as "his [crypto-Jewish] pretense was turning out useless, he [Rodríguez] admitted the deceit, gave up resistance, and confessed according to the sacraments" ("salía inútil su fingimiento, declaró el engaño, se redujo y confesó sacramentalmente"; Gracia Boix 470; see also Roth, "An Elegy of João Pinto Delgado" 360n1).

Barrios might have subsequently confused Beatriz (Raquel) Núñez Fernández for the third of the three "wicked" ("protervos") heretics, Leonor María Enríquez, given that both *relaciones* mention Núñez Fernández only in their catalogs of defendants and sentences. On the other hand, the account of Lara includes Enríquez, not Núñez Fernández, in the group of three to be burned alive as unrepentant Judaizers. With no lack of exaggeration, the friar then claims how the case of the 24-year-old Enríquez was "one of the rarest and most uncommon that the world has wondered at since Adam to today" ("uno de los más raros e inauditos, que ha admirado el mundo desde Adán hasta hoy"; Gracia Boix 479). Before the auto itself, Enríquez, "obstinate in her unrepentant purpose" ("pertinaz en su propósito negativo"; Gracia Boix 479), refused the entreaties, some of them tearful, of religious and nonreligious authorities that she forswear Judaism. Friar Lara then describes and judges her death with great specificity, noting how "the smoke and flames rose to the stars, perhaps to complain of such extreme stubbornness, and the soul went down to its deserved suffering, in sad and unending punishment" ("subió el humo y el fuego a las estrellas, quizá a querellarse de tan escandalosa dureza y el alma bajó al merecido suplicio, en triste y nunca terminable escarmiento"; Gracia Boix 484). The strength of conviction of Enríquez, perhaps combined with her youth and gender, clearly compelled Lara to vilify her and narrate her death in this dramatic manner.

Regardless of this possible confusion regarding Beatriz (Raquel) Núñez Fernández and Leonor María Enríquez, Barrios clearly knew of their tribulations when writing *Contra la verdad* during the following years. As such, in the introductory pages preceding the play, he made Abraham, Jacob, and Raquel the subject of two sonnets and also wrote two *décimas* glorifying Raquel.[26] While limitations of space preclude a discussion of all these texts, a brief analysis of one, the sonnet "¿Qué tres cometas brillan en el cielo?" ("Which Three Comets Shine in the Sky?"), shows how Barrios poeticizes for distinct reasons the same fiery images that Friar Lara incorporates in his account:

> Which three comets shine in the sky?
> Which three new stars does the earth see?
> Which three miracles make war on what is false?
> Which three rainbows announce peace to the heavens?
>    They are those which in thundering Etna,
> those which as soon as dust buries them
> follow the good that encloses them in glory,
> attain the good that horror means to bury.
>    Oh, rare chain of souls
> become torches of the starry firmament,
> you illumine the human with the divine!
>    Guiding in the angriest storm
> those who seek the crystalline port
> because in the sea of the world all is drowned.
>
>    ¿Qué tres cometas brillan en el cielo?
> ¿qué tres nuevos luceros ve la tierra?
> ¿qué tres milagros dan al error guerra?

---

26   Scholberg notes that these two sonnets and the two *décimas* appear on pp. 11, 12, and 14–16 of the original edition of *Contra la verdad*; he includes them on pp. 242–45 of his anthology (*La poesía religiosa* 349n100). All citations to the play are from the edition of the play that Scholberg prepared and included in this work.

¿qué tres Iris anuncian paz al cielo?
    Son los que en el trinante Mongibelo,
son los que en cuanto polvo los entierra
siguen el bien que en glorias los encierra,
alcanzan el que horror destina al suelo.
    ¡O vínculo de almas peregrino!
ya antorchas de la máquina estrellada
a lo humano alumbráis con lo divino.
    Guiando en la tormenta más airada
los que buscan el puerto cristalino
porque en el mar del mundo todo nada. (242–43).

In the first quatrain, the poet transforms the three martyrs from the smoke and fire of Lara's account into comets and stars. He elevates their status further by comparing them with Iris, rainbow goddess and a divine messenger in Greco-Roman mythology, and by equating their ashes with those from the Sicilian volcano Etna. Instead of being scattered to the four winds, such ashes rising to the heavens appear to symbolize immortality that the soul achieves through salvation from God. From their celestial perch, these ashes guide humans looking for a port in life's stormy seas. Barrios adapts this oft-used Golden Age storm/port dichotomy to deliverance of the three martyrs, suggesting that their divinely guided ascent symbolizes hope for crypto-Jews forced to navigate a figurative sea of living in "lands of idolatry." Finally, the repetition of questions in the first quatrain; the learned references to Iris and Etna; and the wordplay of "nada" in the final tercet, as "nothing" juxtaposed with "everything" ("todo") and as a form of the verb *nadar* ("to swim"), situate the sonnet within Baroque poetics, even as Barrios introduces a Jewish subtext without saying so overtly.

### Act 1: The Martyrs of Córdoba as Exemplars of Judaism in Conflict with Christianity

Writing for a readership of former conversos returned to Judaism, Barrios dramatizes this history of conversos still in Iberian lands who have died for their Judaism to invest the characters of *Contra la verdad* with an immediacy beyond abstract allegory. The principal conflict of the play, that between Lie and Free Will, shows the force arrayed against free expression of Judaism and the depth of will that resists this force. Thus, in their first meeting of act 1, after Error deliberately extinguishes the lights on stage, Lie tempts Free Will with her beauty, prompting the latter to declare:

Only you, sweet killer (*To Lie*),
in happy ascent
hand me over to passion
to return me then to life:
if you, preferred even to heaven,
obstruct (goddess of souls)
how much your glorious light sees you,
what will you make of my liberty,
that with more brightness
imagines you more beautiful?

Sólo tú, dulce homicida (*A la Mentira*),
en gustosa elevación
me entregas a la afición
para volverme a la vida:
si aun al cielo preferida
ciegas (de las almas diosa)
cuanto te ve tu luz gloriosa,
¿qué harás de mi libertad
que con más claridad
te imagina más hermosa? (253–54, lines 149–58)

Lie tries to convince Free Will to abandon Israel, i.e., Judaism, through a series of fanciful promises regarding the movement of the sun and moon, while in the face of such gifts, Understanding warns him, "without the Law, without Understanding, / thirsty in your passions, / you drink the poisons of forgetfulness" ("sin ley, sin Entendimiento, / en tus pasiones sediento, / bebes ponzoñas de olvido"; 255, lines 220–22). Truth enters the darkened scene in a pillar of fire and scolds Free Will for his lack of faith by comparison with that of the three crypto-Jewish martyrs of Córdoba. In this first reference of the play to Abraham Atías, Jacob Rodríguez de Cáceres, and Raquel Núñez Fernández, Truth contrasts the depths of their faith with the fickleness of Free Will and urges him to see as inspiration the example of their fiery sacrifice: "All three in Spain confessing / only to the God of Israel, running over / those [gods] of stick and stone" ("Todos tres en España confesando / sólo al Dios de Israel, atropellando / a los de palo y piedra"; 258, lines 331–33).[27]

---

27  By describing Raquel here as "if young in years, mature in her naivety" ("si en edad verde, en candidez madura"; 258, line 330), Truth provides another indication that Barrios may have confused her for Leonor María Enríquez, since Lara states in

Barrios emphasizes the historicity informing his allegorical characters by introducing Virtue, Vice, and Anger as voices that frame the struggle of the previous scene between Judaism and Christianity through their descriptions of Raquel, Abraham, and Jacob, respectively. By using an ally and two enemies of the Jewish faith to provide this information about the three martyrs, including their places of origin, the poet emphasizes their literally undying commitment, as in this example of words that Vice, referring to Abraham, speaks to Lie:

> The audacious Abraham Atías,
> who by denying obedience
> to your singular majesty [that of Lie]
> devotes himself to dangers.
> . . . . . . . . . . .
> Made prisoner by me in Écija,
> he shows himself to be [prisoner] of the Law,
> revealing that [the Law] is his spouse
> when I am his chain.
>
> El osado Abraham Atías,
> que por negar la obediencia
> a tu excelsa majestad
> a los peligros se entrega.
> . . . . . . . . . . .
> En Écija de mí preso
> de la Ley estarlo muestra,
> divulgando que es su esposa
> cuando yo soy su cadena. (267, lines 657–60, 669–72)

Although Vice attempts to bolster Christianity by depicting Abraham as imprisoned by both the Inquisition and the temerity of crypto-Judaism, his words show that the bonds of faith between Abraham and his "spouse," the Law, strengthen the older man to resist the suffering that such faith occasions. Not even the subsequent boast of Error that "I will give them turns [of the cord] / that in the infernal dungeons / . . . / give freedom to their punishments" ("vueltas [de cuerda] le[s] daré de modo / que en las estigias cavernas / . . . / den libertad a sus penas"; 267, lines 681–84) dissuades the

---

his *relación* that Enríquez was twenty-four and Beatriz (Raquel) Núñez Fernández fifty-nine (Gracia Boix 493, 494).

three, because Virtue, Zeal, and Truth declare to Appetite, Error, and Lie that each will stand with one of the three crypto-Jews against these antagonists. Likewise, while Error presumes to show his power by threatening torture, he increases the prestige of Abraham, Jacob, and Raquel in the eyes of Barrios's public, which knew of Inquisitorial prisons, and in cases such as that of Orobio de Castro, had experienced them and torture by the rack, or *potro*, about whose function Error gloats here.

Given that Zeal, Truth, and Virtue on one side, and Error, Vice, and Anger on the other try to convince each other of the superiority of their respective faith, the first group of allegorical figures uses the three martyrs to argue for the Law of Moses. For example, when in the second act Understanding appears on stage to support Free Will, he elevates the significance of their sacrifice by making clear to Error that

> Those who most have taken great pains
> in defending the Truth,
> now exposed to cruelty,
> suffer a double martyrdom.
> 
> ....................
> 
> Another Abraham, peerless,
> another Jacob, without equal,
> another Raquel, heavenly,
> the three, wonders of the world.
> 
> Los que más se han esmerado
> en defender la Verdad,
> ya expuestos a la crueldad,
> tienen martirio doblado.
> 
> ....................
> 
> Otro Abraham sin segundo,
> otro Yahacob sin igual,
> otra Ra[c]hel celestial,
> los tres asombros del mundo. (276, lines 1006–09)

The effort of the three and the cruel price they pay for it ennobles them and the Law for which they have died. Understanding then validates this suffering by affirming the place of Abraham, Jacob, and Raquel of Córdoba as worthy heirs of their biblical namesakes. Similarly, Understanding, representing the perspective of Barrios, a diasporic ex-converso now living openly as a Jew, then lauds the resolve of conversos who, lacking such freedom, suffer the ultimate penalty for making a similar choice:

> With noble determination
> in the battle of their dispute
> they resist tyranny
> by triumphing against ignorance.
> So then for [the sake of] the divine Law
> .....................
> they go against unfaithful ravings
> through their steadfastness in martyrdom
> through their martyrdom to glory.
>
> Ellos con noble constancia
> en la lid de su porfía
> resisten la tiranía
> por triunfar de la ignorancia.
> Conque a la divina Ley
> .....................
> van contra el infiel delirio
> por su firmeza en el martirio
> por su martirio a la gloria. (277, lines 1034–38, 1043–45)

While these praises of martyrdom attempt to signify the triumph of Judaism, they also serve an immediate purpose within the play of fortifying Free Will, whose commitment to Judaism has wavered due to efforts of Lie and Error to convince him of the superiority of Christianity.

### Act 2: Motivated by the Martyrs, Free Will Rejects Lie for Truth

Throughout the second act, Lie continues to disparage Judaism as she harangues Free Will to come to her side through declarations of her power. After promising a fiery death to followers of Truth, she boasts of her unshakable pursuit of Free Will, such that "when you pay me less [attention], / I want you more" ("cuando me pagas menos / entonces te quiero más"; 281, lines 1174–75). This desire on the part of Lie juxtaposed with the attraction Free Will feels towards her as a religion despite the conflict that such allure provokes recreates the tensions in the myth of Ulysses and Circe, prompting one of the two choruses backstage, that of truth, to observe,

> In Circe desire grows
> and in Ulysses sorrow
> because in her sweetest spell
> her most far-reaching poison is found.
>
> En Circe crece el deseo
> y en Ulises el pesar,
> porque en su más dulce hechizo
> su mayor ponzoña está. (281–82, lines 1207–08)

Then, just as Understanding previously cited the three martyrs as evidence of Judaism's superiority to Christianity, Lie asserts that their death symbolizes the weakness of their religion:

> Do you know that of Israel I am
> (and of that new Abraham
> who in vigilant zeal
> offers in sacrifice another Isaac,
> with those two marvels
> who trying to imitate him
> in the hands of death
> seek eternal life)
> such mistrust, such fright,
> that before coming across me,
> they want to come across fire?
>
> ¿Sabes que soy de Israel
> (y de aquel nuevo Abraham
> que en el celante fervor
> da al sacrificio otro Ishac,
> con aquellos dos prodigios
> que intentándole imitar
> en las manos de la muerte
> buscan la vida inmortal)
> tan recelo, tan espanto
> que viendo la claridad,
> primero que dar conmigo
> quieren con el fuego dar? (283, lines 1267–83)

While Abraham, Jacob, and Raquel, as well as the Spanish-Portuguese converso diaspora that celebrates them, regard their martyrdom as an affirmation of faith, Lie suggests that it symbolizes hard-headedness and weakness. Indeed, towards the end of the same speech, she declares of the Law, i.e., Judaism,

> it [Judaism] still cannot compete [with] me,
> because I am so unequal
> that compared with me
> it is a fountain, and I am the sea.
>
> aún no puede competirme
> porque soy tan desigual
> que comparada conmigo
> ella es fuente y yo soy mar. (284, lines 1291–94)

As both characters temporarily exit the stage, these words confer upon Lie an advantage over Free Will, as they show her ability to exploit his equivocation.

However, the direction of the play turns when Free Will, conversing with Virtue, Understanding, Zeal, and Appetite, decides to repent of his prior indecision and lack of Jewish faith. The example of the three martyrs motivates this decision, especially after Appetite, the *gracioso*, or provider of comic relief, jokes sarcastically that he will stoke the fire consuming them so that it will produce more sparks (290).[28] Free Will then says to Truth, who has recently reentered the stage, "I with a longing to imitate them [the martyrs], / turning my soul to your eyes, / bend my lips to your feet" ("Yo con ansia de imitarlos, / volviendo el alma a tus ojos, / inclino a tus pies los labios"; 290, lines 1532–34). In a speech of nearly three hundred lines that follows, the longest such monologue in the play, Free Will confesses and repents of his idolatry, repeating words of Truth herself in which she expresses censure, disbelief, and the command that he turn away from Lie. The subtext

---

28  The ill-placed attempt at humor by Appetite reminds this writer of words that Mexican poet Juan de Dios Peza (1852–1910) attributed to Tomás Treviño de Sobremonte when the stake was lit after the auto de fe of 1649 in Mexico City (loosely): "Throw on more wood, because I am paying for it" ("Echen más leña, que mi dinero me cuesta"; Peza 64; see also Warshawsky, *The Perils of Living the Good and True Law* 95). These apocryphal words do not appear in Treviño's Inquisitorial trial record.

of Ulysses and Circe dramatizes how much Free Will had fallen under the influence of Lie:

> Drinking the cup of her propensity
> was so intoxicating
> that those who found me changed
> thought I was someone else.

> Tanto me embriagó el beber
> de su inclinación el vaso
> que me tenían por otro
> los que me hallaban trocado. (291–92, lines 1591–94)

Thanks to the intercession of Understanding, who as symbol of *desengaño* enters the palace of Lie to disabuse Free Will of his flirtation with idolatry, the latter character beseeches of Truth either forgiveness or a deserved death. Perhaps not unsurprisingly, at the moment when Truth orders the prostrate figure to his feet in the embrace of her restored love, Lie and Error, having been scorned, proclaim offstage that they will burn the three martyrs. Yet three voices, presumably those of the martyrs themselves, remain firm in their faith and prepared to endure the consequences of their steadfastness, given that "we hail one God alone" ("A un solo Dios aclamamos"; 297, line 1812).

### ACT 3: AUTOS DE FE IN FACT AND FICTION TO SHOW THE TRIUMPH OF JUDAISM

Martyrdom as a sign of unwavering Jewish beliefs becomes a central theme of the play during the third act. Thus, in a second example of deus ex machina, Virtue descends in a cloud to say first that "the harshness of the Romans" ("el rigor de los romanos"), or the Inquisition, has condemned Abraham, Jacob, and Raquel to the stake, and then to order Zeal to appeal to the courage of the three to die, "so that they live forever" ("porque vivan para siempre"; 310, lines 2267, 2274). At this point, as Free Will lauds the constancy of the three martyrs and regrets having doubted the Law of Moses, a voice offstage chants the *Shema* (311), the central prayer of Judaism (Deut. 6.4), showing how Barrios uses the *auto sacramental* to assert the oneness of God instead of the mystery of transubstantiation. Free Will personalizes the message of the *Shema* that declares God's unity and glory through a sonnet of repentance in whose tercets he affirms his complete devotion to God:

> I, so distinct from the person I was, hail you,
> burning in the love of your Law,
> that in order to reach you I flee from myself.
> In you alone I trust, great king,
> see that to your devotion I go such that
> by being in you I am not in myself.
>
> Ya os aclamo tan otro del que fui,
> ardiendo en el amor de vuestra Ley,
> que por llegar a vos huyo de mí.
> En vos solo confío, inmenso Rey,
> ved que a vuestra piedad de modo voy
> que por estar en vos en mí no estoy. (314–15, lines 2428–33)

Just as the *Shema* tells the Jewish people that God alone is God and blesses the name of God's kingdom eternally, Free Will in effect says there is no other divine being but God and that, thanks to God's love and mercy, he dedicates himself entirely to this being.

At this point Barrios represents within the play itself an auto de fe to dramatize the constancy of the real-life martyrs and the allegorical figures, especially the newfound faith of Free Will. The Inquisitorial tribunal includes Lie as inquisitor (judge) and Error and Anger as prosecutors (*fiscales*), while Appetite tries to add humor saying that the accused dressed in penitential sackcloth, or *sacos benditos* (often shortened to *sambenitos*), "boast about San Benito" ("del San Benito hacen gala"; 317, line 2535). Free Will, Understanding, and Virtue represent Abraham, Jacob, and Raquel, respectively, voicing the fearlessness with which each real-life individual faced death at the stake. Free Will expresses his own faith and that of the martyrs when he proclaims to his accusers,

> I am a Hebrew, enemies,
> my spouse is the sacred Law,
> my God, the God of Israel alone,
> my honor, to die for the cause of God.
> Seize me, throw me to the fire,
> which, so that his fire may be
> my triumphal car, already is
> my watchfulness of Elijah.

Hebreo soy, enemigos,
mi esposa es la Ley sagrada,
mi Dios, sólo Él de Israel,
mi honor, morir por su causa.
Prendedme, echadme al incendio,
que porque sea su flama
mi carro triunfal, ya es
de Elías mi vigilancia. (319, lines 2578–85)

Connections with historical autos de fe and their representation in other texts add to the impact of these words as a declaration of faith. In one example of such a link, Barrios reworks similar verses of the "Romance al martirio y felicísimo tránsito de don Lope de Vera y Alarcón" by Antonio Enríquez Gómez discussed in chapter 3. Just as Vera y Alarcón, now calling himself Judah the Believer, subverts Inquisitorial control by asserting from the stake his unrepentant Jewish faith, so Free Will undermines the auto de fe as the most visible public site of this control by pronouncing the same sentiment.[29] A second reference to an auto de fe outside *Contra la verdad* occurs when Free Will, comparing himself to Elijah, says that just as the prophet ascended to heaven in a chariot of fire, so too shall his fiery death bring him to that exalted place. Barrios later developed this theme in his sonnet to Tomás Treviño de Sobremonte, a Spanish crypto-Jew burned after the Auto Grande de Fe of 1649 in Mexico, in which he celebrates Treviño as "Elijah of the Indies."[30]

By linking these two autos de fe with the one at Córdoba in 1665 that *Contra la verdad* allegorizes, Barrios inserts its victims into a larger struggle for freedom of conscience. Doing so enables him to dramatize the third of

---

29 Compare the words of Albedrío above with those that Enríquez Gómez assigns to Lope de Vera in the "Romance": ". . . I am a Hebrew / I am a Castilian Jew, / I profess the Law of Moses" (". . . yo soy hebreo / Judío soy castellano, / la Ley de Moséh confieso"; Brown 168, lines 300–04).

30 *Triumpho* 569. The biblical episode occurs in 2 Kings 2.11–12. Barrios compares Treviño with Elijah in the second tercet of his sonnet commemorating the latter's martyrdom: "Now Elijah of the Indies, by going up to heaven / in the flaming cart that lifts him up / leaves the cape of his dust on the ground" ("Ya Indiano Elías, por subir al cielo / en el carro voraz que le levanta, / deja la capa de su polvo al suelo"; Scholberg 242). As I wrote in *The Perils of Living the Good and True Law* 109, I believe that Barrios confuses Treviño with Francisco Maldonado de Silva, a crypto-Jew condemned to the stake in Lima in 1639. See Leibman, "Poetics of the Apocalypse" 45–50, for a different interpretation of this sonnet, based on her compelling claim that the "poem relies on number symbolism" (47).

these autos for an audience removed from it and to voice a perspective regarding the Inquisition and the elect status of Israel that would have resonated with this community of conversos returned to Judaism. Thus, after Lie orders the arrest of Free Will for his self-identification with Abraham Atías and unequivocal declaration of Jewish identity, Zeal descends onto the stage accompanied by a bugle to accuse the Inquisition of rapaciousness:

> Tormenters of innocence,
> who with insatiable pressure
> you drown their lives and their honor,
> you consume their possessions and their reputation.
>
> Verdugos de la inocencia,
> que con hidrópica instancia
> ahogáis su vida y su honra,
> bebéis su hacienda y su fama. (321, lines 2654-57)

These words speak to the reality that the Inquisition inventoried and sequestrated, or impounded, the property of individuals whom it detained. The tribunal then sold some or all these goods to pay the costs of detention and often confiscated them as punishment when the accused were judged guilty (Kamen, *The Spanish Inquisition* 196).[31] Not only did this process impoverish many such detainees, but the public shaming they suffered as accused heretics, regardless of the court's final judgement, often cost them and family members their good name.

When Lie subsequently accuses God of not heeding Israel by permitting defendants—and here she must be thinking of the three at Córdoba—to suffer the cruelty of the stake, Zeal defends this action as a sign of God's privileging of the Jewish people:

> Leaving him/her [Israel] in distress
> is justice, not cruelty,
> because it thus punishes Israel's mistake
> to reward afterwards its zeal.

---

31  Zeal's accusation of Inquisitorial avarice confirms an observation of Kamen about the court's financing, especially during its early years: "Not surprisingly, many ordinary Spaniards came to the conclusion that the Inquisition was devised simply to rob people" (*The Spanish Inquisition* 197).

> Dejarle en el desconsuelo
> es justicia, no rigor,
> pues castiga así su error
> por premiar después su celo. (323, lines 2748–51)

Through this explanation, Zeal contrasts Inquisitorial and New Christian perspectives regarding error. According to the Inquisition, insincere converts to Christianity erred by secretly practicing Jewish beliefs, whereas some conversos, especially those inclined to crypto-Judaism, felt guilt for the "mistake" of living as Christians, even if their survival compelled such observance. Of course, the play aims to show that God will reward the zeal for Judaism of the three allegorical characters, and thus, the capital sentence they receive at trial strengthens their determination, as it does for their counterparts in Córdoba. For this reason, when Lie as inquisitor condemns the allegorical figures to the stake and declares that they will find out if their God will free them, the three respond as one, "Our glory / is to die by following Him" ("La gloria / nuestra es morir por seguirlo [a Dios]"; 327, lines 2902–03).

Perhaps no action confirms this resolve more than the conversion to Judaism of Appetite, a character who plays the *gracioso* of Spanish theatrical comedy, in which role he has, until this moment, freely disparaged Free Will and conversos who would live as Jews. This conversion situates Appetite in the company of other Golden Age *graciosos* who, notwithstanding the comic relief they provide, perform a more serious function. For example, in *El burlador de Sevilla* (*The Trickster of Seville*, ca. 1620s) by Tirso de Molina, the jester Catalinón frequently comments upon the depredations of Don Juan, as when his master contemplates dishonoring the fisherwoman Tisbea: "Those of you who feign [sincerity] and deceive / women in that way / will pay for it with your death" ("Los que fingís y engañáis / las mujeres desa suerte, / lo pagaréis con la muerte"; Molina 61). Similarly, throughout most of *Contra la verdad*, Appetite prefers material goods to faith and lightheartedly scorns Free Will for the latter's equivocation about not embracing Christianity. Thus, when Lie laments that Free Will may leave her for "una antigua", that is, an older law meant to symbolize Judaism, Appetite responds, "Do you want more revenge / than that he [Free Will] marries an old woman?" ("¿Quieres más venganza que / con una vieja se casa?"; 313, lines 2386–87).

Later, during the mock auto de fe, the call by Appetite that the three defendants, whom he scornfully calls "these Jews" ("estos judíos") (327, line

2898), be dispatched to the stake without delay contrasts with his advocacy for Judaism at the end of the play, when he declares to Truth:

> The three who die for you,
> it is certain that they are in the right;
> I agree to marry [myself to] you
> because if you give me to God,
> I will thus see heaven opened.
>
> Los tres que mueren por vos,
> cierto es que están en lo cierto;
> con vos casarme concierto
> porque si me dais a Dios,
> así veré el cielo abierto. (329, lines 2973–77)

This surprising change of heart demonstrates how the forbidden faith of crypto-Jews affects those who persecute them, or at least facilitate such persecution, as Appetite previously did. Likewise, when Appetite declares, "I am a Hebrew of the nation" ("Hebreo soy de nación"; 329, line 2983), Barrios suggests his own awareness of how Spanish-Portuguese society conflated the religion and ethnicity of conversos, even in diaspora. Not only did Old Christians view New Christians as a distinct racial entity despite the Catholicism of the latter, but conversos themselves increasingly identified with this ethnic differentiation. Through the *gracioso*, Barrios makes space within the "Nation" for the reassertion of Judaism, a claim all the more powerful because the one making it is an Old Christian.[32]

This about-face by Appetite reverses the hierarchy of a typical Inquisition trial, dovetailing with the recognition by Lie, the allegorical inquisitor, of her inability to compel Free Will, Understanding, and Virtue to renounce their Judaism. Virtue testifies to this reversal by asserting that Lie and her two prosecutors, Error and Anger, will have to answer to God with their lives: "this celestial sword, / comet of heaven itself / . . . / will slay you" ("Muerte os dará / . . . / esta querúbica espada, / cometa del cielo mismo"; 331, lines 3035–38). Speaking these words through a defendant undeterred by Inquisitorial authority, Barrios adroitly supplants the sword prominent on the shield of the Holy Office with a divinely wielded one that will strike

---

32   See Bodian, *Hebrews of the Portuguese Nation* 6–17, for an explanation of the origin and evolution of the terms *os da nação* and *portugueses de la nación hebrea* ("those of the Nation" and "Portuguese of the Hebrew Nation").

down the court. As if on cue for a third example of this realignment of authority, Zeal descends from heaven mounted on a lion and, to the sound of thunder, lightning, and a shofar, proclaims directly to God that the three demonstrate their fortitude "by defending your love, by giving a sign / that they fear your zeal more than death at the stake" ("por defender tu amor, por dar indicio / que más temen tus celos que el suplicio"; 332; lines 3073–74). Through these words, Zeal links the three martyrs of Córdoba to an exalted group of Spanish-Portuguese crypto-Jews who have sacrificed their lives for a Jewish understanding of God.

Subsequently referring to twelve such individuals, Zeal confirms that diasporic conversos and former conversos celebrated their brethren who died sanctifying the Law of Moses. Indeed, as in the "Memorial of Martyrs" of *Triumpho del govierno popular*, this catalog shows that Barrios knew the teaching in rabbinic Judaism of *kiddush ha-Shem*, or "sanctification of the [Divine] Name," including by martyrdom, if necessary, so that an individual not contravene the commandment against idolatry (Jewish Virtual Library; Litovsky 103–04). The poet thus substitutes *kiddush ha-Shem* for the sacrament of the Eucharist that culminates many *autos sacramentales*, such as at the banquet of Sin/Circe in *Los encantos de la culpa* discussed earlier in this chapter. Just as Penitence redeems Humanity from the temptations of Sin through the gift of the host symbolizing the sacrifice of the body and blood of Christ, so Zeal celebrates the twelve martyrs for their sacrifice effecting their own redemption and that of Judaism.[33] Through the rapturous eulogizing of Zeal, Barrios shows how the fiery demise of these individuals consecrates the name of God, as in the example of the "unconquered ("invicto") Abraham Núñez Bernal, who "when most zealous / he extinguished his life in the cruel flame, / he most inflamed his spirit in God" ("cuando más celante / apagaba la vida en llama impía, / el espíritu en Dios más encendía"; 334, lines 3146–48).

These descriptions of the martyrs permit Barrios to assure that their deaths, far from being in vain, have served a holy purpose. As testament to this assurance, he claims that each victim, being a "pillar of living fire" ("pilar de fuego vivo"; 335, line 3198) will lead one of the twelve tribes of Israel. Then,

---

33  I would like to acknowledge Scholberg for helping me see how Barrios contrasts "the apotheosis of the sacrament of the Eucharist" ("la apoteosis del sacramento de la Eucaristía"; *La poesía religiosa* 119) in *autos sacramentales* with the role of *kiddush ha-Shem* as a declaration of Judaism. Swetschinski also notes this reworking by the poet: ". . . Barrios gave a distinctly Iberian and typically Catholic form an unmistakably Jewish content." (*The Portuguese Jews* 64).

as Free Will, Understanding, and Virtue meet the same end as, respectively, Abraham, Jacob, and Raquel at Córdoba, a voice backstage says that their suffering will precipitate a new beginning: "Come, come, come, because in me you will find / eternal life in exchange for the one which you lose" ("Venid, venid, venid, que en mí hallaréis / la vida eterna por la que perdéis"; 337, lines 3279–80). Truth announces that "nothing can stand up to the truth" ("contra la verdad no hay fuerza"; 338, line 3317), confirming this belief with the help of Zeal and Appetite, as together they overcome Lie, Vice, and Error in a skirmish offstage. The work culminates with Celo proclaiming the redemption of the Jewish people through the promise of divine restoration of Jerusalem, and Appetite asking listeners "to take refuge in the *Shema*" ("[que] se aferren con la *Semah*"; 341, line 3386), thus confirming the intent of Barrios to show the primacy of this prayer.

Conclusion: Making Space for Judaism in the Spanish Baroque
By concluding *Contra la verdad* with this privileging of Jerusalem and the *Shema*, Barrios uses his familiarity with the genre of *autos sacramentales* to extol Judaism and those who died for its forbidden beliefs. Through allegorical representations of Jorge Méndez de Castro (Abraham Atías), Domingo (Jacob) de Rodríguez de Cáceres, and Beatriz (Raquel) Núñez Fernández, the playwright also made accessible to an audience in Amsterdam these historical figures who could not live openly as Jews. Besides resisting the erasure that the Inquisition tried to inflict on these (and other) crypto-Jews, the work argues that Judaism is the true Law of God and, as Truth states, that God rewards those who follow it (340, lines 3379–80). For these reasons, the play creates space within Spanish Baroque literature for the worldview of Spanish-Portuguese New Christians returned to Judaism beyond the Iberian Peninsula and persecuted for their refusal to abandon their faith within that land. Likewise, as a returnee to Judaism who followed closely Spanish literary customs, Barrios shows that one could be a fully Jewish and Spanish writer despite the contradictions these identities otherwise suggested. Finally, the presence of the auto de fe at Córdoba as subtext of an allegorical play shows how *Contra la verdad* represents Catholic Christianity and the Iberian Inquisition as antagonists of Judaism in ways that resonated throughout the Spanish-Portuguese Jewish diaspora of the 1600s.

# 6
# "Your Grace, Lord, Will Sustain Me": A Transatlantic Perspective on Psalms in *Espejo fiel de vidas* of Daniel Israel López Laguna

AN IN-DEPTH STUDY of *Espejo fiel de vidas que contiene los Psalmos de David en verso, obra devota, útil y deleitable* (*Faithful Mirror of Lives That Contains the Psalms of David in Verse, a Devout, Useful, and Pleasing Work*) of Daniel Israel López Laguna shows the influence of a *converso* worldview on his paraphrase of Psalms written when he lived openly as a Jew in Jamaica. López Laguna and his poem encapsulate the transatlantic reach of the Spanish-Portuguese Jewish diaspora fully two centuries after the expulsion and conversion of Iberian Jews during the 1490s. Born in Portugal or France in the mid-1600s, raised in the latter country, educated in Spain, and apparently prosecuted by the Holy Office of the Inquisition of Spain or Portugal for Jewish heresy, López Laguna wrote the earliest literary work by a Jew in Jamaica, which he took to London for publication in the large Sephardic community of that city. Written in a Spanish illustrative of the poet's absorption of Baroque literary trends, *Espejo fiel de vidas* reflects this geographic and spiritual trajectory by illuminating the importance of resilience and redemption in his reworking of Psalms.

This chapter explores these themes by analyzing passages that show the hybrid nature of the poet as an emergent or "New" Jew, possibly raised as a crypto-Jewish New Christian, who uses the literary language of Catholic Spain to communicate his experience of the converso mindset. Examples of this mindset include a geographic and spiritual wandering represented in the *peregrino*, or wanderer; praise of the elect status of the Israelite people; entreaty of God to protect conversos against enemies representative of the Inquisition and gratitude for doing so; and disparagement of talebearers, a clear reference to the *malsín*, or Inquisitorial informant. Through his paraphrase of Psalms, López Laguna offers readers intimate access to how these elements of the converso worldview informed his practice and understanding of Judaism. In turn, such access broadens American Jewish historical narratives to include an early modern Sephardic voice that sheds light on the hopes and fears of New Christians who resisted efforts of the Iberian Inquisition to prevent them from recovering their Jewish identity.[1]

Additionally, the chapter builds upon the work of other scholars who have studied how *Espejo fiel* represents the Jewish identity of a diasporic former New Christian after 1492. For example, among more recent analyses of the work, Ronnie Perelis suggests that the autobiographical nature of Psalms permits López Laguna to "express his own sentiments and reflect on his own life of tumult and salvation" without focusing on himself as a first-person speaker (323; see also 322). Laura Leibman situates *Espejo fiel* within messianic and typological currents of the Sephardic diaspora during the 1600s and early 1700s, arguing that, through the image of a mirror, López Laguna "rewrites [Psalms] to reflect the dispersed conversos' experiences," producing not a "faithful translation" of the Psalms but one that "paraphrases or 'reflects'" the biblical precursor ("Poetics of the Apocalypse" 51). In her study of *Espejo fiel*, Ruth Fine calls attention to the work "as a testimonial narrative of persecution and Sephardic exile" and demonstrates how it recovers Psalms for diasporic conversos previously unfamiliar with the biblical work (47). Fine also compares specific passages of *Espejo fiel* with the Vulgate, the Ferrara Bible, and the so-called Bear Bible by Casiodoro de Reina in order to argue that López Laguna may have used the original Hebrew of Psalms and to show how he "transfers the biblical text to his contemporary context and personal life experience, especially in registering the mark of trauma" (56).[2] Informed by the work of these and other scholars, the following analysis

---

[1] This chapter builds, in part, upon research conducted in 2020 with University of Portland students Catherine Wojda and Joshua Henderson through the Summer Undergraduate Research Experience (SURE) of the College of Arts and Sciences and published in *International Journal of Undergraduate Research and Creative Activity* (see Wojda, Henderson, and Warshawsky). I wrote the present chapter subsequent to our SURE project while also expanding content I contributed to our jointly authored article.

[2] Published in 1553 in the Italian city of its namesake, the Ferrara Bible made the Hebrew original accessible to the post-1492 Sephardic diaspora as a translation into Ladino, or Judeo-Spanish, written in the Roman alphabet. See Lazar for an edition of this work. A convert from Catholicism to Protestantism, Casiodoro de Reina helped publish in Switzerland in 1569 a translation of the Bible into Castilian Span-

situates *Espejo fiel* within the context of its publication and then, through a previously unexplored study of López Laguna's voice in eight Psalms from his paraphrase, shows how Baroque Spanish literary customs and Iberian Inquisitorial society forged his literary worldview.

## López Laguna as (ex-)Converso Avatar in the Early Modern Transatlantic World

Biographical information about López Laguna is limited beyond that which he provides in an acrostic poem in the extensive introductory text of *Espejo fiel de vidas* (Wojda, Henderson, and Warshawsky 1-2). This poem consists of four ten-line strophes, or *décimas*, divided into two columns; the initial letters of each line, when read in descending order on the left column and then the right, spell out the following words of a title that precedes the text: "To the zealous reader, the assistance of King David is now equal. And if the sign of the Law gives a light, only the Torah enriches life" ("Al celoso lector, ya equivalen auxilios del rey David. Y si el aviso de Ley le da luz, sólo Torá enriquece la vida"; n.p., 60 in PDF).³ The first *décima* and the beginning of the second one establish the literary proclivity and some of the whereabouts of López Laguna, while also raising as many questions as they answer:

> Inclined towards the Muses
> I have been since my childhood;
> [My] adolescence in France
> [A] sacred school gave me;
> In Spain the arts polished
> My youth somewhat;
> Opening my eyes in virtue,
> I escaped from the Inquisition.
> Today Jamaica in song
> Gives the Psalms to my lute.
> In my prison I took up the desire
> Of creating this work.

---

ish, called the *Biblia del Oso* (Bear Bible) for an image on its cover of a bear reaching for honey in a tree.

3   The introduction to the work covers more than fifty pages but is not numbered; the lines cited here come four pages before the end of this section. Citations throughout the chapter to López Laguna's paraphrase of Psalms are from this work. The translation of the fragment of the acrostic poem is by Wojda, Henderson, and Warshawsky.

> A las musas inclinado
> He sido desde mi infancia,
> La adolescencia en la Francia
> Sagrada escuela me ha dado,
> En España algo han limado
> Las artes mi juventud,
> Ojos abriendo en virtud,
> Salí de la Inquisición
> Hoy Jamaica en canción
> Los salmos da a mi laúd.
> En mi prisión los deseos
> Cobré de hacer esta obra. (n.p., 60 in PDF)

Historical context allows one to fill in some gaps of this life story.[4] López Laguna was born to a converso family, probably of Portuguese origin, in the 1650s and grew up in France, perhaps in Bayonne or Peyrehorade, towns in the southwest corner of that country where Iberian New Christians established communities in exile.[5] Despite having expelled its own Jews in 1394, France, especially this border region, served as a destination of Spanish and Portuguese New Christians for several centuries after the expulsion and forced conversions of Jews on the Iberian Peninsula during the 1490s. Starting in 1550, these conversos, many of whom were secret Jews, purchased *Lettres Patentes*, or "'Letters of Naturalization and Dispensation' that granted the 'Portuguese merchants' the right to settle and trade in the territories of the Bordeaux Parliament" (Gerber, *The Jews of Spain* 191). Regardless of the circumstances of López Laguna's adolescence in France, by the 1600s, while New Christians such as his family "were tacitly recognized by the surrounding population as Jewish, they were also well integrated into mainstream life,

---

4   My online inquiries did not locate an extant record for López Laguna in the collections of either the Archivo Histórico Nacional in Madrid or the Arquivo Nacional da Torre do Tombo in Lisbon, the repositories of Inquisition trial records in Spain and Portugal, respectively.

5   Cecil Roth stated that the poet was born in Portugal ("Laguna, Daniel Israel López" 438–39). One of the sources whom Roth cites does not specify the birthplace of the poet; see Mayer Kayserling, "The Jews in Jamaica and Daniel Israel Lopez Laguna." Stanley Mirvis asserts that the family of López Laguna settled in Bayonne after leaving Portugal (36–38).

able to trade and circulate in Catholic society with relative ease" (Gerber, *The Jews of Spain* 192).⁶

The fact that López Laguna studied in Spain confirms the hold of Spanish-speaking culture on individuals whose forebears had been forced into exile from the Iberian Peninsula. Likewise, it testifies to the reality that, starting in the early 1600s, the Spanish monarchy permitted and even encouraged Portuguese New Christians to enter and leave Spain, in many cases thanks to their willingness to pay large sums of money to do so. Traveling to Spain for an education in a Spanish milieu, López Laguna differed from many conversos living in southwest France whose reasons for a similar journey were principally commercial, especially if they did not intend to settle in the Iberian Peninsula permanently (Graizbord 79–89). Nevertheless, the fact that conversos experienced greater ease of movement during the 1600s did not safeguard them from Inquisitorial prosecution for Judaizing heresy, as the experiences of López Laguna and others, such as Antonio Enríquez Gómez, the subject of chapter 3, show. In fact, after the downfall in 1643 of Gaspar de Guzmán, Duke of Olivares, who as *valido* of Felipe IV had facilitated the immigration of Portuguese converso businessmen to Spain, the Inquisition uprooted most crypto-Judaism in the country (Gitlitz, *Secrecy and Deceit* 45).

Although it is possible that the Inquisition absolved López Laguna or suspended its case for lack of evidence, a more likely outcome, especially in the absence of a trial record, is that the court convicted him for Judaizing heresy and then reconciled him to Catholicism. If this latter outcome occurred, the penance that the tribunal designated must have left him with enough means to escape the Inquisition for Jamaica rather than suffer confiscation of goods that frequently left reconciled crypto-Jews in various states of destitution. López Laguna reached Jamaica in approximately 1680 and became a naturalized citizen in 1693.⁷ In 1655, the English had captured Jamaica from Spain, at which time they found conversos already living there, some of whom likely were crypto-Jews whose ancestors had arrived as early as 1530. The English permitted these New Christians, their descendants, and subsequent Portuguese arrivals to live openly as Jews at the same time as they

---

6   It seems reasonable to suppose that this description by Gerber of the situation of New Christians in southwestern France would have applied to the family of López Laguna.

7   For possible outcomes of Inquisitorial trials, see Kamen, *The Spanish Inquisition* 248–60. For these dates and other biographical information about López Laguna, see Fine 46; and Kayserling, "The Jews in Jamaica."

readmitted Jews to England after having expelled them in 1290. Many settled in Port Royal, making it the largest Jewish community in Jamaica during the second half of the 1600s.

Aided by connections with other outposts of the Portuguese Nation throughout the Caribbean, most Jews in Jamaica worked in commerce, a circumstance that contributed to "the common perception that Jews were devious smugglers who were intent on monopolizing foreign trades" and that prompted a subsequent "Jews' Tribute," or tax (August 305). The resentment directed towards Jewish merchants occasioned laws denying Jews rights to vote and hold office until 1831, showing that they "could be first-class merchants but second-class citizens" (Arbell 246). López Laguna does not specify his role in this economy, but despite the prejudice and limitations he and other Jews of early colonial Jamaica faced, the freedom to worship in a synagogue and to write without fear of Inquisitorial prosecution was surely a salve. He brought *Espejo fiel* to the well-established Portuguese Sephardic community of London in 1720—then known as the Spanish and Portuguese Jews' Congregation and by its Hebrew name, Kahal Kadosh Shaar Asamaim ("Holy Congregation The Gates of Heaven")—and published it thanks to the patronage of Mordejay Nunes Almeyda. Shortly thereafter he returned to his wife Ri[v]ka (Rebecca) and their children David, Jacob, and Isaac in Jamaica, where he died in approximately 1730.[8]

*ESPEJO FIEL DE VIDAS*: AN EMERGENT JEWISH WORLDVIEW IN BAROQUE SPANISH LITERATURE

Members of the London community contributed laudatory texts to the extensive prefatory pages of *Espejo fiel* demonstrating its positive reception and the importance of its publication. Abraham Henriques Pimentel wrote a preface that described the hardships endured by crypto-Jewish New Christians in the Iberian sphere, including López Laguna. He affirms the faithfulness to Judaism of these individuals in the shadow of the Inquisition and their desire to live openly as Jews once they could. Abraham's father, Jahacob Henriques Pimentel, authored an *aprobación*, or approval, of the work after

---

8   The translation of the community's Hebrew name is from the website of the Spanish and Portuguese Sephardi Community [of London], sephardi.org.uk/bevis-marks/visit-bevis-marks/. López Laguna and his family would have visited the synagogue there, completed in 1701 and called Bevis Marks for its location off of the street by this name. It is possible that David accompanied López Laguna to London, given that he praised his father and *Espejo fiel* in a poem included in the prefatory pages (see López Laguna, *Espejo fiel*, n.p., 44 in PDF).

editing its spelling. In his preface, Abraham praises his friend for producing, in Castilian Spanish, a work accessible to fellow conversos who were "fleeing the persecutions of such tyrannical and cruel lands" ("huyendo las persecuciones de tan tiranas, y crueles tierras") so that, given their unfamiliarity with Hebrew, "all the[se] devout souls better understand what they read, and all the music aficionados have something in which to take pleasure singing these divine and sacred songs" ("para que todos los devotos entiendan lo que lean, y todos los aficionados a la música tengan en qué recrearse cantando estas divinas y sagradas canciones"; n.p., 50 in PDF). He also describes the experiences of conversos able to live openly as Jews beyond Inquisitorial reach by praising "our holy Law," [which] . . . brings us out of hard captivity and redeems us from wretched slavery" ("nuestra santa Ley . . . nos saca de duros cautiverios y nos redime de míseras esclavitudes"; n.p., 51 in PDF). Finally, Abraham asserts that López Laguna spent twenty-three years writing the work "and as many more of sleeplessness, between persecutions of wars, fires, and hurricanes, in order to perfect and give you this mirror" ("y otros tantos de desvelo, entre persecuciones de guerras, incendios y huracanes, para perfeccionar y darte este *Espejo*"; n.p., 52-53 in PDF). If such chronology is accurate, then the poet worked on *Espejo fiel* from the time he arrived in Jamaica to his voyage to London to publish it.

Like other New Christian authors, López Laguna wrote for (New) Jewish readers using Golden Age poetics. *Espejo fiel* exemplifies this evocation of Jewish literature of Baroque Spain. López Laguna announces his intention to appropriate the language of the very society that persecuted him by indicating the verse form of each psalm between its prefatory verses and the text itself. As a result, the twenty poetic forms that he uses to rewrite the Psalms make the work seem "a bit like a primer of Golden Age poetics," as Leibman has noted ("Poetics of the Apocalypse" 54).[9] For example, the *canción* ("song"), a composition containing stanzas of varying length whose lines consist of seven and eleven syllables, appears ten times in the work, and its subcategory, the *lira*, in which the stanzas are always five lines long, occurs five times.[10] Other stylistic features typical of Baroque Spanish poetry include hyperbaton, or interchanged word order, and synalepha, or the blending together of vowel sounds at the end of one word and the beginning of the

---

9   See Leibman, "Poetics of the Apocalypse" 62n67, for a list of the different forms, such as *romances* and *décimas*, and the frequency with which they are used.

10   See McCaw and Thornton Spinnenweber 30–32 for more information about some of these forms and the poets who used them.

following one. These two features enable the text to adhere to requirements of rhyme and verse length, respectively, of the various poetic forms.

It is also likely that López Laguna was familiar with works of Spain's most prolific Golden Age playwright, Lope de Vega Carpio (1562–1635), including perhaps the *Arte nuevo de hacer comedias en este tiempo* (*New Art of Writing Plays at This Time*) of 1609, where Lope indicates when to use a number of forms that appear in *Espejo fiel*:

> Compose verses with care
> for the subjects that you are treating:
> *décimas* are good for complaints;
> the sonnet is good for those who are waiting;
> narratives call for *romances*,
> although in *octavas* they make an impression in extreme;
> tercets are for weighty matters,
> and for those of love, *redondillas*.
>
> Acomode los versos con prudencia
> a los sujetos de que va tratando:
> las décimas son buenas para quejas;
> el soneto está bien en los que aguardan;
> las relaciones piden los romances,
> aunque en otavas lucen por extremo;
> son los tercetos para cosas graves,
> y para las de amor, las redondillas. (148, lines 305–12)

We can only speculate about the reasons for López Laguna's choice of forms, although it is possible that he wished to show off his poetic virtuosity.

Even as *Espejo fiel* exemplifies Spanish poetry stylistically, the influences on the work show that its relationship to this literature is both "in and out." López Laguna and the fellow ex-conversos whom he cites in his prologue identified with their Spanish-Portuguese origins while living in diaspora as members of a separate "nation," distinct even within Judaism. The first of these individuals, Jacob Judah (Aryeh) León (ca. 1603–75), spent most of his life in Amsterdam, where he taught in the school for the sons of the Portuguese-Jewish community, became a rabbi, and wrote treatises about and drew models of the Tabernacle of Moses and the Temple of Solomon. The models traveled throughout Europe, including England, and became so well known that his son Solomon added the descriptor "Templo" to the family name León (Leibman, "Sephardic Sacred Space" 16; Shane 120).[11] In 1671, Jacob Judah León Templo translated the Psalms from Hebrew into Spanish as *Las alabanzas de la santidad* (*Praises of Holiness*), a text that inspired and guided López Laguna, as he acknowledges in the prologue to *Espejo fiel*:

> Since it's only right to admit
> What should not be denied,
> I won't refrain from saying
> That for a long time my pen is very bold.
> The only excuse for my zeal
> Is incompetence.
> To make up for lack of skill
> I've let my ship be steered
> By Jacob Judah León,
> Temple of sacred excellence.

> Si es licito confesar
> Lo que negar no se debe,
> Decir que ha mucho se atreve
> Mi pluma, no he de excusar;
> Solo podrá disculpar
> Mi celo, la insuficiencia,
> Supliendo faltas de ciencia,
> Regir mi nave el timón,
> Por Jacob Yehudah León,
> Templo de sacra excelencia. (n.p., 56 in PDF)

In the following stanza, López Laguna recognizes the influence of another luminary of the Spanish-Portuguese Jewish community of Amsterdam on *Espejo fiel*, saying that he "faithfully follows the true teaching of the *Eterna Ley Divina* (*Eternal Divine Law*)" of Menasseh ben Israel (1604–57). Born Manoel Dias Soeiro to converso parents in Portugal, Menasseh ben Israel moved during his childhood to Amsterdam, where he became a leading intellectual as a rabbi, printer, and author of religious texts. One of these works was *The Humble Address*, a pamphlet in which, during his visit to London in 1655, he tried to convince Protestant leader Oliver Cromwell to let Jews return to England after their exile of more than 350 years. Cromwell

---

11   Shane writes that Jacob Judah León added Hebreo to his surname in literary works and that descendants after Solomon León also called their progenitor Templo.

did grant such permission, at least informally, but Menasseh died shortly before the restored English monarchy permitted the return of Jews starting in 1660 (Gerber, *The Jews of Spain* 202–04; see also Leibman, "Sephardic Sacred Space" 16–17). Meyer Kayserling, the first scholar to write about López Laguna, noted that Menasseh included *De la divinidad de la Ley de Moseh* (*On the Divinity of the Law of Moses*) in a list of unpublished works, but that López Laguna would most likely not have been familiar with this text ("The Jews in Jamaica" 714). Kayserling argued that López Laguna likely consulted *Conciliador* (*Conciliator*), a four-volume work that Menasseh wrote over two decades in which he proposed to explain inconsistencies in the Hebrew Bible (Nadler 60–63).

A POETIC RESPONSE TO INQUISITORIAL OPPRESSION

Frequently throughout the Psalms, the speaker entreats God for protection against cruel enemies and retribution against them for their iniquities, and then expresses gratitude for such divine providence. For this reason, the book may have seemed propitious for a New Christian author who suffered at the hands of an unjust oppressor and turned to God for refuge and redemption. López Laguna was not the only New Christian to find comfort in the psalter. For example, discussing the paraphrase of Psalms in Spanish written by David Abenatar Melo, another Portuguese converso who became an openly practicing Jew after leaving the Iberian Peninsula, Miriam Bodian notes that "Psalms were central prayers to crypto-Jews in the [Iberian] Peninsula, where they were available from Latin bibles, the Books of Hours, and other Catholic devotional writings" (*Hebrews of the Portuguese Nation* 176n35; see also 34–36). In Portugal, Abenatar Melo, known as Fernão Álvares Melo, dealt in textiles and owned a vineyard. Like López Laguna, he suffered Inquisitorial imprisonment and trial as an accused Judaizing heretic, despite his insistence that he was a faithful Christian. At the end of this two-year ordeal, Álvares Melo abjured *de vehementi* (on strong suspicion of heresy) at the auto de fe of July 31, 1611, in Lisbon.

Less than six months later, realizing that "Portugal had nothing more to offer him," Álvares Melo traveled to Amsterdam, where he was circumcised and called himself David Abenatar Melo within the Spanish-Portuguese Jewish community (Salomon 114-16, quote 122). He set up a printing press in 1617 that published several prayer books in Spanish to make Jewish liturgical works more accessible to former conversos. Melo left Amsterdam with his wife Isabel (Abigail) Rodrigues after the death of their only son, Duarte

(Eliahu), at the age of fifteen in 1622 (Salomon 139–40, 152–54).[12] The paraphrase of Psalms that he published in Hamburg in 1626 contains a highly personal dedication to el Dio Bendito (the Blessed Lord, abbreviated as D. B.) in which the poet laments not having been a faithful Jew earlier in his life. As part of this repentance, Melo describes a journey to God whose result is his paraphrase of Psalms, including the following description of a spiritual awakening while a prisoner of the Inquisition:

I knew myself, I knew thee,
And I tore my chest before Thee.
In it Thou sawest my heart
Full of contrition. (Melo, translated by Salomon 161)

In his own reworking of Psalm 94, López Laguna similarly applies an Inquisitorial context to his interpretation of the biblical framework of an evil people insulting or damaging "those worthy of your grace" ("a los de tu gracia dignos"; Ps. 94.3, 184):

Your people, God, they mistreat,
In their tribunal, in such a way
That they bring death to the wanderer
And kill the orphan and widow.

Tu pueblo, Señor, maltratan,
En su tribunal, de suerte
Que al peregrino dan muerte
Y al huérfano y viuda matan. (Ps. 94.5, 184)[13]

This strophe describes the previously unspecified oppressors as an Inquisitorial court that prosecutes crypto-Jews, who frequently represented themselves as geographical and spiritual wanderers. By 1720, New Christians of Iberian origin had established a nearly global diaspora with offshoots throughout northern Europe, the Mediterranean basin, the Americas, and

---

12    Salomon is the principal source of biographical information about David Abenatar Melo in this chapter.

13    The portion of *Espejo fiel* containing the paraphrase of Psalms by López Laguna is paginated; hence citations to his work here and subsequently refer to page numbers in the text of *Espejo fiel* rather than to the overall location of these excerpts in the PDF.

even India. This exile from lands to which they still felt an affinity despite experience of Inquisitorial persecution coexisted with a spiritual exile of guilt due to conversion and a desire of many to demonstrate commitment to Judaism however they could.[14] The inclusion of a tribunal in this *redondilla* (four-line strophe) also differentiates the text from that of León Templo on which it is based, given that the first two lines of the translator at Amsterdam state, "Those who act unjustly / crush your people and cause pain to your inheritors" ("… todos los obrantes de iniquidad. A tu pueblo, A., / majan, y a tu heredad afligen"; 271).[15] This distinction confirms the impact of the Inquisition on how López Laguna represents Psalms.

As a result, in subsequent *redondillas* of Psalm 94, López Laguna depicts God respectively consoling individuals perhaps symbolic of conversos and punishing others representative of the Inquisitorial apparatus that would ill-treat them. Echoing the psalmist, the poet describes this protection broadly and individually:

> Blessed God will not forsake
> His people;
> . . . . . . . . . . . . . . . . .
> [The wicked] gather and arrange themselves
> Against the soul of the just,
> And to obtain their pleasure
> They condemn innocent blood.
> But God has always been my protection
> Against that one who would hurl me down,
> God whom I always held
> As a rock of my remedy.
>
> Que no desamparará
> A su pueblo el Dios bendito;
> . . . . . . . . . . . . . . . . .
> Estos se juntan y ordenan
> Contra el ánima del justo,
> Y por conseguir su gusto,

---

14  See chapters 2 and 3 of this book for examples of the *peregrino* in the works of João Pinto Delgado and Antonio Enríquez Gómez, respectively.

15  The second "A." appears to stand for Adonai, a word meaning Lord in Hebrew. The author viewed this fragment of *Alabanzas de la santidad* in a PDF of a microfiche from the series Sephardic Editions, 1550–1820.

Sangre inocente condenan.
Mas siempre ha sido mi amparo
Contra aquel que me despeña
El Dios que siempre por peña
Le tuve de mi reparo. (Ps. 94.14 and 21–22, 185)[16]

López Laguna dramatizes these dual roles of God as protector and avenger through the antithesis between *"peña"* and *"despeña"*: God is a rock (*peña*) who protects the speaker against one who attempts to throw him from the rock by making this latter person fall (the verb form is *despeña*). This contrast between God as protector and avenger represented the worldview of crypto-Jewish conversos and then New Jews outside Spain and Portugal during the post-1492 era who took comfort believing that God recognized their attempts to live as Jews and exacted retribution against those who persecuted them for doing so. To a certain extent, such persecution grew out of a belief commonly held in Inquisitorial Spain that, notwithstanding their conversion, the blood of New Christians, that is, their lineage, was impure. By adding a reference to blood absent from the original psalm to describe the unjust acts of those who would persecute the speaker, perhaps the poet censures Spanish-Portuguese society for othering conversos as a distinct ethnicity.[17]

Divine protection of an unnamed people likely signifying New Christians together with punishment of their oppressors occurs frequently in the writing of conversos seeking to resist such othering, albeit with circumspection. Thus, for example, in the poem "On Leaving Lisbon" ("A la salida de Lisboa"), João Pinto Delgado, the subject of chapter 2, imagines the following retribution visited upon the Inquisition:

---

16   Another verse about divine support in this section of the psalm is the source of the first part of the title of the present chapter: "As although I say, on complaining / That my foot has slipped, / Your grace, despite evil, / Lord, will sustain me" ("Pues aunque digo, al quejarme / Que ya mi pie dio en resbalo, / Tu gracia, a pesar del malo, / Señor, ha de sustentarme"; Ps. 94.18, 185).

17   See the translation of Psalm 94.21 in *The Jewish Study Bible*, which is referenced throughout this chapter: "They band together to do away with the righteous; / they condemn the innocent to death." The differentiation of Spanish-Portuguese conversos as a racial if not religious other led some New Christians eager to escape the stigma of their so-called impure blood to fabricate genealogies purporting to alter their origins. For purity of blood statutes in late medieval Spain and after the expulsion of 1492, see Gitlitz, *Secrecy and Deceit* 38, 41–43, and *passim*.

> And although your delight is born
> of seeing so many perish,
> that day which you made others
> suffer will also dawn for you. (translated by Oelman 55)

> Y aunque nace tu alegría
> viendo a tantos perecer,
> si a muchos lo hiciste ver,
> también has de ver tu día. (Oelman 54)

Subsequently addressing the Israelite people in the poem, who most certainly represent New Christians unable to live as Jews because of the danger of doing so, Pinto Delgado urges,

> Hold fast to his holy precepts [those of God, "your king"],
> for amid the hostile squadrons
> and the ravening lions
> you are bound to gain your purpose. (translated by Oelman 61)

> Sigue sus santos precetos,
> que en medio los escuadrones
> entre rabiosos leones,
> has de alcanzar tus efetos. (Oelman 60)

The similarity between the worldview of these two poets who wrote nearly a century apart shows how Pinto Delgado and López Laguna affirmed an incipient Jewish identity rooted in God as a redemptive force that would make the Inquisition account for its cruelty towards New Christians.

López Laguna reflects Psalms through his worldview as a converso escaped from the Inquisition by adapting biblical censure of those who speak injuriously of their neighbors to his criticism of the *malsín*, or Inquisitorial informant. The derivation of this word from the Hebrew *malshin* (slanderer) showed, ironically, the influence of a prayer from Jewish liturgy on the same Inquisitorial apparatus that aimed to uproot all traces of Judaism. *Malshinim* (the plural of *malshin*) is part of *Birkat ha-Minim*, the twelfth of eighteen prayers in the Amidah ("Standing Prayer") that observant Jews recite daily: "*ve la-malshinim al tehi tikvah*" ("May slanderers have no hope").[18] The In-

---

18  For more on the prayer in the daily Amidah where the word *malshin* is found, see "Birkat ha-Minim." See also Langer 4–6.

quisition depended on *malsines* for denunciations and facilitated their collaboration by shielding their identity from the people whom they accused of heresy. As trial testimonies make clear, such informants could be neighbors, colleagues, and, frequently, individuals facing their own trials for Judaizing, including friends and family members. This testimony was not always reliable, given the various types of animus unrelated to religion that could have motivated it. As a result, the accused could attempt to discredit these witnesses through the use of the *tacha* ("defect" or "imperfection"), by which they would try to name those who spoke against them and the unjust motives for doing so (Gitlitz, *The Lost Minyan* xii).[19]

The frequency throughout *Espejo fiel* with which López Laguna scorns those whose words hurt others suggests his own experience as a victim of informants. For example, in his paraphrase of Psalm 15, the poet, directing himself to God, answers the question, "Who will live in your tent?" ("¿Quién, gran Señor, habitará en tu tienda?"; Ps. 15.1, 19), by stating,

> He who speaks truth according to how he understands it
> In his faithful heart free of despicable matter,
> Not forging deceits with his lip
> That can cause grievance to his neighbor.

> Y el que hablare verdad según la entienda
> En su fiel corazón limpio de escoria,
> No forjando quimeras con su labio
> Que a su prójimo puedan ser de agravio. (Ps. 15.2–3, 19)

The poem serves as a guide to those who will "find the door of the eternal Temple open" ("del Templo eterno hallar la puerta abierta"), in contrast to individuals who, in addition to spreading calumnies, resort to usury and bribery (Ps. 15.4–5, 20). This promise of divine protection perhaps helped secret Jews withstand marginalization from Old Christians and the threat of Inquisitorial punishment for dedicating themselves to a forbidden faith.

López Laguna intensifies his call for divine punishment of the Inquisitorial informant in Psalm 109, where the verses inserted before the paraphrase align David with conversos and the antagonist who would persecute David, Doeg the Edomite, with talebearers. The poet foregrounds this call by writing how the psalmist, "persecuted by slanderers" ("perseguido / . . . de sus

---

19   For a contemporaneous definition of *tacha*, see Real Academia Española, *Diccionario de Autoridades*, vol. 6, https://apps2.rae.es/DA.html.

calumniadores"), implores God to punish "perfidious traitors" ("pérfidos traidores"; Ps. 109, 216), thus using language a New Christian might have used to describe accusers sheltered by the tribunal's promise of anonymity for witnesses. In so doing, López Laguna continues the thread of Psalm 52, where the voice of David speaks directly to Saul's herdsman, Doeg, accusing him of treacherously serving Saul and endangering David:

> You loved evil more than good,
> Since you became accustomed
> Always to speak deceit
> Against faithful justice.

> Amaste mal más que bien,
> Pues siempre a hablar falsedad
> Contra la fiel justedad
> Te acostumbraste también. (Ps. 52.5, 99)[20]

Doeg first appears in 1 Samuel 21.8 and in 22.9–11 betrays David's whereabouts to Saul. At the king's command, Doeg subsequently kills the priests of God, whom Saul believes are conspiring with David against him (22.16–19). This biblical framework permits López Laguna to represent the story of someone wicked speaking ill of a good person through an Inquisitorial context in which a spy defames a New Christian:

> Thus you [God] see how
> The evil one provokes me [David],
> Opening his mouth against me,
> Soliciting my harm
> With lips of wickedness, a tongue of deceit,
> Friends who reveal themselves to be flattering,
> Being false enemies,
> As with snares of deceit they encircle me
> Always, and fight against me without cause.

> Pues ves cuál me provoca
> El malo, abriendo contra mí su boca,

---

20 Commentary in *The Jewish Study Bible* by Shimon Bar-Efrat to 1 Samuel 21–22 and by Adele Berlin and Marc Zvi Brettler to Psalm 52 has helped me understand the importance of David and Doeg to the worldview of López Laguna.

Procurando mi daño
Con labios de maldad, lengua de engaño,
Lisonjeros que amigos
Se muestran, siendo falsos enemigos,
Pues con lazos de engaño me rodean
Siempre, y sin causa contra mí pelean. (Ps. 109.2, 216)

The psalm itself contains the most extended curse of any text in the psalter, which may explain its appeal to someone who wished God to exact justice against persecutors.[21] Beyond wishing that an impugner of others die and that his family become orphaned and destitute, this malediction urges God to perpetuate the shame of such a person across generations, perhaps reflecting the desires of a survivor of the Inquisition. This wish also reflects an awareness of how the Holy Office publicized the heresies of its victims by compelling them to wear the *sambenito*, or penitential sackcloth inscribed with symbols representing various levels of punishment. To compound such ignominy, the tribunal then displayed these garments in churches, with the names of the guilty affixed. Just as the talebearer contributed to this shame, so here López Laguna desires that one who offends with words suffer similar humiliation:

May God not cast into oblivion the crime
Of his father, and grandparents, and of his mother,
May his sin never be forgiven.
As he has imitated their evil habits,
May his guilt become permanent
In front of the great judge of the living.

No eche Dios en olvido de su padre
Y abuelos el delito, y de su madre,
Nunca el pecado sea perdonado.
Pues sus malas costumbres ha imitado,
Sus culpas puestas sean permanentes
Delante del gran juez de los vivientes. (Ps. 109.14–15, 117)

Lamenting that individuals such as this maligner have humiliated and impoverished him, the speaker beseeches divine help, imagining an outcome

---

21  Berlin and Brettler, Psalm 109 footnote, in *The Jewish Study Bible*, 1393. Here they mention the commonality of these curses throughout the Bible.

that contrasts with his present tribulation. As a result, by the end of the psalm, those who have caused him anguish will be covered in shame and grief, whereas he will praise God for protecting him against those who would "usurp worldly goods, reputation, and glory ("usurparle hacienda, honor y palma"; Ps. 109.31, 219). These words describe the situation of individuals prosecuted by the Inquisition, which robbed victims of their good name and then sequestered their possessions, some or all of which it sold to pay the cost of trial and imprisonment. As a result, destitution frequently afflicted those made to endure penances including compulsory attendance at mass, fines, imprisonment, exile, and servitude rowing on galleys.[22]

## God as Protector and Redeemer of New Christians against All Calamities

While *Espejo fiel* does not describe Jamaica in any detail, in his rewriting of Psalm 46 López Laguna uses divine protection described in the biblical text as a source of comfort in light of the earthquake of June 7, 1692, which destroyed Port Royal, where he might have been living. The poet personalizes his understanding of God as a port in a storm after surviving this most impactful experience of the natural world as a destructive force:

> The sovereign creator of earth and heaven
> Is our protection, refuge, and stronghold,
> Whose aid and succor, in our anguish
> He, being merciful, grants us immeasurably.
> Therefore, we will never fear ruin,
> When the earth moves, even though
> The obelisks may slide to the bottom of the sea.
> And although upon bellowing, the roaring waves
> Make the towering mountains tremble,
> He who builds up his breath in God does not fear
> The harshness of water, earth, fire, and wind.
>
> El soberano autor de tierra y cielo
> Es nuestro amparo, asilo y fortaleza

---

22  Part of the notoriety of the Spanish Inquisition rests in the indelible spectacle of victims being burned at the stake after their sentencing at the conclusion of the auto de fe. For descriptions from primary sources of public autos in 1486 and 1680 showing the evolution of the act of faith into a more visually performative event, see Kamen, *The Spanish Inquisition* 255–59.

Cuyo favor y ayuda, en nuestra angustia
Nos otorga piadoso inmensas veces.
Por eso, nunca estragos temeremos
En moverse la tierra, aunque resbalen
Al profundo del mar los obeliscos.
Y aunque al bramar sus ondas rugidoras,
Hagan temblar los encumbrados montes,
Que no teme quien funda en Dios su aliento,
Rigores de agua, tierra, fuego y viento. (Ps. 46.2–4, 84–85, translated by Wojda, Henderson, and Warshawsky, 3)

Just as God accompanies New Christians forced to live their Judaism secretly and in isolation, so God, more powerful than nature, protects them from earthquakes and other calamities. The content that López Laguna then adds at this point reflects his perspective on the theme of exile and the promise of Jerusalem as symbol of its end: "Because today, although scattered, we wait, / Persevering, to see the end of our captivity" ("Porque hoy, aunque esparcidos, esperamos / Constantes ver al fin del cautiverio"; Ps. 46.4, 85, translated by Wojda, Henderson, and Warshawsky, 3). In this context, scattering describes the diaspora of crypto-Jewish conversos, while captivity, sometimes literal, evinces their living conditions under the Spanish-Portuguese Inquisitions.

For López Laguna in subsequent verses, Jerusalem as the dwelling place of God, irrigated by a life-giving river, contrasts with the ruinous display of nature just described and provides a vision of hope as a physical and spiritual refuge. Describing Jerusalem in this way, he evokes Ezekiel 47.1–12, where the prophet describes a great stream that flows from under the place where the new Temple will be built and that will sustain the land around it.[23] López Laguna then emphasizes divine might by stating that "all the (Gentile) nations will roar" ("rugirán las gentes, todas") and "the monarchies will bellow" ("bramarán las del orbe monarquías") upon witnessing the destruction of "their arrogant pretentiousness" ("su altiva pompa"; Ps. 46.7, 85) at the sound of God. Repeating the verbs (*rugirán, bramarán*) with which he described

---

23  As Berlin and Brettler observe in their notes on Psalm 46.5, the image of such a river in Jerusalem is invented and may serve as a means of comparing the city to the Garden of Eden, "watered in a positive way" (1319). In the same place, they also point out that Ezekiel 36.35 makes this comparison describing Jerusalem and the surrounding area: "And men shall say, 'that land, once desolate, has become like the Garden of Eden; and the cities, once ruined, desolate, and ravaged, are now populated and fortified.'"

the earthquake-induced tsunami, the poet suggests that God exercises dominion over nature and humanity, surely a reaffirming message for a survivor of a natural cataclysm and Inquisitorial oppression.

In at least one instance, López Laguna inserts the title of the work, *Espejo fiel de vidas*, within the text itself, following a tradition of Spanish Golden Age playwrights who regularly did likewise. Perhaps he does so as a way of presenting events of his own life without having to narrate them directly. Through this partial revelation of his identity, López Laguna demonstrates, as Ronnie Perelis has noted, how "the dialectic of hiding at the heart of much Baroque poetry, in particular, lends itself perfectly to the discomfort of many former conversos as they reflect upon their experiences" (322). Psalm 119, the longest poem in the psalter, shows this discomfort by enumerating the converso worldview of López Laguna at the same time as it leaves the reader wondering about events informing this perspective. For example, the poet has the first-person narrator identify himself as "wanderer, Lord, I am in the land" ("peregrino, Señor, soy en la tierra"; Ps. 119.19, 235), thus repeating the epithet *peregrino* by which many New Christians understood their geographic and spiritual mobility.[24] Whereas the biblical text then says, "For Your decrees are my delight, / my intimate companion" (Ps. 119.24), López Laguna writes, "Also your testimonies, like [a] *Faithful / Mirror of Lives*, offer me their advice" ("También tus testimonios, cual *Espejo / Fiel de vidas*, me ofrecen su consejo"; Ps. 119.24, 235), thus suggesting the possibility of an autobiographical connection in subsequent verses of the psalm through their subtle reflection of the author's own experiences.[25] In so doing, he broadens the reach of biblical verse 54, "Your laws are a source of strength to me / wherever I may dwell," to include the Inquisitorial prison:

> Your laws were psalms sung to me
> (Perhaps accompanied by laments)
> In the house that my tragedies and
> Wanderings call [a house] of prisons.
>
> Eran a mí tus psalmeamientos
> (Tal vez acompañados de lamentos)

---

24  I thank one of the anonymous reviewers of *American Jewish History* for commenting that Spanish-Portuguese conversos returned to Judaism also used the term *peregrino* as a translation of the Hebrew *ger tzedek* ("righteous convert").

25  See also Berlin and Brettler 1402–03, where they note that Psalm 119 is the longest chapter in the Bible.

> En la casa que llaman de prisiones
> Mis tragedias y peregrinaciones. (Ps. 119.54, 238)

The presence of God there surely animated López Laguna to maintain his identity as a crypto-Jew during a time of sorrow amidst figurative and literal darkness. Likewise, changing the tense of the verb "remember" from present to past time in the subsequent verse—"I remembered your name at night, / Being all my glory the keeping of your Law" ("De tu nombre en la noche hice memoria, / Siendo el guardar tu Ley toda mi gloria; Ps.119.55, 238)—the poet emphasizes his faithfulness while imprisoned. Finally, López Laguna adds an Inquisitorial context to the psalm's affirmation of constancy despite persecution:

> Those who make war on the just
> Almost reduced me to nothing on earth,
> But I, away from their pacts,
> Never slackened from your commands.[26]

> Casi me aniquilaron en la tierra
> Los que al justo dan guerra.
> Mas yo lejano de sus alianzas,
> Nunca aflojé de tus encomendanzas. (119.87, 241)

Here the poet identifies himself with "the just" and suggests that the Holy Office prosecuted a "war" against him, but that such tribulation did not lessen his faith.

The last five psalms of the collection, Psalms 146–50, begin and end with the command "Hallelujah" (praise) and indeed praise God for deliverance of the Israelite people. In his rewriting, López Laguna exalts God as redeemer of the Israelites to vindicate the adversity that New Christians have faced and to emphasize their connection with the elect status of the Jewish people, regardless of whether they live openly Jewish lives. Thus, the David who speaks in his Psalm 146 represents the catalog of this redemption through a worldview that reflects the author's struggle with the Inquisition:

> Those locked up with shackles
> God sets free from prison.

---

26   The biblical text reads, "Though they almost wiped me off the earth, / I did not abandon your precepts."

> ..........
> God loves all the righteous
> And protected the wanderer.
> ..........
> God will reign forever,
> Forging Zion again.
>
> Y a encarcelados en grillos
> Redime [Dios] de la prisión.
> ..........
> A todos los justos ama,
> Y al peregrino amparó.
> ..........
> Reinará Dios para siempre,
> Volviendo a fraguar a Zion. (Ps. 146.7–10, 281)

Inquisitors typically assumed guilt of the accused, detained them as long as proceedings dictated, hid the identity of incriminatory witnesses, and delayed revealing the charges, all in order to extract confessions and the names of other potential heretics. Under these conditions, the promise of divine deliverance from imprisonment held special urgency for the poet, as did his belief in God's protection of the "wanderer" (*peregrino*) with whom displaced conversos identified rather than the "stranger" of the biblical text. López Laguna rewrote the end of the psalm so that besides affirming God's eternal sovereignty, as in the original, it also ascribes to God the "reforging" of Zion, a rebuilding that spoke to the diasporic condition of conversos as exiles from the Holy Land as well as from Judaism itself.

In the penultimate psalm, Psalm 149, López Laguna conflates praise of God as redeemer and avenger of the Israelites, dual roles that are compatible in the converso worldview despite their apparent contradictoriness. The prefatory verses foreground these roles through the exhortation of David to the Israelites to praise God:

> For the eternal and exalted glory that
> God holds prepared for them on high,
> And for the hope
> That God will exert just revenge
> On cruel inhuman kings,
> Who, persecuting them, so harass them as tyrants,

That, boasting to be judges of the soul,
They take from them life, honor, wealth, and renown.

Por la gloria que eterna y sublimada
Le tiene en las alturas preparadas;
También por la esperanza
De la que les dará justa venganza
De los que crueles reyes inhumanos,
En perseguirlos corren tan tiranos
Que ostentando ser jueces de las almas,
Les quitan vida, honor, riqueza y palmas. (Ps. 149.284)

These lines repeat an earlier lament of the poet regarding good name, possessions, and life itself that victims of Inquisitorial prosecution stood to lose, even as the tribunal promised them reconciliation with the Catholic Church, justifying the vengeful divine retribution described here. The "inhuman kings" surely reflect inquisitors whom López Laguna disparages for claiming to care about the souls of accused heretics while meting out punishment including death at the stake for those whom it deemed impenitent and/or recidivist heretics.[27] The paraphrase of the psalm itself contrasts with the rejoicing of the Israelites at their divine deliverance, as vengeful justice is inflicted on their oppressors. The speaker thus expresses a wish that the Israelites praise God with musical instruments and dance for the redemption they have received, which will bring them delight as they sing God's glory.

At the same time, a representative individual will praise God while taking up a two-edged sword, an action perhaps meant to dramatize divine retaliation against Inquisitorial society:

> So that vengeance on the Gentiles
> He (God) may carry out against the one who outraged Him,
> Punishing in the nations
> Cruelties of the Inquisition.

---

27   Despite its reputation as an implacable arbiter, the Inquisition imposed a capital sentence at rates approximately equal to or less than those of secular courts of the time in Spain and elsewhere in Europe, although the majority of the condemned were New Christians of Jewish or Muslim background; see Kamen, *The Spanish Inquisition* 254. The number of such victims was less than 4% of the total number of Inquisitorial trials for heresy in Spain and its colonies; see Gitlitz, *Lost Minyan* xii; and Gitlitz, *Secrecy and Deceit* 32n56.

> Para que venganza en las gentes
> Haga de quien le ultrajó,
> Castigando en las naciones
> Crueldades de Inquisición. (Ps. 149.7, 285)

For López Laguna, Inquisitorial abuses will occasion God's wrath towards *las gentes*, a term used by ex-conversos returned to Judaism to describe Old Christians in order to emphasize their view of themselves as a distinct and divinely privileged group.[28]

It is also possible that the subject of these actions is the person armed with the two-edged sword himself. In this case, the words of this speaker praising God join with his sword to punish antagonists of Israelites.[29] Here, López Laguna conflates the inquisitors with Sihon, Og, and Pharaoh as examples of such enemies and the conversos of his era with biblical Jews who suffered at the hands of these rulers. Praise of God by the Israelites will thus bring about

> Imprisonment of kings
> As God did to Sihon and Og,
> . . . . . . . . . .
> To render justice on them,
> As God did with Pharaoh.

> Para encarcelar sus reyes,
> cual hizo a Sihón y a Og,
> . . . . . . . . . .
> Para hacer en ellos juicio,
> Como hizo con Faraón. (Ps. 149.8–9, 285)

In Numbers 22.21–35 and Deuteronomy 2.26–37, the Israelites, on their journey from Sinai to Canaan, defeat the forces of Sihon and Og after these kings have refused to let them pass through their respective kingdoms in

---

28 Similarly, e.g., Isaac Cardoso, the subject of chapter 4 of this book, wrote in *Las excelencias de los hebreos* that the Israelites are "one people among many, although scattered ... chosen by God, and separate from all" ("una gente entre muchas, una aunque esparcida ... escogidos de Dios, y apartados de todos"; 24)

29 I acknowledge Berlin and Brettler, footnote on Psalm 149.6, 1434, for the idea that the two-edged sword may symbolize "the power of the words of praise; they can achieve the retribution of the following verses."

what is today the Jordanian side of the Dead Sea. These episodes connect to the converso worldview of López Laguna by establishing a link between divinely supported retribution against biblical kings who opposed Israelites and inquisitors who have opposed New Christians.

## Conclusion: *Espejo fiel* as Reflection of a Contradictory Experience of Judaism

Informed by his youth in France (and possibly Portugal), education and Inquisition trial in Spain, settlement in Jamaica, and interaction with the Spanish-Portuguese Jewish community of London, López Laguna illuminates in *Espejo fiel de vidas* the transatlantic character of Sephardic Jewry in the Americas three hundred years ago. In the absence of information about its author's Jewish practices in Iberian lands and Jamaica, *Espejo fiel de vidas*, while not a biography per se, shows the depth of his beliefs, the impact of Inquisitorial society on their formation, and the efficacy of Psalms in reflecting them. His interpretation of Psalms shows the hybrid and at times contradictory nature of this experience of Judaism: López Laguna wrote as an ex-New Christian of Spanish-Portuguese origins living as a Jew in diaspora who proudly used Spanish literary language to vindicate an identity prohibited in Spain. The work challenges American Jewish historical narratives by focusing on an early-1700s Sephardic voice in Jamaica that expresses a keen understanding of displacement and suggests the possibility of divine redemption. Bearing witness to a worldview often unseen despite the longstanding presence of secret and then openly practicing Jews of converso origin in the Americas, the voice of López Laguna reclaiming a once forbidden Judaism resonates today for its triumph over forces that would have silenced it.

# Conclusion

> ... Throughout those generations there was a constant movement of conversos throughout Portugal and Spain, as well as a regular migration of the exiles in Europe from one Jewish community to another. It was a virtually endless history of restlessness. Despite the shadow of the Inquisition, Iberia gave to Jewish and converso exiles a common bond that made them all "men of the nation."
>
> KAMEN, *The Disinherited* 30[1]

FROM *NEW CHRISTIANS TO New Jews: Seventeenth-Century Spanish Texts in Defense of Judaism* has argued that Isaac Orobio de Castro, João Pinto Delgado, Antonio Enríquez Gómez, Isaac Cardoso, Miguel (Daniel Levi) de Barrios, and Daniel Israel López Laguna broaden the reach of Baroque Spanish literature to include diasporic New Christians who expressed various levels of Jewish identity in texts that follow Spanish literary customs. At the same time, the analysis has shown the lasting influence of Inquisitorial Spain and Portugal on the six writers, given that their works typically praise crypto-Jews and the faith for which they suffered, represent Catholic Christianity as the antagonist of Judaism, lament societal ills to which conversos were especially attuned, and express a spiritual and geographic wandering, all in ways that resonated throughout the Sephardic world post-1492. These texts also bring readers today closer to the bifurcated worldview of writers who convey a recovered Jewish identity or at the very least, a converso one, using their literary formation in a Spanish-Portuguese Catholic milieu. Finally, the works show how sites of refuge beyond the Iberian Peninsula provided a setting for conversos to embrace or reflect the influence of the faith formerly denied them. As chroniclers of this transformation, each writer testifies to distinct possible levels of this faith in texts

---

[1] Kamen wrote these words at the end of a section of *The Disinherited* discussing the case of Isaac Cardoso, whom he calls "the most significant converso figure of the seventeenth century" (28).

that also maintain connections with the Iberian society that had forbidden its expression.

The book has also attested to the "virtually endless history of restlessness" that in the words of Kamen characterized the converso diaspora and fostered a sense of belonging among its members precisely because of its dispersed nature. The displacement of all six authors across borders and in some cases, seas, compelled them to form communities with other New Christian immigrants rooted in an experience of ethnic and religious difference. Indeed, a desire to perpetuate this difference that led them away from the Iberian Peninsula in the first place explains how diasporic New Christians adapted to host societies without necessarily assimilating to them, at least during the 1600s. Likewise, the restlessness emblematic of the journeys of the six authors and other conversos found its parallel in a spiritual restlessness that in many cases had prompted them to become geographic *peregrinos* (wanderers). This sense of wandering, evident in the life stories and literary themes of all six authors, contributed to the cultural cohesion of New Christians and in many cases, led them to return to Judaism in defiance of its erasure in Spanish-Portuguese lands. One may even argue that not only "despite the shadow of the Inquisition," in Kamen's words cited in the epigraph, but precisely because of it, these authors and their brethren strengthened their self-identity as "those of the Nation" (*os de la nação*), validated by a literature whose protagonists resisted the tribunal, even at the cost of their lives.

The texts of Orobio, Pinto Delgado, Enríquez Gómez, Cardoso, Barrios, and López Laguna continue to speak to readers today because of their modernity and urgency. In different ways they affirm the power of belief in an omniscient and ultimately forgiving God who offers humans a way forward, especially in moments when they must contend simultaneously with hope and despair. Thus, for example, the potential for divine forgiveness through humility, repentance, and taking responsibility for one's actions, mitigates the desolation of Jerusalem that Pinto Delgado describes in *Lamentaciones del profeta Jeremías*. Likewise, belief in the promise of divine salvation justifies the choice of Lope de Vera y Alarcón, the three martyrs in Córdoba, and all the other crypto-Jews who died sanctifying the name of God rather than forswear their conscience. Regardless of the drastic results of their unbending will, each of them lived (and died) in what Enríquez Gómez, describing his own situation in the prologue to *Academias morales de las musas* with words applicable to all six writers, called "the justification of my truth" (la justificación de mi verdad"; 10v). Faith in this truth, a truth that in many instances the six authors manifest as freedom of conscience to beseech and, hopefully, effect divine redemption, helps them confront any barrier, whether imposed by Inquisitorial prosecution, the argument of an opponent in a theological polemic, disillusionment in light of societal ills, or even an earthquake.

Opened in 2012, the Isaac Cardoso Interpretation Center of Jewish Culture (Centro de Interpretação da Cultura Judaica Isaac Cardoso) in Trancoso, Portugal, memorializes its namesake and the Jewish legacy of the town, especially during the Inquisition era, in exhibits that describe the secret Jewish faith of many conversos there, the persecution they suffered for the charge of Jewish heresy, and their subsequent diasporic journeys. On a visit in April 2022, the author learned from a staff member that local descendants of these conversos insisted the center include a synagogue so that they would have a place to pray openly as Jews. Thus, in addition to commemorating the Jewish and then converso presence in Trancoso, the center, through its Beit Hayim Mayim (House of Living Waters) synagogue, asserts the existence of Judaism as a living faith, in defiance of the forced conversion of Portuguese Jewry in 1497 and Inquisitorial prosecution of New Christians in the kingdom starting in 1536. Just as this history speaks to the strength of Iberian Judaism well into the twenty-first century, so the texts of the writers studied in this book testify to its resilience and redemption, especially since all were written at least 150 years after the expulsion and conversions of the 1490s. Through their works, Orobio, Pinto Delgado, Enríquez Gómez, Cardoso, Barrios, and López Laguna resoundingly counter the events of that decade and the Inquisitorial project of using religious orthodoxy to silence and erase crypto-Judaism amongst conversos. Whether identifying with Jewish teachings or declaring Judaism outright in their texts, these authors challenge the official story of Inquisition-imposed silence and erasure of crypto-Judaism amongst conversos, while opening a space in Spanish Golden Age letters for the literary legacy of a forbidden faith and the culture that accompanied it.

## Works Cited

Alonso, Álvaro, editor. *Fray Luis de León: Poesía*. Penguin Random House, 2016.
Amelang, James S. *Parallel Histories: Muslims and Jews in Inquisitorial Spain*. Louisiana State UP, 2013.
Amit, Yairah, editor. Note to Judges 13.1–25. *The Jewish Study Bible*, p. 526.
Arbell, Mordechai. *The Jewish Nation of the Caribbean: The Spanish-Portuguese Jewish Settlements in the Caribbean and the Guianas*. Gefen, 2002.
Artigas, María del Carmen. Introduction. *Sansón Nazareno, poema épico*, by Antonio Enríquez Gómez, Editorial Verbum, 1999, pp. 9–52.
August, Thomas G. "An Historical Profile of the Jewish Community of Jamaica." *Jewish Social Studies* vol, 49, no. 3/4, 1987, jstor.org/stable/4467393. Accessed 7 June 2022.
"Auto sacramental." *Diccionario de la lengua española*, Real Academia Española, 2021, dle.rae.es/auto?m=form#8ldQbaH. Accessed 31 Mar. 2022.
Baer, Yitzhak. *A History of the Jews of Christian Spain*, vol. 2. Jewish Publication Society, 1992.
Bar-Efrat, Shimon, editor. Note to 1 Samuel 21–22. *The Jewish Study Bible*, pp. 587–90.
Barrios, Miguel. *Coro de las musas*. Brussels, Baltazar Vivien, 1672. *Google Books*, books.google.com.
———. *Triumpho del govierno popular y de la antigüedad holandesa*. Amsterdam, n.p., 1683. Edition from the Bibliotheca Rosenthaliana, Amsterdam (Ros., 19G11). Digitized 7 Mar. 2016. *Google Books*, books.google.com.
Barnett, L. D. "Two Documents of the Inquisition". *The Jewish Quarterly Review*, vol. 15, no. 2, 1924, pp. 213–39.
Bartolomé-Pons, Esther. "Comentario y texto del poema 'Lamentación fúnebre en la muerte de mi padre,' del judío español Daniel Leví de Barrios (1635-1701)." Ribera, pp. 197–221.
Ben Israel, Menasseh. *Segunda parte del Conciliador, o De la conveniencia de los lugares*. Amsterdam, Nicolaus de Ravesteyn, 1641. *Google Books*, books.google.com.
Berlin, Adele. Introduction to Lamentations. *The Jewish Study Bible*, Jewish Publication Society Tanakh Translation. Oxford UP, 2014, pp. 1581–83.
———. Introduction to Esther. *The Jewish Study Bible*, pp. 1619–21.

Berlin, Adele, and Marc Zvi Brettler, editors. Notes to Psalms 52 and 109. *The Jewish Study Bible*, pp. 1326, 1393.

"Birkat ha-Minim." *The New Encyclopedia of Judaism*, edited by Geoffrey Wigoder, Fred Skolnik, and Shmuel Himelstein, New York UP, 2nd ed., 2002.

Blecua, José Manuel, editor. *Poesía de la Edad de Oro*. Castalia, 1984. 2 vols.

Bodian, Miriam. *Dying in the Law of Moses: Crypto-Jewish Martyrdom in the Iberian World*. Indiana UP, 2007.

———. "The Formation of the Portuguese Jewish Diaspora." *The Jews in the Caribbean*, edited by Jane S. Gerber, Littman Library of Jewish Civilization, 2014, pp. 17–27.

———. *Hebrews of the Portuguese Nation: Conversos and Community in Early Modern Amsterdam*. Indiana UP, 1997.

Bodian, Miriam, and Ide François. "From the Files of the Portuguese Inquisition: Isaac de Castro Tartas's Latin Ego-Document, 1645." *Jewish Quarterly Review*, vol. 107, no. 2, 2017, pp. 231–46. *Project MUSE*, https://doi.org/10.1353/jqr.2017.0013.

Brown, Kenneth. *De la cárcel inquisitorial a la sinagoga de Amsterdam (edición y estudio del "Romance a Lope de Vera" de Antonio Enríquez Gómez)*. Consejería de Cultura de Castilla-La Mancha, 2007.

Brown, Kenneth, and Cyndi Valerio. "Nuevas calas sobre la persona y la obra de Antonio Enríquez Gómez." Diputación Provincial de Cuenca, *Revista Cuenca*, vol. 44, 1996, pp. 47–65.

Calderón de la Barca, Pedro. *Los encantos de la culpa*. Edited by Juan Manuel Escudero, Edition Reichenberger, 2004.

Cardoso, Isaac. *Las excelencias de los hebreos*. Amsterdam, David de Castro Tartas, 1679. *Google Books*, books.google.com.

Cash, Annette G., and James C. Murray, editors. *Anthology of Medieval Spanish Poetry*. Cervantes & Co., 2010.

Cassius Dio Cocceianus, Lucius. *Roman History*. Translated by Earnest Cary, vol. 8, Harvard UP, 1925, 1995.

Cervantes, Miguel de. *Don Quixote*. Translated by Edith Grossman, Ecco, 2005.

Chazan, Robert. *From Anti-Judaism to Anti-Semitism: Ancient and Medieval Christian Constructions of Jewish History*. Cambridge UP, 2016.

Colbert Cairns, Emily. "Esther in Inquisitorial Iberia and the Sephardic Diaspora." *Hispanófila*, vol. 175, 2015, pp. 183–200.

Cross, Harry E. "Commerce and Orthodoxy: A Spanish Response to Portuguese Commercial Penetration in the Viceroyalty of Peru, 1580-1640." *The Americas*, vol. 35, no. 2, 1978, pp. 151–67.

Davidi, Einat. "The Corpus of Hebrew and Jewish *Autos Sacramentales*." *European Journal of Jewish Studies*, vol. 13, 2019, pp. 182–226.

Den Boer, Harm. *La literatura sefardí de Amsterdam*. Instituto Internacional de Estudios Sefardíes y Andalusíes, Universidad de Alcalá, 1995.

Dent-Young, John, editor and translator. *Selected Poems of Luis de Góngora: A Bilingual Edition*. U of Chicago P, 2007. *ProQuest Ebook Central*, ebookcentral.proquest.com/lib/up/detail.action?docID=408458.

Dille, Glen F. *Antonio Enríquez Gómez*. Twayne, 1987.

———. "Antonio Enríquez Gómez's Honor Tragedy *A lo que obliga el honor*." *Bulletin of the Comediantes*, vol. 30, no. 2, 1978, pp. 97–11.

Egido, Aurora. Introduction. Calderón de la Barca, *Los encantos de la Culpa*, pp. 7–106.

Elliott, J. H. *The Count-Duke of Olivares: The Statesman in an Age of Decline*. Yale UP, 1986.

*Elogios que zelozos dedicaron a la felice memoria de Abraham Núñez Bernal, que fue quemado vivo santificando el Nombre de su Criador en Cordova a 3 de mayo 5415*. Amsterdam, 1655. *Google Books*, books.google.com.

Enríquez Gómez, Antonio. *Academias morales de las musas*. Bordeaux: Pedro de la Court, 1642.

———. *La inquisición de Lucifer y visita de todos los diablos*. Edited by Constance Hubbard Rose and Maxim P. A. M. Kerkhof, Rodopi, 1992.

———. *Romance al divín mártir Judá Creyente (don Lope de Vera y Alarcón) martirizado en Valladolid por la Inquisición*. Edited by Timothy Oelman, Fairleigh Dickinson UP, 1986.

———. *Sansón Nazareno, poema épico*. Edited by María del Carmen Artigas, Editorial Verbum, 1999.

———. *El siglo pitagórico y vida de don Gregorio Guadaña*. Edited by Charles Amiel, Ediciones Hispanoamericanas, 1977.

———. *El siglo pitagórico y vida de don Gregorio Guadaña*. Edited by Teresa de Santos. Cátedra, 1991.

Fine, Ruth. "*The Psalms of David* by Daniel Israel López Laguna, a Wandering Marrano." Translated by William Childers, *The Conversos and Moriscos in Late Medieval Spain and Beyond*, edited by Juan Ignacio Pulido Serrano and Kevin Ingram, Brill, 2016, pp. 45–62.

Fishlock, A. D. H. "The *Lamentaciones* of João Pinto Delgado." *Atlante*, vol. 3, 1955, pp. 47–61.

———. "The Shorter Poems of João Pinto Delgado." *Bulletin of Hispanic Studies*, vol. 31, no. 1, 1954, pp. 127–40.

García Valdecasas Andrada, José Guillermo. *Las "Academias morales" de Antonio Enríquez Gómez: críticas sociales y jurídicas en los versos herméticos de un "judío" español en el exilio*. Anales de la Universidad Hispalense, 1971.

Gerber, Jane S., editor. *The Jews in the Caribbean*. Littman Library of Jewish Civilization, 2014.

———, *The Jews of Spain: A History of the Sephardic Experience*. The Free Press, 1992.

Gitlitz, David M. *The Lost Minyan*. U of New Mexico P, 2010.

———. *Secrecy and Deceit: The Religion of the Crypto-Jews*. 1996. U of New Mexico P, 2002.

Goldstein, Jonathan A., editor and translator. *2 Maccabees*. Anchor Yale Bible Series, Yale UP, 2007.
Gottheil, Richard, and Samuel Krauss. "Fulvia." *The Jewish Encyclopedia*, edited by Cyrus Adler and Isidore Singer, vol. 5, KTAV, 1964, www.jewishencyclopedia.com/articles/6423-fulvia.
Gracia Boix, Rafael. *Autos de fe y causas de la Inquisición de Córdoba*. Diputación Provincial de Córdoba, 1983.
Graizbord, David. *Souls in Dispute: Converso Identities in Iberia and the Jewish Diaspora, 1580-1700*. U of Pennsylvania P, 2004.
Green, Otis H. *Spain and the Western Tradition: The Castilian Mind in Literature from* El Cid *to* Calderón, vol. 4, U of Wisconsin P, 1966.
Henriques Pimentel, Abraham. Preface. López Laguna, n.p., pp. 49–54 in PDF.
Homer. *The Odyssey*. Translated by Robert Fitzgerald, Anchor Books, 1963.
Horace. *Q. Horati Flacci opera*. Edited by Edward C. Wickham and H. W. Garrod, Oxford UP, 1989.
Israel, Jonathan. "Sephardic Immigration into the Dutch Republic, 1595–1672." *Studia Rosenthaliana*, vol. 23, no. 1 (fall), 1989, pp. 45–53.
*The Jewish Study Bible*. Edited by Adele Berlin and Marc Zvi Brettler, 2nd edition, Oxford UP, 2014.
Kamen, Henry. *The Disinherited: Exile and the Making of Spanish Culture, 1492–1975*. HarperCollins, 2007.
———. *The Spanish Inquisition: A Historical Revision*. 4th ed., Yale UP, 2014.
Kaplan, Gregory B. *Arguments against the Christian Religion in Amsterdam by Saul Levi Morteira, Spinoza's Rabbi*. Amsterdam UP, 2017.
———. *The Origins of Democratic Zionism*. Routledge, 2019.
Kaplan, Yosef. *From Christianity to Judaism: The Story of Isaac Orobio de Castro*. 1989. Translated by Raphael Lowe, Littman Library of Jewish Civilization, 2004.
———. "The Intellectual Ferment in the Spanish-Portuguese Community of Seventeenth-Century Amsterdam." *Moreshet Sepharad: The Sephardi Legacy*, vol. 2, edited by Haim Beinart, Magnes Press, Hebrew University, 1992, pp. 288–314.
———. "Wayward New Christians and Stubborn New Jews: The Shaping of a Jewish Identity." *Jewish History*, vol. 8, no. 1–2, 1994, pp. 27–41. *JSTOR*, https://www.jstor.org/stable/20101189.
Kayserling, Meyer. "The Jews in Jamaica and Daniel Israel López Laguna." *Jewish Quarterly Review*, vol. 12, no. 4, 1900, pp. 708-17, https://doi.org/:10.2307/1450701.
———. "Une histoire de la littérature juive de Daniel Levi de Barrios." *Revue des études juives*, vol. 18, 1889, pp. 276–89.
"Kiddush Ha-Shem and Hillul Ha-Shem." Jewish Virtual Library, jewishvirtuallibrary.org/kiddush-ha-shem-and-x1c24-illul-ha-shem. Accessed 28 Jan. 2022.
*The Ladino Bible of Ferrara, 1553: A Critical Edition*. Edited by Moshe Lazar, Labyrinthos, 1992.
Langer, Ruth. *Cursing the Christians? A History of the* Birkat Hamanim. Oxford UP, 2012.

Leibman, Laura. "Poetics of the Apocalypse: Messianism in Early Jewish American Poetry". *Studies in American Jewish Literature*, vol. 33, no. 1, 2014, pp. 35–62, muse.jhu.edu/article/541024. Accessed 7 June 2022.

———. "Sephardic Sacred Space in Colonial America," *Jewish History*, vol. 25, 2011, pp. 13–41. https://doi.org.10.1007/s10835-010-9126-7. Accessed 7 June 2022.

León Templo, Jacob Judah. *Las alabanzas de santidad: traducción de los Psalmos de David por la misma frasis y palabras del hebraico*. Amsterdam, 1671. Sephardic Editions, 1550–1820.

Lieberman, Julia Rebollo. "*Contra la verdad no hay fuerza*, comedia alegórica de Miguel (Daniel Leví) de Barrios." Ribera, pp. 181–96.

———. *El teatro alegórico de Miguel (Daniel Leví) de Barrios*. Juan de la Cuesta Hispanic Monographs, 1996.

Litovsky, Haydee. *Sephardic Playwrights of the Seventeenth and Eighteenth Centuries in Amsterdam*. University Press of America, 1991.

López-Ibor, Marta. *Los judíos en España*. Anaya, 2006.

López Laguna, Daniel Israel. *Espejo fiel de vidas que contiene los Psalmos de David en verso, obra devota, útil y deleitable*. London, 1720. *Google Books*, books.google.com/.

McCaw, R. John, and Kathleen Thornton Spinnenweber, editors. *Anthology of Spanish Golden Age Poetry*. Cervantes and Co., 2007.

McGaha, Michael. "Antonio Enríquez Gómez and the 'Romance al divín mártir, Judá Creyente.'" *Sefarad*, vol. 48, no. 1, 1988, pp. 59–92.

———. "Biographical Data on Antonio Enríquez Gómez in the Archives of the Inquisition." *Bulletin of Hispanic Studies*, vol. 49, 1992, pp. 127–39.

———. "'Divine' Absolutism vs. 'Angelic' Constitutionalism: The Political Theories of Quevedo and Enríquez Gómez." *Studies in Honor of Bruce W. Wardropper*, edited by Dian Fox, Harry Sieber, and Robert Ter Horst, Juan de la Cuesta, 1989, pp. 181–92.

———. "El prólogo a las *Academias morales de las musas* de Antonio Enríquez Gómez." *Homenaje a Alberto Porqueras Mayo*. Edition Reichenberger, 1988, pp. 307–15.

———. Introduction. *The Perfect King (El rey más perfeto)*, by Antonio Enríquez Gómez. Bilingual Press/Editorial Bilingüe, 1991, pp. vii–xlix.

———. "Is There a Hidden Jewish Meaning in *Don Quixote*?" *Cervantes: Bulletin of the Cervantes Society of America*, vol. 24, no. 1, 2004, 173–88.

McMichael, Steven J. *Was Jesus of Nazareth the Messiah? Alphonso de Espina's Argument against the Jews in the* Fortalitium Fidei. Scholars Press, 1994.

Menocal, María Rosa. *The Ornament of the World: How Muslims, Jews, and Christians Created a Culture of Tolerance in Medieval Spain*. Little, Brown & Co., 2002.

Mirvis, Stanley. *The Jews of Eighteenth-Century Jamaica: A Testamentary History of a Diaspora in Transition*. Yale UP, 2020.

Molina, Tirso de. *El burlador de Sevilla y el convidado de piedra*. Edited by R. John McCaw, Cervantes and Co., 2003.

Morffiz González, Arielys, Fabi Zeller-Márquez, and Matthew D. Warshawsky. "From Baroque Spain to 1600s Amsterdam: Emergent Judaism in the Literary Works of Ex-New Christian Miguel de Barrios." *Reinvention: An International Journal of Undergraduate Research*, vol. 15, no. 1, 2022, reinventionjournal.org/index.php/reinvention/article/view/892. Accessed 30 April 2022.

Muchnik, Natalia. *Une vie marrane: Les pérégrinations de Juan de Prado dans l'Europe du XVIIe siècle*. Honoré Champion, 2005.

Nadler, Steven. *Menasseh ben Israel: Rabbi of Amsterdam*. Yale UP, 2018.

Nahon, Gérard. "The Hague, Amsterdam, Istanbul, Jerusalem: David de Pinto and the *Jesiba* Magen David, 1750–1767." *The Dutch Intersection: The Jews and the Netherlands in Modern History*, edited by Yosef Kaplan, Brill, 2008, pp. 251–78.

*The New Oxford Annotated Bible: New Revised Standard Version with the Apocrypha*. Edited by Michael D. Coogan et al., Oxford UP, 2018.

*The NIV Study Bible*. Edited by Kenneth Barker et al., Zondervan, 1995.

Oelman, Timothy, editor and translator. *Marrano Poets of the Seventeenth Century: An Anthology of the Poetry of João Pinto Delgado, Antonio Enríquez Gómez, and Miguel de Barrios*. Associated University Presses, 1982. E-book ed., Liverpool UP, 2007.

Orobio de Castro, Isaac. *La observancia de la divina ley de Mosseh*. Edited by Jacobo Israel Garzón, Riopiedras, 1991.

———. *Prevenciones divinas contra la vana idolatría de las gentes*, vol. 1. Edited by Myriam Silvera, Leo S. Olschki, 2013.

Ovid. *Metamorphoses*. Translated by David Raeburn, Penguin, 2004.

Paganini, Gianni. Forward. Orobio de Castro, *Prevenciones divinas contra la vana idolatría de las gentes*, vol. 1, pp. v-xv.

Perelis, Ronnie. "Daniel Israel López Laguna's *Espejo fiel de vidas* and the Ghosts of Marrano Autobiography." Gerber, *The Jews in the Caribbean*, pp. 319–28.

Peza, Juan de Dios. *Leyendas históricas, tradicionales y fantásticas de las calles de la Ciudad de México*. Porrúa, 1992.

Pinto Delgado, João. *Poema de la Reina Ester. Lamentaciones del Profeta Jeremías. Historia de Rut y varias poesías*. Edited by I. S. Révah, Institut Français au Portugal, 1954.

Popkin, Richard H. "The Historical Significance of Sephardic Judaism in 17th Century Amsterdam." *The American Sephardi: Journal of the Sephardic Studies Program of Yeshiva University*, vol. 5, no. 12, 1971, pp. 18–27.

Quevedo, Francisco de. *Lágrimas de Hieremías castellanas*. Edited by Edward M. Wilson and José Manuel Blecua, Consejo Superior de Investigaciones Científicas, 1953.

Rauchwarger, Judith. "Antonio Enríquez Gómez's *Epístolas tres de Job*: A Matter of Racial Atavism?" *Revue des études juives*, vol. 138, 1979, pp. 69–87.

Real Academia Española, *Diccionario de Autoridades*, vol. 6, 1739, https://apps2.rae.es/DA.html. Accessed 21 Dec. 2023.

Révah, I. S. *Antonio Enríquez Gómez: un écrivain marrane (v. 1600–1663)*. Edited by Carsten L. Wilke, Éditions Chandeigne, 2003.

———. "Autiobiographie d'un Marrane: Édition partielle d'un manuscrit de João (Moseh) Pinto Delgado." *Revue des études juives*, vol. 119, 1961, pp. 41–130.

———. "Les écrivains Manuel de Pina et Miguel de Barrios et la censure de la communauté judéo-portugaise d'Amsterdam." *Tesoro de los judíos sefardíes: Estudios sobre la historia de los judíos sefardíes y su cultura*, vol. 8, 1965, pp. 74–90.

———. *Spinoza et le Dr. Juan de Prado*. Mouton, 1959.

Ribera, Josep, editor. *Actes del Simposi Internacional sobre Cultura Sefardita*. Promociones y Publicaciones Universitarias, 1993.

Rivers, Elias L., editor and translator. *Renaissance and Baroque Poetry of Spain with English Prose Translations*. Waveland P, 1966, reissued 1988.

Romero Muñoz, Carlos. "El prólogo al *Sansón Nazareno* de Antonio Enríquez Gómez." *Annali della Facoltà di lingue e letterature straniere di Ca' Foscari*, vol. 23, no. 2, 1984, pp. 219–38.

Rose, Constance H. "Antonio Enríquez Gómez and the Literature of Exile." *Romanische Forschungen*, vol. 85, 1973, pp. 63–77.

———. "The Marranos of the Seventeenth Century and the Case of the Merchant Writer Antonio Enríquez Gómez." *The Spanish Inquisition and the Inquisitorial Mind*, edited by Ángel Alcalá, Columbia UP, 1987, pp. 53–71.

Roth, Cecil. "An Elegy of João Pinto Delgado on Isaac de Castro Tartas." *Revue des études juives*, vol. 121, no. 3–4, 1962, pp. 355–66.

———. "João Pinto Delgado: A Literary Disentanglement." *Modern Language Review*, vol. 30, 1935, pp. 19–25.

———. "Laguna, Daniel Israel López." *Encyclopaedia Judaica*, edited by Michael Berenbaum and Fred Skolnik, 2nd ed., vol. 12, Macmillan Reference USA, 2007, pp. 438–439. *Gale eBooks*, link.gale.com/apps/doc/CX2587511764/GVRL?u=port18814&sid=bookmark-GVRL&xid=5ab948a1. Accessed 21 Dec. 2022.

Salomon, Herman Prins. *Portrait of a New Christian, Fernão Álvares Melo (1569-1632)*. Paris, Fundação Calouste Gulbenkian, Centro Cultural Português, 1982.

Sánchez, José. *Academias literarias del Siglo de Oro español*. Gredos, 1961.

Scholberg, Kenneth. *La poesía religiosa de Miguel de Barrios*. Edhigar, for Ohio State UP, 1962.

———. "Miguel de Barrios and the Amsterdam Sephardic Community." *Jewish Quarterly Review*, vol. 53, no. 2, 1962, pp. 120–59.

Shane, A. L. "Rabbi Jacob Judah Leon (Templo) of Amsterdam (1603–1675) and His Connections with England." *Transactions & Miscellanies (Jewish Historical Society of England)*, vol. 25, 1973–75, pp. 120–36, jstor.org/stable/29778840. Accessed 7 June 2022.

Shepard, Sanford. *Lost Lexicon: Secret Meanings in the Vocabulary of Spanish Literature during the Inquisition*. Ediciones Universal, 1982.

Slavitt, David R., translator. *The Poem of Queen Esther by João Pinto Delgado*. Oxford UP, 1999.

Society for Crypto-Judaic Studies, www.cryptojews.com. Accessed 13 June 2022.

Spanish and Portuguese Sephardi Community [of London], sephardi.org.uk/bevis-marks/visit-bevis-marks/. Accessed 21 Dec. 2022.

Stuczynski, Claude B. "Ex-*Converso* Sephardi New Jews as Agents, Victims, and Thinkers of Empire: Isaac Cardoso Once Again." *Paths to Modernity: A Tribute to Yosef Kaplan*, edited by Avriel Bar-Levav, Claude B. Stuczynski, and Michael Heyd, The Zalman Shazar Center for Jewish History, 2018, pp. 209–31.

Suárez Fernández, Luis, editor. *Documentos acerca de la expulsión de los judíos*. Consejo Superior de Investigaciones Científicas, 1964.

Swetschinski, Daniel M. "The Portuguese Jews of Seventeenth-Century Amsterdam: Cultural Continuity and Adaptation." *Essays in Modern Jewish History: A Tribute to Ben Halpern*, edited by Frances Malino and Phyllis Cohen Albert, Fairleigh Dickinson UP, 1982, pp. 56–79.

———. *Reluctant Cosmopolitans: The Portuguese Jews of Seventeenth-Century Amsterdam*. Littman Library of Jewish Civilization, 2000.

"Tacha." *Diccionario de Autoridades*, Real Academia Española, vol. 6 (1739), apps2.rae.es/DA.html, accessed 24 Mar. 2023.

Thornton Spinnenweber, Kathleen. Introduction to Students. *El divino Narciso*, by Sor Juana Inés de la Cruz. Cervantes and Co., 2021, pp. 9–33.

Tigay, Jeffrey. Notes to Exodus, *The Jewish Study Bible*.

Usque, Samuel. *Consolation for the Tribulations of Israel*. Translated by Martin A. Cohen, Jewish Publication Society, 1964.

"Value of the Guilder versus Euro." International Institute of Social History. iisg.amsterdam/en/research/projects/hpw/calculate.php. Accessed 28 Feb. 2022.

Vega Carpio, Lope de. *Arte nuevo de hacer comedias*. Edited by Enrique García Santo-Tomás, 2nd ed., Cátedra, 2009.

Vernet Pons, Mariona. "The Origin of the Name Sepharad: A New Interpretation." *Journal of Semitic Studies*, vol. 59, no. 2, 2014, pp. 297–313, https://doi-org.ezproxy-eres.up.edu/10.1093/jss/fgu002. Accessed 15 June 2022.

Wachtel, Nathan. *The Faith of Remembrance: Marrano Labyrinths*. 2001. Translated by Nikki Halpern, U of Pennsylvania P, 2013.

Wacks, David A. *Double Diaspora in Sephardic Literature: Jewish Cultural Production before and after 1492*. Indiana UP, 2015.

Warshawsky, Matthew. "A Spanish *Converso's* Quest for Justice: The Life and Dream Fiction of Antonio Enríquez Gómez." *Shofar*, vol. 23, no. 3, 2005, pp. 1–23.

———. *Longing for Justice: The New Christian Desengaño and Diaspora Identities of Antonio Enríquez Gómez*. 2002. Ohio State U, PhD dissertation.

———. "Las múltiples expresiones de identidad judeoconversa en la poesía de Antonio Enríquez Gómez." *Calíope: Journal of the Society for Renaissance and Baroque Hispanic Poetry*, vol. 17, no. 1, 2011, pp, 97–124.

———. *The Perils of Living the Good and True Law: Iberian Crypto-Jews in the Shadow of the Inquisition of Colonial Hispanic America*. Juan de la Cuesta-Hispanic Monographs, 2016.

———. Review of *Prevenciones divinas contra la vana idolatría de las gentes*, vol. 1, by Orobio de Castro, *Sephardic Horizons*, vol. 4, no. 3, 2014, sephardichorizons.org/Volume4/Issue3/warshawsky.html. Accessed 3 June 2022.

Wilson, Edward M. "The Poetry of João Pinto Delgado." *Journal of Jewish Studies*, vol. 1, 1948–49, pp. 131–43.

———. Review of *La poesía religiosa de Miguel de Barrios*, by Kenneth R. Scholberg. *Bulletin of Hispanic Studies*, vol. 40, 1963, pp. 176–80.

Wills, Lawrence M. Notes to Daniel, *The Jewish Study Bible*.

"Yearly Average Currency Exchange Rates." Internal Revenue Service. irs.gov/individuals/international-taxpayers/yearly-average-currency-exchange-rates. Accessed 28 Feb. 2022.

Wojda, Catherine L., Joshua Henderson, and Matthew Warshawsky. "'Mi amparo y Fortaleza': Seeing Psalms through a Trans-Iberian Worldview in *Espejo fiel de vidas* (*Life's True Mirror*)." *International Journal of Undergraduate Research and Creative Activity*, vol. 13, no. 1 2021, pp. 1–10, http://doi.org/10.7710/2168-0620.0307. Accessed 7 June 2022.

Yerushalmi, Yosef Hayim. *From Spanish Court to Italian Ghetto. Isaac Cardoso: A Study in Seventeenth-Century Marranism and Jewish Apologetics*. U of Washington P, 1981.

Yovel, Yirmiyahu. *The Other Within: The Marranos: Split Identity and Emerging Modernity*. Princeton UP, 2009.

———. *Spinoza and Other Heretics, Volume 1: The Marrano of Reason*, Princeton UP, 1989.

Zepp, Susanne. *An Early Self: Jewish Belonging in Romance Literature, 1499–1627*. Translated by Insa Kummer, Stanford UP, 2014.

※

# Index

Abd al-Rahman III, 114
Abraham, 36, 97, 106n38
Acis, 58-60
Ahasuerus, 50-59, 61, 64
Almeida Bernal, Marcos (Ishac) de, 135, 136n9
Alvares de Orobio, Manuel, 26
Alonso, Álvaro, 70n17
Amsterdam, 9, 15-16, 18, 20-23, 25, 27, 29-33, 36, 37, 41, 46-47, 49-50, 51n3, 96, 97n23, 103-04n33, 114n3, 116-17, 132-40, 143nn23-24, 144, 162, 168, 171-72, 174
Amzalak, Moisés Bensabat, 38
Antiochus IV Epiphanes, 102-03, 123-24
Arias Montano, Benito, 35
Asumpção, Diogo d', 124
Atías, or Athias, Abraham (Jorge Méndez de Castro), 132, 143-56, 158, 162
*auto sacramental*, 19, 133, 140-44, 155, 161-62
autos de fe
    auto de fe of 1603 (Lisbon), 124
    auto de fe of 1611 (Lisbon), 172
    auto de fe of 1632 (Madrid), 119
    auto de fe of 1644 (Valladolid), 99, 124
    auto de fe of 1647 (Lisbon), 124
    auto de fe of 1649 (Mexico City), 101n31, 154n28, 157
    auto de fe of 1655 (Córdoba), 135-36
    auto de fe of 1655 (Santiago de Compostela), 135
    auto de fe of 1665 (Córdoba), 19, 132, 136, 144-48, 157-58, 162
    definition and characteristics of, 19n5, 31n18, 180n22
Babylonian siege and captivity, 65-66, 68, 103, 123
Barrios, Miguel (Daniel Levi) de
    biographical information about, 20-21, 133-39
    writings:
    *Contra la verdad no hay fuerza*, 19, 132-34, 136, 140-41, 143-44, 147-62
    *Coro de las musas*, 32-33n19, 132n5, 137-39,
    *Estrella de Jacob sobre flores de Lis*, 134, 135n8, 139n16
    "Lamentación fúnebre en la muerte de mi padre Yahacob Leví de Barrios," 134, 139n16

"¿Qué tres cometas brillan en el cielo?," 147-48,
*Maskil el Dal*, 134n5
"Memoria de los mártires," 96, 135-36, 159
*Relación de los poetas y escritores españoles de la nación judaica amstelodama*, 50n2, 96
*Triumpho del govierno popular*, 96, 135-36, 138, 139, 143, 157, 161
Barrios, Simón (Jacob Levi) de, 134
Basurto, Isabel, 83, 91n16
Bautista Pérez, Manuel, 115n5
*beatus ille*, 86
Ben Israel, Menasseh, 171-72
*Biblia del Oso* (Oso Bible), 164-65n2
Bordeaux, 15, 23, 82, 83, 84n6, 85, 166
Brussels, 134n5, 135-37
Calderón de la Barca, Pedro, 71n18, 140-43
Cardoso, Isaac (formerly Fernão or Fernando)
    biographical information about, 113-16
    writings:
    *Las excelencias de los hebreos*, 19, 112, 116-31, 186n28
Cardoso, Abraham (formerly Miguel), 113, 115-16
Carvajal, Luis de, the Younger, 124
Castro Tartas, Isaac de, 124, 143-44
Castro Tartas, David de, 116, 143-44
Catholic Christianity
    criticisms of by converso authors, 18, 25, 40-45, 100-01, 187
    influence of on formation of converso authors, 46, 75, 76, 112n3, 114, 121, 137-38, 143, 161n33, 162, 163, 172, 189
    Trinitarian understanding of God in, 41-42
Cervantes, Miguel de
    *Don Quixote de la Mancha*, 42n27, 73n20
    possible converso origin of, 21n7
circumcision, 26, 28, 44-45, 97, 115, 116n8, 120, 122
Circe, 139, 142, 152-53, 155, 161
conversos (New Christians)
    definition of, 15, 17, 27, 74, 119
    diaspora of, 15, 16, 20-23, 28, 49, 69n16, 81, 112, 114, 115, 117, 135, 164, 166-67, 170, 173, 184, 191
    efforts of to return to Judaism, 16-19, 28-29, 30, 33, 40, 45-46n28, 49-50, 51, 60, 64-65, 94-96, 97, 113, 114n3, 116, 124, 130-31, 133-34, 148, 152, 158, 161-62, 164, 169, 172, 175, 182, 186, 189-90
    stigma of lineage of, 19-20, 23, 26, 42, 80, 135n7, 160, 175
    tribulations endured by, 62, 74, 87, 89, 106, 107, 112, 118-19, 122-23, 125, 126, 127-28, 129, 130, 132, 145, 159, 168, 174, 176, 177-78, 181, 183, 185n27, 187, 191
*Cristo de la Paciencia* case, 118-19
crypto-Judaism
    definition and practices of, 15, 27-28, 35, 47, 83, 89, 110, 135n7, 150, 159, 167, 191
    greater presence of in Portugal than in Spain, 27, 113-15, 134
Dalestina, 105, 106, 108n43
Daniel, 32-33, 103, 121

David, 61n10, 75-76n22, 85, 126, 163, 165, 177-78, 183, 184
deism, 18, 30-32, 35n22, 36, 47
Delgado, Gonçalo, 49
Democritus, 93
*desengaño*, 71, 73, 77-78, 80, 86, 93, 155
divine Law (of Torah), 25, 29, 33, 35, 36-37, 41, 43-44, 45-46n28, 67, 128, 139, 152
Doeg, 177-78
Dotar society, 23
Duke of Lerma, 21
Egypt, 48, 77-78, 80, 105, 115, 118, 122
elect status of Jews, 30, 34, 37, 40, 41, 75, 99, 117, 118, 119, 121, 130, 158, 163
Elijah, 103, 156-57
Emanuel, father of Samson (Manoah in Bible), 107n40
Enríquez, Leonor María, 146-47, 149-50n27
Enríquez de Mora, Antonio, 85
Enríquez Gómez, Antonio
  biographical information about, 81-85, 88-89
  writings:
  *Academias morales de las musas*, 82, 83, 84, 85-95, 98, 102, 106, 110-11, 119, 190
  *El siglo pitagórico y Vida de don Gregorio Guadaña*, 87n12
  *La inquisición de Lucifer y visita de todos los diablos*, 91, 96n22
  "Romance al martirio y felicísimo tránsito de don Lope de Vera y Alarcón," 20, 82-83, 95-104, 106, 108, 110, 157
  *Sansón Nazareno*, 83, 96, 104-110
Enríquez Villanueva, Diego, 81, 85n8, 91
Espina, Alonso de, *Fortalitium fidei* of, 35, 125-27
Esther, 18, 50-57, 60-62, 65, 80, 123
Eucharist, 18, 100, 130, 140, 142, 163
exile, 16n2, 19, 26, 51, 60, 65-66, 82-83, 86, 88-89, 92-94, 106n39, 110, 119, 145, 164, 166-67, 171, 174, 180, 181
Exodus, 18, 65, 75-76n22, 77-79, 80, 118, 121-22
expulsion of Jews from Spain
  consequences, 87, 114n3, 123, 125, 126, 127-28, 130, 134, 163, 166, 175, 189, 191
  edict of, 61-62, 125, 127, 130
Febos, Bartolomé, 88-89
Felipe IV, 21, 84-85, 89, 114, 115, 167
Fernández de Fonseca, Miguel, 91n16
Fernández Núñez, Mencía, 26
Fernando the Catholic, 15, 61, 113n1, 125, 127
Ferrara Bible (Judeo-Spanish translation), 66, 67, 76, 164
Ferrer, Vicente, 125-26
*finta*, 114
Flavius Clemens, 128
Fonseca, Catalina, 85n8
Fulvia, 128
Gómez, Isabel, 85n8, 91n16
Góngora, Luis de, poetry of, 18, 48, 50, 55-56, 58-59
Haman, 50, 52, 55, 57-60, 62, 64-65
Hannah, 102, 123-24
Hasdai ibn Shaprut, 114, 115n4

Hebrew Bible, 40, 46, 50, 51, 75, 99, 100, 106n38, 123n15, 128, 172
Helios, 56n8
Henriques Pimentel, Abraham, 168-69
Henriques Pimentel, Jacob, 168-69
*herem*, 29
Heraclitus, 93-94
Herrera, Pedro de, 145
Hooghe, Romeyn de, 22
Holy Child of La Guardia, 130
Horace, *Odes* of, 73n20, 86n11
Inquisition, Holy Office of
  efforts to confront its legacy today, 189-91
  in literary texts and lives of authors
    Barrios, Miguel de, 132-33, 143, 150-51, 155, 158-59, 160, 162
    Cardoso, Isaac, 115, 123, 124
    Enríquez Gómez, Antonio, 81-84, 85n8, 89, 91, 94, 95, 96n22, 97-99, 103, 107-09
    López Laguna, Daniel Israel, 20, 163, 164, 165-67, 174, 179-80, 181, 183-85, 187
    Orobio de Castro, Isaac, 26, 28n13, 45-46n28
    Pinto Delgado, João, 49, 51, 55n7, 65, 175-76
  prosecution and judgement of conversos accused of heresy, 19n5, 31n13, 113, 118-19, 123, 127-28, 130, 134, 135n7, 145, 146, 173, 189
  reconciliation of penanced heretics, 26n11, 183
  Suprema (*Consejo de la Suprema y General Inquisición*), 84n5, 102
Isabel the Catholic, 15, 61, 113n1, 125, 127
Israel and Israelites (to refer to Jewish people, in biblical sense), 20, 27-28, 30, 35, 36, 37, 38-39, 41-46, 65-67, 69-75, 77, 78, 80, 85, 101, 102, 105, 106-07, 109-10, 119-23, 136n10, 138, 149, 153, 156-59, 161, 163, 176, 183-87
Jerusalem, 16n2, 65-70, 71, 73-74, 80, 162, 181, 190
Jesus Christ
  as God incarnate (in Christianity), 40, 140, 142,
  criticisms of by converso authors, 38-39, 42-45, 100-101, 120
  appellation of Nazarene of, 105-06
  messiahship of, 43
  redemptive role (in Christianity) of death on cross of, 38-39, 100-01, 161
Job, 89-92, 110
João II, 129
Judah León Templo, Jacob, 170-71, 174
Judaize (and/or Judaizer), 27-28, 29, 81, 85n8, 99, 113, 118-19, 123, 127-28, 145-46, 167, 172, 177
Kethuvim, 51, 65
*kiddush ha-Shem*, 161,
kosher customs, 121
Lamentations, 18, 50n2, 51, 65-67, 76
Lara, Pedro Mateo de, 145-48, 149-50n27

Law of Moses, 30, 40, 83, 104, 115, 144, 151, 155, 157n29, 161
León, Fray Luis de, odes of, 18, 48, 50, 52-53, 54-55, 68n15, 70, 77, 78-79, 86n11
Livorno, 15, 85n8, 95, 96, 136
*locus amoenus*, 54-55, 67, 69-70, 85-86
London, 15, 20, 143n23, 163, 168, 169, 171, 187
López Laguna, Daniel Israel
   biographical information about, 165-68
   writings:
      *Espejo fiel de vidas*, 19-20, 163-65, 168-87
Maccabees, 97, 102-03, 123-24
*Mahamad*, 29, 30-32, 137-38, 139, 144
Maimonides, Moses ben, 114-15
Maldonado de Silva, Francisco, 124, 157n30
*malsín*, 86-87, 95, 108n41, 163-64, 176-77
Manoel I, 15, 27, 113
Manrique, Jorge, 18, 48, 71-73
Manrique, Rodrigo, 72n19
Marranos, 113
Márquez de Moscoso, Bartolomé, 98
Martínez, Ferrand, 125
Maurry, Laurent, 104
Melo, David Abenatar, 172-73
Mordecai, 50, 52, 54, 55, 58, 62-64
Morquecho y Saoba, Gerónimo, 99
Morteira, Saul Levi, 32, 50, 136-37
Mount Etna (Mongibelo), 102, 147-48
Munez, Agnes, 49
Muslims, 30-31, 72, 126

Nation (*nação*, in reference to diaspora of Portuguese *conversos*), 23, 69n16, 114n3, 118, 160, 168, 170, 189-90
Nebuchadnezzar, 103, 123
Nero, 85
New Christians *See* conversos
New Jews, 16-17, 25, 49-50, 60, 116-17, 119, 130, 175
Nunes Almeyda, Mordejay, 168
Núñez Bernal, Abraham, 135-36, 161
Núñez Fernández, Raquel (Beatriz), 132, 143-56, 158, 162
Old Christians, 13, 27, 42n27, 74, 80, 113n2, 115, 124, 160, 177, 186
Olivares, count-duke of (Gaspar de Guzmán), 21, 84-85, 89, 115, 167
oneness of God in Judaism, 41-42, 101, 116, 118, 120, 123, 155
Orobio de Castro, Isaac (formerly Baltasar)
   biographical information about, 20-21, 26-28
   writings:
      "Carta al hijo del doctor Prado," 37
      "Carta apologética," 30, 35-36
      "Epístola invectiva contra Prado," 29, 30n16, 33-35
      *La observancia de la divina ley de Mosseh*, 25, 27-28, 38-40
      *Prevenciones divinas contra la vana idolatría de las gentes*, 25, 40-46,
Ottoman Empire, 15, 21, 38,
Ouderkerk, 28, 137
Ovid, *Metamorphoses* of, 56n8, 58, 141n19

Paul of Burgos (Pablo de Santa María, formerly Solomon Halevi), *Scrutinium Scripturarum* of, 35
Pagnino (Pagnini), Santes (Xantes), *Veteris et Novi Testamenti nova translatio* of, 35
*parnasim*, 29n14
Penso, Ishac, 143
*peregrino* (wanderer symbolic of converso worldview), 20, 79, 91n15, 92-94, 98, 102, 148, 163, 173-74, 182, 184
Persian Jews, 60
Pérez de la Peña, Isabel (Esther), 26
Pharaoh, 55, 65, 78, 186
Phaethon, 56n8
Philistines, 105, 106-10, 128
phoenix, 103
Pina Fonseca Dias, Abigail de, 137
Pinto family (of Amsterdam), 117-18
Pinto Delgado, João (Mosseh)
  biographical information about, 20-21, 49-50
  writings:
  *Canción, aplicando misericordias divinas y defetos proprios a la salida de Egipto hasta la Tierra Santa*, 48, 77-80
  *Lamentaciones del Profeta Jeremías*, 48, 65-77, 80, 119, 190
  *Poema de la Reina Ester*, 48, 50-65, 69n16, 80
Polyphemus, 58-60
Port Royal, Jamaica, earthquake of 1692, 180-81
Portuguese as synonym for converso, crypto-Jew, and Jew, 23, 115, 145, 160n32

Prado, David de, 37
Prado, Juan (Daniel) de, 18, 25, 29-37, 40, 46-47
Purim, 51-52
purity of blood (*limpieza de sangre*), 26, 87, 175n17
Quevedo, Francisco de, 67n14, 71n18
rejudaization of conversos, 16, 28-29, 50, 112n3
Reyna, Casiodoro de, 66, 76, 164-65n2
Rodríguez de Cáceres, Yahacob, or Jacob (Domingo), 132, 143-56, 158, 162
Rouen, 15, 48, 49-50, 55n7, 89, 91, 95, 104
Sabbath, 44-45, 116n8, 121-22, 131, 137
Salinas, Francisco de, 77n24, 78-79
*sambenito*, 26, 145, 156, 179
Samson, 83, 104-10
Saul, 85, 178
Seneca, 85
Sephardim (origin of term in the word *Sepharad*), 16n2
Seville, 31, 81, 83, 84n5, 104
Spanish Golden Age (Baroque) poetry, characteristics of, 17, 50, 52-59, 69-71, 77, 139, 140, 148, 159, 169-70, 182
Spinoza, Benedict (Baruch), 31
storm/port dichotomy, 68-69, 147-48, 180-81
*Tierras de idolatría*, 124, 135, 137, 148, 169
Torquemada, Tomás de, 127
Trancoso, Portugal, 113, 191

Treviño de Sobremonte, Tomás, 103n32, 124, 154n28, 157
Ulysses, 141, 152-53, 155
University of Salamanca, 55n7, 78, 82, 99
Váez, Débora, 136
Valle, Sebastiana (Sara Levi) del, 134-35
Vashti, 51, 53, 54
Vega, Garcilaso de la, 55, 56n8, 88
Vega Carpio, Lope de, 170
Vera y Alarcón, Lope de, 10, 20, 82-83, 95-104, 110, 124, 157, 190
*vivir muriendo*, 78, 90
Vulgate, 66, 67, 76
Zeus, 56n8
Zevi, Sabbatai, 38, 115-16, 139
Zion, 63, 64, 67, 70, 71-72, 74, 76, 184

www.ingramcontent.com/pod-product-compliance
Lightning Source LLC
Chambersburg PA
CBHW021355300426
44114CB00012B/1234